THE INTERNATIONAL TENNIS FEDERATION

A CENTURY OF CONTRIBUTION TO TENNIS

WRITTEN BY CHRIS BOWERS

EDITED BY EMILY FORDER-WHITE

New York · Paris · London · Milan

First published in the United States of America in 2013
by Rizzoli International Publications, Inc.
300 Park Avenue South
New York, NY 10010
www.rizzoliusa.com

2013 2014 2015 / 10 9 8 7 6 5 4 3 2 1

Distributed to the U.S. trade by Random House, New York

Designed by Brave
www.studiobrave.co.uk

Printed in Italy

ISBN-13: 978-0-8478-3990-2

Library of Congress Control Number: 2012948687

CONTENTS

FOREWORD

FRANCESCO RICCI BITTI, PRESIDENT OF THE INTERNATIONAL TENNIS FEDERATION

As an amateur historian – but one whose knowledge and appreciation of the work of the ITF is extensive – I was determined that the centenary of our organisation would serve as a catapult to celebrate the many things we have accomplished in the past as well as a look ahead to what we will achieve in the future. A key element in this celebration is the publication of this volume that details the history of the ITF and key moments in our sport against the backdrop of the 20th and 21st centuries.

The ITF was founded in 1913, just before the tumult of the First World War, to reflect the need for a uniform way of playing tennis, but it was not just about establishing rules. Before the ITF's foundation, Davis Cup was already a full-fledged international success, tennis was part of the Olympic Games, and the sport was making headlines and growing in popularity year on year. The foundation of the ITF therefore was a way of guiding and growing the sport, which is what we continue to do 100 years later.

We are justifiably proud of the growth of our flagship competitions, Davis Cup by BNP Paribas and Fed Cup by BNP Paribas, and the interest that they generate around the world. Because they are important, every bit of news about them attracts comment, good and bad, but it is inarguable that these two competitions are a force in tennis, with almost every top player from every nation participating on a regular basis. But it is not just about winning Davis Cup and Fed Cup; it is about the structure in place that is vital to the growth of tennis. This structure brings top-quality tennis to countries around the world, stimulating interest in tennis itself and bringing in vital funds for national associations which allow for the development of the sport.

Similarly, when Victoria Azarenka or Gustavo Kuerten win Grand Slam titles, how many people stop and look at what has allowed players from countries without a deep-rooted tennis tradition to reach the very top? Without support from the ITF development department and the Grand Slam Development Fund, these two household names, and many other players, would probably not have reached No. 1 in the rankings. Their success breeds further success among the youth of their nations who are inspired by the glow of a homegrown champion, so the effort put in by the ITF is multiplied in its effectiveness.

On our 100th birthday, I hope the full range of the ITF's involvement in tennis can be recognised. Much as we highlight the successes of the Azarenkas and Kuertens, it is important to recognise that growing tennis is not just about developing top players, it is about getting people to play at all levels. We at the ITF look after grassroots tennis, juniors, the professional circuits, wheelchair tennis and seniors. It is a wide remit, but we are assisted in this important work by our 210 member nations and six regional associations. Each of these activities is highlighted in this history, and I hope that you will take time to learn a bit more about the unseen ways the ITF works to develop tennis at every level.

Finally, I would like to make one comment about what makes tennis a successful sport. It is the millions of volunteers who work tirelessly on behalf of tennis. The strength of the sport lies in these unsung heroes, and it is to them that this book is dedicated. The ITF's centenary is their celebration.

TIMELINE

1873   Walter Wingfield markets 'Sphairistike' by selling boxed sets of rackets, balls and a net, spawning the modern form of tennis

1887   First Wimbledon championships

1881   First US national championships (later US Open)

1891   First French national championships (later French Open)

1896   First modern Olympic Games which includes tennis

1900   Longwood Cricket Club in Boston, MA, hosts the first Davis Cup competition; tennis player Charlotte Cooper becomes the first woman in history to win an Olympic gold medal

1905   First Australian national championships (later Australian Open)

1913   International Lawn Tennis Federation founded

1922   First uniform set of rules for lawn tennis agreed

1924   First uniform set of rules for lawn tennis comes into effect under the ILTF

1925   French national championships opened up to non-French nationals for the first time

1926   Suzanne Lenglen becomes first female player to turn professional

1927   ILTF votes not to stage a tennis tournament at the 1928 Olympics, starting a 64-year absence for tennis from the Olympic movement

1938   Donald Budge wins all four major championships in the same year, spawning the term 'Grand Slam'

1940   ILTF secretariat moved from Paris to London, largely to protect value of ILTF funds from the ravages of war in France

1957   First international association for veterans tennis established by independent group VITA

1960   Motion to admit professionals to official tournaments and make tennis open narrowly defeated in Paris

1963   50th anniversary of ILTF celebrated by inaugurating the first multi-nation team competition for women, the Federation Cup (later Fed Cup)

1967   Lamar Hunt launches the World Championship Tennis tour for professionals; Wimbledon controversially stages an eight-man pro tournament

1968   ITF approves tennis going open, following strong pressure from Wimbledon and USTA

1970   ITF launches first 'Grand Prix' men's tour, culminating in year-ending Masters in New York; the tiebreak makes its debut at the US Open

1972   As television coverage increases, yellow tennis balls are introduced to improve visibility on screen; Davis Cup Final Round instituted; formation of the Association of Tennis Professionals

1973   81 male players boycott Wimbledon; ILTF appoints its first member of staff (Basil Reay as secretary); first official men's computer rankings come into effect, with Ilie Nastase as No. 1; Women's Tennis Association founded

1974   Formation of Men's International Professional Tennis Council following 1973 Wimbledon boycott; South Africa becomes first non-Grand-Slam nation to win Davis Cup in the final that was never played because of India's boycott

1975   Professional Code of Conduct introduced

1976   First fact-finding mission to Africa (under Gil de Kermadec); ILTF establishes own men's circuit; Federation Cup gains first title sponsor in Colgate-Palmolive

1977   Philippe Chatrier elected ILTF president; decision taken to drop 'Lawn' from Federation's name, henceforth ITF; ITF launches Junior World Rankings circuit; point penalty system adopted in the U.S. on an experimental basis

1978   ITF announces its first World Champions; ITF instructs South Africa to withdraw indefinitely from Davis Cup and Fed Cup over issues relating to apartheid

1979   ITF takes over formal responsibility for Davis Cup from the Davis Cup Nations; veterans tennis incorporated into the ITF

1981   Restructuring of Davis Cup into World Group and feeder zones; NEC becomes Cup's first title sponsor; first seniors world individual championships takes place and the ITF introduces seniors rankings

1982   ITF stages first Worldwide Coaches Workshop

1984 Structuring of ITF into four major departments: men's tennis, women's tennis, administration and development; ITF establishes own women's circuit; tennis reappears at the Olympic Games as a test event in Los Angeles

1985 Chatrier voted off presidency of MIPTC in favour of the ATP's Mike Davies; first ITF international junior team competition, World Youth Cup, takes place; Wimbledon donates £100,000 to the ITF, which is the launch pad for the Grand Slam Development Fund

1986 First tennis drug testing programme drawn up by MIPTC

1987 ITF moves offices from Wimbledon to Barons Court; wheelchair tennis is accepted into the Stoke Mandeville Games

1988 Tennis returns to the Olympics; ATP declares it will run its own tour from 1990, thereby ending the role of the Grand Slams and ITF in the regular men's tour; ITF adopts wheelchair tennis's two-bounce rule into the official rules of tennis, and the sport's acceleration gives birth to the International Wheelchair Tennis Federation (IWTF)

1989 Brian Tobin becomes ITF's first elected salaried officer as executive vice-president; ITF seniors department established; following pressure from the IOC, South Africa is suspended as a member nation by the ITF over issues relating to apartheid

1990 Formation of Grand Slam Committee; ITF and Grand Slam tournaments found Grand Slam Cup

1991 Tobin elected as first ITF president on a four-year term as de facto chief executive

1992 Wheelchair tennis makes Paralympics debut; South Africa is readmitted to the ITF and to Davis Cup, Fed Cup and Olympic competition

1993 The Tennis Anti-Doping Programme is established, with the ITF, ATP and WTA managing testing at their own events

1995 Federation Cup name changed to Fed Cup, moves from week-long event to home-and-away format with qualifying rounds

1996 ITF technical department established

1997 ITF/ATP/WTA come together to form joint certification scheme for officials, run by the ITF

1998 ITF moves from Barons Court to the Bank of England sports ground in Roehampton, which also becomes home of the ITF 'lab', the world's most advanced tennis-specific research facility; the IWTF is subsumed into the ITF, making wheelchair tennis the first disabled sport to achieve such a union at international level

1999 Restructuring of ITF into five departments; Davis Cup celebrates 100th anniversary; World Anti Doping Agency (WADA) founded

2000 ITF cooperates with ATP to launch first Tennis Masters Cup; first ITF Tennis Science & Technology Congress takes place in London

2001 Wheelchair tennis celebrates first quarter century with launch of the Silver Fund, its own development programme

2002 BNP Paribas takes over from NEC as Davis Cup title sponsor; World Youth Cup renamed Junior Davis Cup and Junior Fed Cup

2004 ITF launches tennis's first out-of-competition drug testing programme; Junior Tennis School established; the Davis Cup final between Spain and USA in Seville is attended by the largest-ever crowd for an official tennis match (27,200) in history; ITF launches IPIN (International Player Identification Number) enabling players to manage their tournament schedules online

2005 BNP Paribas becomes title sponsor of Fed Cup

2006 ITF takes over administration of joint drug testing programme from ATP; electronic line-calling review makes official debut at Hopman Cup; ITF technical department renamed science and technical

2007 ITF takes over administration of joint drug testing programme from WTA, meaning the Tennis Anti-Doping Programme is now exclusively managed by the ITF; Tennis Play & Stay campaign launched, a recruitment and retention programme aimed at start-up players; wheelchair tennis staged at all four Grand Slams for the first time; ITF launches 'Tennis iCoach'

2008 ITF Beach Tennis Tour founded; ITF Junior Tennis School opens up online

2009 New Tennis Anti-Corruption Programme comes into effect, operated by the Tennis Integrity Unit; ATP Ranking points awarded for Davis Cup for the first time; ITF announces new role of Player Welfare Officer

2010 The inaugural Youth Olympic Games takes place in Singapore

2012 Mixed doubles returns to the Olympic fold; Spain and Czech Republic contest the 100th Davis Cup final

2013 ITF celebrates its centenary; Fed Cup turns 50

"YOUR PRESENCE HERE MAY BE SAID
TO BE THE CONSECRATION OF THE
INTERNATIONAL ASSOCIATION,
AND THE DATE OF THE 1st OF MARCH
WILL REMAIN A MEMORABLE ONE
IN THE ANNALS OF LAWN TENNIS."

HENRY WALLET
ITF CO-FOUNDER

CHAPTER 01

AN INTERNATIONAL UMBRELLA FOR LAWN TENNIS

THE FOUNDATION AND DEVELOPMENT OF THE ITF

THE FOUNDATION OF THE ITF IS TRACEABLE TO THE MINUTE.
AT 2 P.M. ON 1 MARCH 1913, REPRESENTATIVES FROM 13 NATIONS MET IN THE
PARIS OFFICE OF THE FRENCH SPORTS UNION, THE UNION DES SOCIETES FRANCAISES
DE SPORTS ATHLETIQUES, TO FOUND THE INTERNATIONAL LAWN TENNIS
FEDERATION (ILTF). INVITATIONS HAD GONE OUT TO 18 NATIONS: 15 SAID THEY
WANTED TO JOIN, AND VOTES WERE SET ASIDE FOR THE REMAINING THREE.

THAT MEETING WAS THE CULMINATION OF 18 MONTHS OF BEHIND-THE-SCENES
HARD WORK, STARTED BY A MAN WHO WAS ARGUABLY THE GODFATHER OF THE ITF
BUT WHO WASN'T AROUND TO SEE HIS LABOURS COME TO FRUITION BECAUSE
HE HAD DROWNED WHEN THE TITANIC HIT AN ICEBERG.

THE GROWTH OF 'LAWN TENNIS'

Tennis has existed in some form since the 13th century, and possibly for much longer. Early versions were played without rackets, such as the French game known as *jeu de paume*, literally 'game of the palm (of the hand)', and the Italian *giuoco della palla*, or 'game of the ball'. Tennis became popular among Europe's royal families in the 16th and 17th centuries when rackets were first used and the game was played largely indoors, with players allowed to bounce the ball off the walls. The variant played then is still around, generally under the name 'real tennis' (a corruption of 'royal tennis') or 'court tennis'. (The word tennis is thought to have come from the French *tenez* or 'hold'.)

The development of the Italian *giuoco della palla* into *pallacorda* (ball and string) in the 18th century reflects the presence of a string across a hall or street representing what is now the net. The first attempts to take the sport outdoors came in the late 18th century, but it wasn't until the 1870s – by which time the sport that had been played by the royals was pretty moribund – that today's tennis took off.

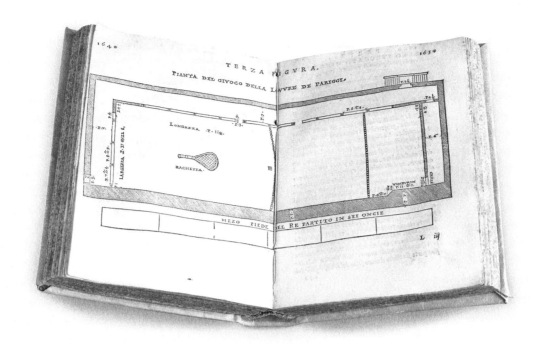

Trattato del Giuoco della Palla, the first book written about tennis, published in 1555 and written by theologian Antonio Scaino. The book discusses five variant ballgames but with a focus on tennis. Pictured is the layout of the royal tennis court at the Louvre in Paris, where Henry II played *giuoco della palla.* Scaino was prompted to write the book after a dispute of rules over a game of tennis.

A depiction of lawn tennis in the 1870s. The pastime was enjoyed mainly by the social elite and grew rapidly in popularity.

The 1877 Marylebone Cricket Club rulebook for 'The Games of Lawn Tennis and Badminton'

In what was one of the most brilliant sales-and-marketing exercises of the 19th century, an English army major, Walter Clopton Wingfield, designed, patented and manufactured the equipment for playing tennis on a flat lawn, and sold it in boxes costing five guineas (about $8 at today's exchange rate). It quickly became the must-have item among affluent families. In fact, his invention was a massive success in all but one respect: the name Wingfield gave it. He called it Sphairistike from the Greek word for 'ball games', but had helpfully subtitled it 'lawn tennis', and fortunately that was the name that stuck. (The 'International Sphairistike Federation' just doesn't have the same ring to it.)

Lawn tennis's first governing body was the Marylebone Cricket Club in London, which was in charge of English cricket. It changed a number of Wingfield's rules, including the abandonment of the 'first to 15 points' scoring system in favour of the one we know today with deuce and advantage. It also gave players two serves instead of one. In the late 1870s, the All England Croquet Club, which had angered its members by staging a tennis tournament (the first Wimbledon) in 1877, took over from the MCC as the new sport's governing body.

1874. Monday July 6

The Countess Waldegrave
    Strawberry Hill
    Twickenham
1 Large Ser Tenn 10 10 0
   Tomorrow Paid JB.

The Lady Hamilton
   38 Upper Brook Street
   Grosvenor Square
to Berkhamsted House &c &c
1 Ser Tennis 5 5 —

The Lord Cawdor
   74 South Audley Street
1 Ser Tennis 5 5 —
    Paid JB.

The Earl of Galloway
   17 Upper Grosvenor Street
1 Large set 10 10 —
1 Extra Net 15 —
   Paid JB. 11 5 —

Captain Eccles
   Fair Oak N Bishopstoke
1 2 dn Balls 10 —
   Paid JB.

Lawrence Latter Esqr
   50. High Street Borough
1 Ser Tennis 5 5 —
   Paid JB.

G Hardy Esqr
   7 Carlton House Terrace
1 Set 5/5/0 Balls 5/ 5 10 —
   Paid JB.

1874 Monday July 6

Lt Colonel F Maitland Wilson
  To Plowlands Hall &c Bury St Edmunds
  40 Upper Brook Street
1 Large Set 10 10 —

Mr Lionel Ashley
  23 Portman Square
1 Ser Tennis 5 5 0
1 2 Bats 30/- Ball 2/6 1 12 6
1 2 Presses 1 10 —
   Paid JB. 8 7 6

The Hon W H B Portman M.P.
  By Cash 6.5.0. &c

Lord Ashburton
  By Cash 10.10.0 June 22

Messrs J & H Harrison
  44 Grey Street
  Newcastle on Tyne
1 2 sets Tennis 10 10 0
   10 0/0 1 1 —

A/c for	9 9 0
June 1. 8 Sets	14 3 6
10 3 do	14 3 6
15 1 do }	±± 3 6
Aug 6 2 do }	4 18 6
	42 10 6
July 18. By Cheque	20 — —
	22 10 6

(what was sent for 6 July?
what is booked for 6 July?)

The 1888 US National Championships – today's US Open – at the Newport Casino, which is now home to the International Tennis Hall of Fame

The winner's medal for the first-ever US Open, the 1881 US National Championships. Richard Sears would be the recipient.

With Wingfield's boxes finding their way into mainland Europe and across the Atlantic, tennis tournaments began springing up all over the place. There was certainly a tournament in Nahant, Massachusetts, in 1876, but there may well have been a slightly earlier one. In 1881 the United States National Lawn Tennis Association – today the USTA – was founded and promptly staged its first national championships (the forerunner of the US Open) in Newport, Rhode Island. In 1891 the French national championships were held for the first time, and Hamburg hosted Germany's first national tournament in 1896. The first tournament in Australia was the 1879 Victorian national championships,

before Australia was a united country; the seven colonies came together in 1901, and the first Australasian national championships (now the Australian Open) took place in 1905.

The growth of tennis was also reflected in the foundation of the Davis Cup in 1900. Originally a USA v Great Britain invitation event, it expanded to include Belgium in 1903, Australasia (Australia and New Zealand) in 1905, and other nations after that. Each of these countries had its own governing body, but there was no uniformity. The idea of forming a transnational umbrella organisation to oversee the sport's development along similar lines across the world began to take root.

TOP
The 1892 Wimbledon Championships at Worple Road, the original site of the All England Lawn Tennis Club (AELTC)

BOTTOM
Army & Navy's reinvention of the Sphairistike set, c.1880, featuring the Marylebone Cricket Club/AELTC rules and measurements for a rectangular, not hourglass-shaped court

Charles Barde

Duane Williams

Henry Wallet

AN INTERNATIONAL ORGANISATION

The man credited with having both the idea of an international umbrella organisation and the means to turn his vision into some form of reality was Duane Williams. An American lawyer who had been living in Geneva since 1891, he got together with Henry Wallet, the president of the Commission Centrale de Lawn Tennis (which was responsible for lawn tennis in France as the French Tennis Federation hadn't yet been founded), and Charles Barde, honorary secretary of the Swiss association. Over several unofficial meetings, they managed to convene the gathering of a dozen nations in Paris on 1 March 1913.

As part of the shuttle diplomacy that led to the ILTF's foundation, Williams sailed in April 1912 from England to America on the new 'unsinkable' liner, SS Titanic. He died after the ship hit an iceberg off Newfoundland, the collapsing forward funnel crushing him as he tried to swim to safety. His son, Richard Norris Williams, who was with him and apparently witnessed his father's death, was rescued in the nick of time and persuaded medical staff not to amputate his badly frozen legs. A good job too, as the younger Williams went on to win the US national championships and the Davis Cup several times.

Had Duane Williams survived, it's possible the USA would have been among the founding members of the ILTF. As it was, the Americans didn't join until 1923. The USA's accession helped the Federation become truly international, because until then it was predominantly European, with only Australasia and South Africa coming from outside Europe.

CHRONIQUE LOCALE

C. Duane Williams

On nous écrit :

« C'est avec un chagrin profond que l'on a appris à Genève que M. C. Duane Williams figurait au nombre des victimes de la catastrophe du *Titanic*.

« M. Williams, en effet, ne comptait que des amis dans notre ville. Citoyen de la grande république nord-américaine, il aimait passionément Genève, à tel point qu'il y vint dans l'intention d'y passer quarante-huit heures et qu'il y demeura dix neuf ans. A une franchise et une cordialité qui lui gagnaient la sympathie de tous, il joignait un tact et une générosité rares ; il était de ceux qu'aucun ennui, aucune misère d'autrui ne laissent indifférents. Un détail caractéristique : Williams se plaignait de n'avoir pas assez d'impôts à payer dans une ville où il se considérait comme chez lui.

« Père de l'aimable champion de tennis Richard N. Williams, il fut chez nous le grand promoteur de ce sport, et c'est incontestablement à lui qu'est due la merveilleuse extension que le jeu de tennis a prise à Genève depuis quelques années.

« Ceux qui ont eu le privilège de connaître cet homme de bien n'oublieront pas cette figure sympathique, ces yeux pleins de malice et de bonté, cette poignée de main franche comme lui, et le joyeux : « Helloh, my boys » par lequel il nous accueillait. Sa mort met en deuil une ancienne et vénérée famille de Philadelphie et, du même coup, de nombreux membres de la famille genevoise.

"It was with a deep sorrow that we learnt in Geneva that Mr. C. Duane Williams was amongst the victims of the Titanic.

Indeed, Mr. Williams only had friends in this city. He was a citizen of the great republic of North-America; he passionately loved Geneva, so much that he came here for two days only and in fact spent nineteen years of his life. His frankness and warmth turned everyone around him into friends, and he was also a tactful and generous man to a rare level. He was a man who never was indifferent to anybody's trouble or misery. This is a detail that will tell you a lot about him: he complained that he did not pay enough taxes in a city where he felt at home.

His son was the nice tennis champion Richard N. Williams; Mr. Williams Sr. promoted this sport in this country, and no one can deny that it is thanks to him that tennis wonderfully spread in Geneva in the last years.

Those who had the privilege to know this man of good will never forget this nice character, his sparkling eyes full of bounty, the way this honest man frankly clutched your hands, the joyful "Hello my boys!" he welcomed us with. His death brings mourning to an ancient and respectable family from Philadelphia and, at the same time, to many members of the Geneva family."

LETTER SENT BY A 'W .M.' TO *JOURNAL DE GENEVE*, 25 APRIL 1912 (TRANSLATED)

A tribute to Duane Williams in the *Journal de Geneve*. The ILTF visionary died in the Titanic sinking at age 51. He had joined the liner in Cherbourg and travelled in first class.

WAS THE ITF REALLY INTENDED?

While it's generally accepted that there were three movers and shakers responsible for the ILTF's foundation – Duane Williams, Henry Wallet and Charles Barde – the exact circumstances of the threesome coming together are the subject of some speculation.

One account has Williams approaching Barde, as they lived close to each other in French-speaking Switzerland, and Barde then approaching Wallet because he knew he needed some serious backup. In those days of slower travel, Barde was lucky to find Wallet on holiday by the shores of Lake Geneva.

Another account, recounted by Heiner Gillmeister in his book *Tennis: A Cultural History*, has Williams approaching Wallet directly to organise a world championship on clay courts. Wallet liked the idea, so an international organising committee was set up, and this morphed into the ILTF.

Richard Norris Williams, c.1910, before the fateful Titanic trip with his father Duane. He went on to win his first US Championships in 1914.

The numbers of nations represented at the foundation of the ILTF need some explaining. There were 12 representatives, speaking for 13 nations, but with 15 founding members (see panel, page 20). The explanation lies in Australasia being one representative for two nations, and Hungary, Italy and Spain not attending but saying they wanted to join. The other founders were Austria, Belgium, Denmark, France, Germany, Great Britain, Netherlands, Russia, South Africa, Sweden and Switzerland. The Federation's administration was to be run from Paris, with an advisory committee set up to assist the honorary secretary in dealing with business.

Inevitably when a new association is established, the concerns of various members have to be assuaged, and the early minutes of ILTF meetings testify to those worries being laid to rest. Great Britain was given the right to stage 'the world championships on grass – in perpetuity', while France was given the right to stage the 'world hard court championships' until 1916 ('hard courts' meant clay in those days, as clay was a deviation from the sport's core surface of grass, so 'hard courts' became a generic name for all non-grass surfaces). French fears of being linguistically swamped by the English-speaking world were already apparent, so it was agreed that French would be the ILTF's operating language, but with all important documents translated into English. Each national association affiliated to the ILTF was given between one and five votes, depending on their importance in the tennis world, but the British were given six votes in recognition of having been the 'cradle of the game' and because of their influence throughout the tennis-playing world.

The first meeting also committed to the creation of a World Covered Court Championship – which posed an interesting dilemma in the 1960s and 1970s, when purists felt that the proliferation of indoor tournaments was a corruption of the sport. When tennis went 'open' in 1968, all the prestigious events were outdoors, with indoor events viewed by traditionalists as an inheritance from the professional tour. Even today, the four Grand Slam tournaments are all played outdoors. In reality, the first members of the ILTF envisaged an indoor event right from the start.

1913: Queues form on Worple Road for the 'world championships on grass', which is how Wimbledon was formally recognised at the ILTF founding meeting four months earlier

Seven survivors from the ILTF foundation: left to right, Anthony Sabelli (British Isles), Robert Gallay (France), Pierre Gillou (France), RJ McNair (British Isles), Charles Barde (Switzerland), Paul de Borman (Belgium), and Hans Behrens (Germany)

"How has the game managed to spread in this phenomenal way without losing its individuality in the labyrinth of territorial differences and national customs? How is it that one can fly half-way round the world and drop in, as it were, to a Davis Cup match or a garden party game in the comforting knowledge that there will be no local rules to learn? Why has one never heard of Mrs. Wills-Moody, for instance, arguing that a service regarded as correct in Lisbon would be disallowed at Forest Hills? The answer to all these questions is, of course, international co-operation in the administration of the game."

FROM THE OCTOBER 1948 EDITION OF *WORLD SPORTS*, OFFICIAL MAGAZINE OF THE BRITISH OLYMPIC ASSOCIATION

Basil Reay became the ILTF's first paid member of staff in 1973 and served as general secretary for three years.

Despite the Federation's aim of coordinating the development of the sport so it remained recognisable across the world, there were difficulties in the first ten years with national associations accepting the ILTF as having the exclusive right to alter and control the rules of the game. It took until 1922 for an International Rules Board to be established within the Federation, and its first official ILTF 'Rules of Tennis' came into effect on 1 January 1924.

The secretariat remained in Paris until the outbreak of the Second World War. Concerns that a devaluation of the French franc would render much of the Federation's savings worthless prompted a decision to transfer all the ILTF's money to banks in England. That effectively was how the ITF came to be based in London, although there were no paid members of staff until Basil Reay became the first paid secretary in 1973. The word 'Lawn' was dropped from the Federation's title in 1977.

THE FOUNDER NATIONS

Eighteen invitations were sent out to 19 countries for the conference on 1 March 1913 that resulted in the founding of the ILTF. The nations invited were:

Australasia (Australia & New Zealand)
Austria
Belgium
Canada
Denmark
France
Germany
Great Britain
Hungary
Italy
Netherlands
Norway
Russia
South Africa
Spain
Sweden
Switzerland
USA

Of these nations, Canada, Norway and the USA declined to join the new Federation. Hungary, Italy and Spain were not present but had asked to join. The founding nations signed an International Lawn Tennis Agreement with 13 paragraphs dealing primarily with amateurism. By the end of the First World War only ten nations were members, but the ILTF grew rapidly in the years after 1918.

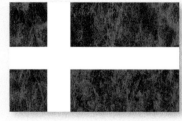

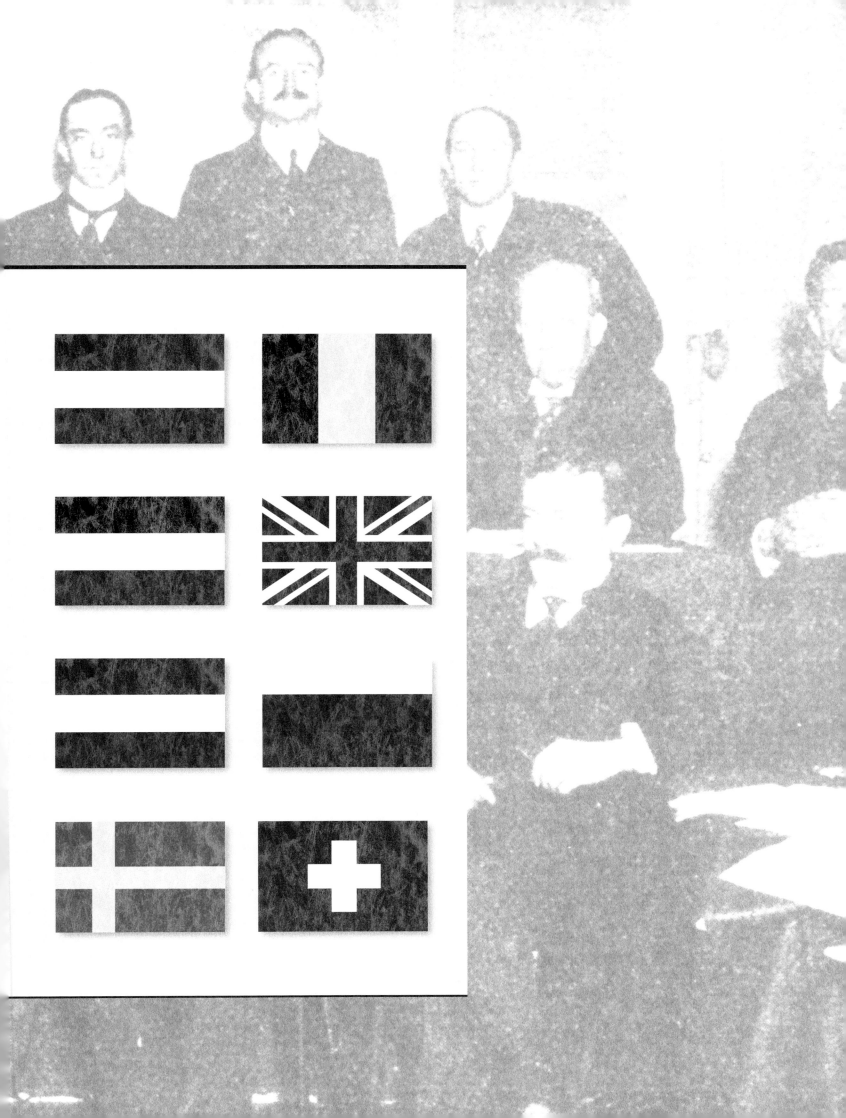

The ban also precluded 'non-Aryans' from filling any roles on lawn tennis committees. Further in the edition, Germany's Davis Cup team is announced and excludes Daniel Prenn, the country's tennis star of Polish-Jewish birth.

The ITF has had to deal with a number of problems in its 100-year history, many of them relating to the changing geography of the global map.

The two world wars forced a suspension of many of the sport's activities, and resulted in the expulsion of various nations at the end of each conflict. For example, Germany and Japan were booted out after 1945, a decision reflecting the power among the sport's decision makers of the victorious countries from the Second World War. Both were reinstated in 1950.

A number of nations have been political hot potatoes, of which Germany was one. In 1933 the case of Daniel Prenn arose, when Germany's new National Socialist (Nazi) government barred him from representing the country because he was racially Jewish (see panel, opposite). It is easy to see the ILTF's unwillingness to stand up for Prenn – especially in light of the letter supporting him by Fred Perry and Bunny Austin – as a sombre chapter in the Federation's history, and viewed from today's perspective its lack of action

does not look good. It wouldn't happen today because the ITF's constitution forbids discrimination on any grounds other than performance, but this event occurred less than 15 years after the end of the Great War, which had wiped out a generation of young men. There were to be more experienced operators than the ILTF's leading figures – notably the prime ministers of Great Britain and France – who were so keen to avoid another war that they failed to recognise the Nazi threat until it was too late to avoid it.

Germany's expulsion at the ILTF's first postwar meeting in 1946 lasted only four years, but the organisation's rules forbade two member associations from one country, so when East Germany applied to join in the early 1950s, it was turned down since the West German 'Deutsche Lawn Tennis Bund' had been admitted. It took until 1964 for East Germany to convince the Federation that it was a separate nation (and it was recognised as such until the Germany reunification in 1990).

RIGHT

This extract shows how much the leading tennis nations were largely on one side during the Second World War. Note the title 'Enemy and Satellite Nations'. The decision was taken to expel Austria, Bulgaria, Finland, Germany, Hungary, Italy, Japan, Libya, Romania and Siam, although it is pointed out that Austria could not be expelled as it was not a member (having been annexed by Germany in 1938). It is also interesting to note that the chairman, the ILTF's president Charles Barde, said his country, Switzerland, would not vote as it had been neutral in the war.

ENEMY AND SATELLITE NATIONS -

The Chairman said that the meeting now had to decide upon the attitude to be taken up by the Federation in regard to the Lawn Tennis Associations of Austria, Bulgaria, Finland, Germany, Hungary, Italy, Japan, Libya, Romania and Siam.

The recommendation of the Committee of Management was that those countries should be dealt with in the same manner as that which was applied in 1919 to the Lawn Tennis Associations of the Central Empires.

Sir Ernest Cooper pointed out that Austria was not a member and could not therefore be expelled. The Chairman agreed that that was the case and Austria would have to renew her application.

A general discussion ensued. Mr. Russell B. Kingman said that a very plausible case had been made out for the admission of Italy. He did not suggest that she should come back, but he wondered whether some differentiation might be made between the various nations.

The Chairman said that his country as a neutral, would not register its vote.

FROM ANNUAL GENERAL MEETING ON 5 JULY 1946 AT THE SAVOY HOTEL, LONDON

LEFT
Germany's Gottfried von Cramm
(left) and Daniel Prenn (right)
(with teammate Gustav Jaenecke
obscured) on their way to the Davis
Cup Europe Final in Milan in 1932.
They defeated Italy 5–0.

THE CASE OF DR. PRENN

In 1932 Daniel Prenn became Germany's hero when he beat Fred Perry of Great Britain in a live fifth Davis Cup match to see Germany through to the European final. Somewhat dramatically, Prenn had saved a match point at 2–5 in the fifth set – he was rescued by a baseline judge who called him for a foot fault as Perry struck what he thought was the winning return of serve.

But two months after Hitler came to power in January 1933, the German Tennis Federation passed a resolution stating that 'No Jew may be selected for a national team or the Davis Cup'. As Prenn was a Jew by blood, albeit non-practising, he was excluded from his national team. He was supported by Perry and Great Britain's other leading player, Bunny Austin, who together wrote a letter to *The Times* of London, published on 15 April 1933, saying: 'We have always valued our participation in international sport because it was a human activity that countenaced no distinction of race, class or creed. For this reason, if for none other, we view with great misgivings any action which may well undermine all that is most valuable in international competitions'.

Yet the ILTF refused to take any action against the German Tennis Federation, and Germany continued in Davis Cup without Prenn. Prenn emigrated to England shortly after, became a British citizen and died four days before his 87th birthday in 1991.

GERMANY AND THE DAVIS CUP

TO THE EDITOR OF THE TIMES

Sir,—We have read with considerable dismay the official statement which has appeared in the Press that Dr. D. D. Prenn is not to represent Germany in the Davis Cup on the grounds that he is of Jewish origin.

We cannot but recall the scene when, less than 12 months ago, Dr. Prenn before a large crowd at Berlin won for Germany against Great Britain the semi-final round of the European Zone of the Davis Cup, and was carried from the arena amidst spontaneous and tremendous enthusiasm.

We have always valued our participation in international sport, because we believed it to be a great opportunity for the promotion of better international understanding and because it was a human activity that countenanced no distinction of race, class, or creed. For this reason, if for none other, we view with great misgivings any action which may well undermine all that is most valuable in international competitions.

Yours faithfully,

H. W. AUSTIN.
April 13.   FRED PERRY.

South Africa proved another hot potato, largely because of its policy of racial segregation – known as apartheid – that was only abolished in the early 1990s. In the 1960s South Africa was represented within the ILTF by the South African Lawn Tennis Union (SALTU), but this was a whites-only organisation. In 1964 the ILTF was approached by a multi-racial body, the South African Sports Association, asking to be recognised because it represented tennis players of all racial backgrounds. But the ILTF's rule of accepting only one association per country prohibited this, and whenever the matter came to the vote, SALTU always won.

In 1968 and 1969 Hungary and the Soviet Union refused to play against South Africa in Davis Cup, and in 1970 – at the height of boycotts of South Africa in other sports – the ILTF persuaded South Africa not to play. The country was reinstated in 1972, but the number of countries that refused to play against South Africa grew, culminating in the 1974 Davis Cup final that never took place, as India refused to travel to Johannesburg. Thus, the first Davis Cup title to be won by a non-Grand Slam nation – a real milestone in the competition – was decided on an anticlimactic walkover. South Africa was banned from Davis Cup after 1978 and only returned to the fold in 1992 after apartheid came to an end.

TOP
Demonstrations outside a USA v South Africa Davis Cup tie in 1977

BOTTOM
Dennis Brutus, founding secretary of the multi-racial body, the South African Sports Association. The SASA challenged the whites-only South Africa Lawn Tennis Union, a member of the ILTF, and also called for South Africa's expulsion from the Olympic Games.

Croatians Goran Prpic and Goran Ivanisevic both played under the Yugoslav flag until the onset of the Serbo-Croat war in 1991. It wasn't until Croatia earned an outright place in the Davis Cup structure in 1993 that the two men returned to the competition.

Among other countries to pose problems was China, which was admitted to the ILTF in 1938 but withdrew in 1970, when the ILTF approved the accession of the Republic of China, otherwise known as Formosa or Taiwan and now officially Chinese Taipei. Members of the Chinese government escaped to the island of Taiwan during the cultural revolution of the 1960s that swept the communists to power in what became the People's Republic of China. Having proclaimed itself the legitimate government of China, the regime in Taiwan was inevitably on a course of antagonism with mainland China, so when Taiwan was admitted to the ILTF, mainland China left. It was readmitted in 1978.

The breakups of the former Soviet Union (USSR) and Yugoslavia in the early 1990s created a redrawing of the global map with dozens of new countries. This swelled the ITF's membership but sometimes caused problems, especially when a new nation replaced an existing one in Davis Cup. For example, Yugoslavia began to disintegrate into six constituent states in 1991, the year its Davis Cup team reached the semifinals.

Serbia was the central Yugoslav state, but its leading players that year were two Croats, Goran Ivanisevic and Goran Prpic. As a result, Croatia was given Yugoslavia's place in the Davis Cup structure (by then it was in Euro-African Zone I, as it was then called, not the World Group), while Serbia had to begin at the bottom of the Davis Cup ladder.

By the start of its 100th year, the ITF could boast 210 member national associations (of which at least four had considerably more money than the ITF itself).

PROFESSIONALISING THE FEDERATION

The arrival of open tennis in 1968 provided a catalogue of growing pains for the ILTF. Up to then it was largely run by a network of hard-working, well-meaning volunteer administrators, who earned certain privileges in return for their input into the functioning of the tennis world. But when the global tennis circuit became professional, it required a professionalising of the sport's administration, and this created a number of challenges that the old guard didn't always respond to with a clarity we can admire four decades later (see chapter 3).

In 1977 the ILTF was fortunate in finding, at its time of greatest need, a new president in Philippe Chatrier, who saw the importance of a fully professionalised governing body and had diplomatic links to both the old world and the new. Chatrier's background in one of the Grand Slam nations (he also served as president of the French Tennis Federation from 1973 to 1993), as well as his contacts with Jack Kramer and other figures in the new commercial world of tennis, were crucial for the welfare of both the ITF and the modern form of tennis. Without him, or at least someone playing the role he played, the sport may have lost some of the traditions that are still valued today.

VOLUNTEERS AND PAID STAFF

Astonishingly, the ITF didn't have a paid member of staff until it was 60 years old. For its first six decades, the Federation was run by volunteers serving on an advisory committee, working with a secretary who was also unpaid.

The ILTF secretary from 1948 to 1973 was Basil Reay, an old-school Englishman who was honorary secretary in partnership with a succession of co-secretaries. In 1973 Reay became the ILTF's first paid official as secretary on his own. He was replaced in 1976 by David Gray, who became the ILTF's general secretary.

Until 1976 the ILTF president was elected for a two-year term and was largely a figurehead. When Philippe Chatrier became president in 1977, he doubled the term to four years, and effectively made the president the chief executive as well as chairman of the board. But Chatrier was never paid by the ITF, as he continued as president of the French national association, the FFT.

The role of general secretary (known in some companies as chief operating officer) became a general manager role in the 1980s, with the incumbent answering to the president. But in 1989 it was taken by a member of the board, Brian Tobin, whose title became executive vice-president (he thereby became the first board member to receive a salary from the ITF). When Tobin became president in 1991, he was replaced by Mike Davies (1991–95) and later Doug MacCurdy (1995–98), but as neither was a board member, they kept the title general manager. In 1999 MacCurdy was replaced by Juan Margets, who is a member of the board so took the title executive vice-president.

In 2001 Tobin's successor as president, Francesco Ricci Bitti, initiated a change in the ITF constitution which required any ITF president to resign from being president of his/her national association or regional association.

The Formation of Zonal Associations

In order to bridge the gap between the national associations and the headquarters of the I.L.T.F. we suggest that the I.L.T.F. recommend the formation of 6 supra-national associations in the following zones:

Europe, Asia, Africa, North America, South America and Australia.

Each zonal association shall be financially self supporting, their objective being to promote and strengthen the game within their respective zones, within the jurisdiction of the I.L.T.F.

FROM ANNUAL GENERAL MEETING HELD ON 9 JULY 1975 AT THE PALACIO DE CONGRESOS, BARCELONA

THE VOTING SYSTEM

Voting at ITF annual general meetings is carried out according to a weighted system, whereby the largest nations get the most votes. The current system is as follows:

5 nations have 12 votes (Australia, France, Germany, Great Britain, USA)

14 nations have 9 votes (among them Argentina, Russia, Switzerland and Sweden)

7 nations have 7 votes (among them Croatia, New Zealand and Thailand)

12 nations have 5 votes (among them Belgium, Chile, Israel and Uzbekistan)

22 nations have 3 votes

85 nations have 1 vote

The ITF headquarters today, based in Roehampton, South West London and housing over 80 staff

The first ITF directors with president Philippe Chatrier (seated, centre). Standing left to right, Doug MacCurdy (Development), Mike Davies (Marketing), Thomas Hallberg (Men's). Seated left and right, Barbara Wancke (Women's) and Sally Holdsworth (Administration).

Perhaps the biggest development in the ITF's history was the sponsorship of Davis Cup in 1981 by the Japanese electronics giant NEC. It was both a milestone in the commercialisation of the sport and an enabling measure to professionalise the Federation. With the income from NEC (which also sponsored the Federation Cup), the ITF was able to expand its administration from a modest secretariat with small offices above the Wimbledon Museum into a proper governing body with clearly established departments. In 1984, following the death of the ITF's General Secretary David Gray, three new departments were created: men's tennis, women's tennis and development. Thomas Hallberg became the director of men's tennis, Barbara Wancke was his equivalent in women's tennis, and Doug MacCurdy formalised his development work by taking over the development department. Gray was succeeded by Shirley Woodhead, who headed up a new administration department. The job of president also became full time – albeit unpaid until 1991 (see panel, opposite).

The ITF continued to grow, with such important milestones as the creation of an anti-doping programme in 1986, a veterans department in 1989 and a technical department in 1996.

"THE IMPORTANT THING
IN LIFE IS NOT TO TRIUMPH
BUT TO COMPETE."

PIERRE DE COUBERTIN

FOUNDER OF THE MODERN OLYMPIC GAMES

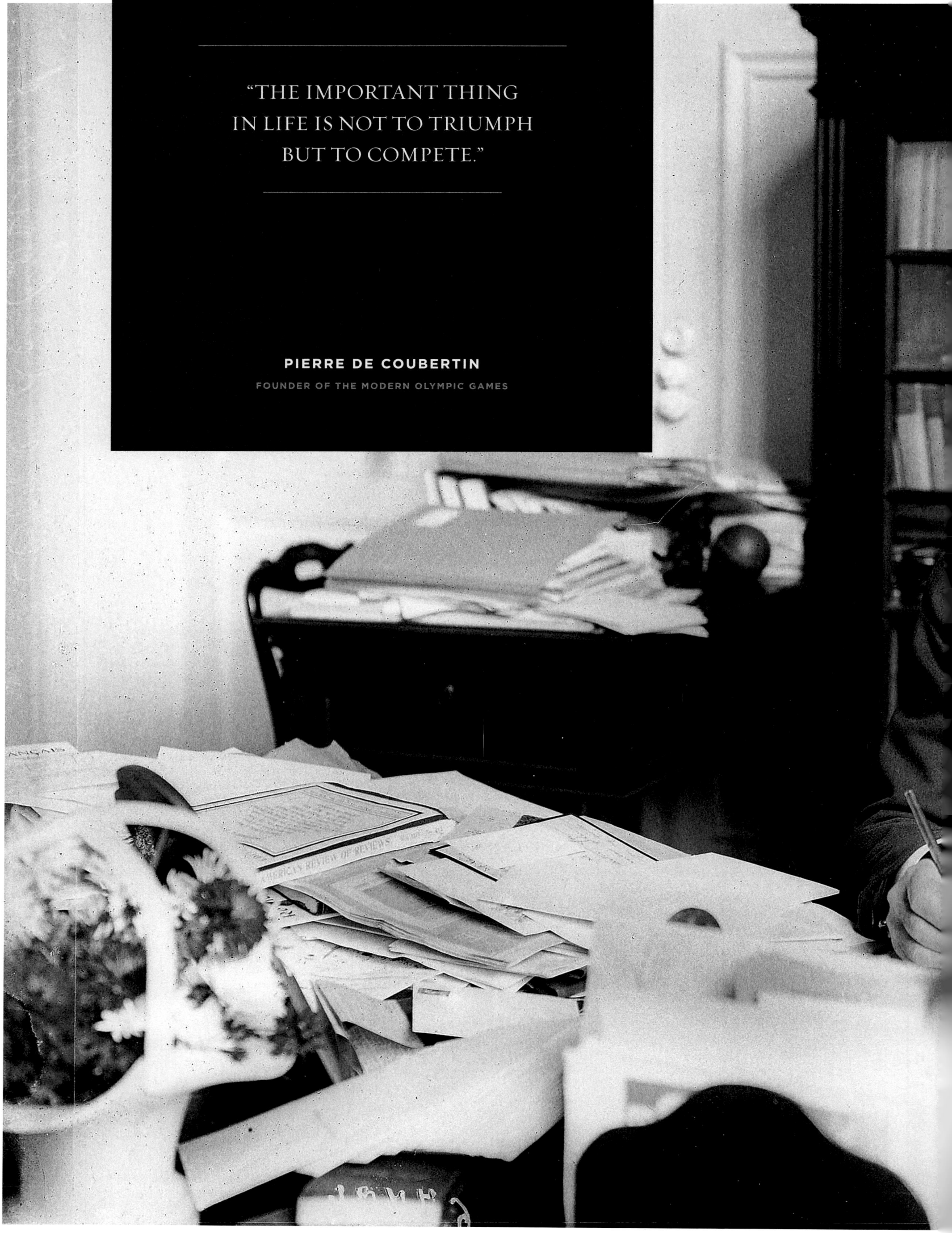

CHAPTER 02

RINGS OF FIRE

TENNIS IN THE OLYMPICS

THERE ARE THREE ELEMENTS TO THE STORY OF TENNIS'S INVOLVEMENT IN
THE OLYMPIC GAMES. THE FIRST IS HOW IT CEASED TO BE AN OLYMPIC SPORT
AFTER 1924. THE SECOND IS HOW IT GOT BACK INTO THE OLYMPIC FOLD IN 1988.
AND THE THIRD IS ABOUT THE INCREASED STATUS OF THE OLYMPICS WITHIN
THE TENNIS WORLD IN THE SIX OLYMPIADS SINCE TENNIS RETURNED.
THE ITF HAS PLAYED A CENTRAL ROLE IN ALL THREE PHASES.

THE GREAT FALLOUT

When the French baron Pierre de Coubertin organised the first modern version of the ancient Olympic Games in Athens in 1896, he included sports beyond the traditional track and field events. Tennis was an obvious candidate and provided some notable Olympic milestones. Women weren't allowed to compete in 1896, so John Peers Boland became tennis's first Olympic gold medallist. (He later became a member of the British parliament, thus epitomising de Coubertin's ideal of the scholar-athlete.) By winning the women's singles in the Paris Games of 1900, Charlotte Cooper became the first female athlete in any sport to claim a gold medal.

Tennis was played at the Olympics in St. Louis in 1904 (though there was no women's event), London in 1908 (there was an indoor event at the Queen's Club and an outdoor event at Wimbledon), Stockholm in 1912, Antwerp in 1920 and Paris in 1924 (there were no Games in 1916 because of the First World War). The tennis event at Antwerp was somewhat chaotic – there were no towels and no hot water in the locker rooms, and the accommodation was more than ten kilometres from the courts – but with Belgium having been occupied during the war, much was forgiven. And with Suzanne Lenglen winning the women's gold, the tennis event had at least put on its medal rostrum one of the global icons of sport. As a result, everyone expected better at the 1924 Olympic tennis in Paris. Alas, it was not to be.

TOP
Members of the International Olympic Committee during the 1896 IOC session at the Olympic Games in Athens. It was here that Baron Pierre de Coubertin (seated left) replaced Demetrius Vikelas of Greece (seated centre) as president.

MIDDLE
A tennis match at the 1896 Athens Olympic Games

BOTTOM LEFT
Tennis at the 1900 Paris Games features on the front cover of leading French sporting magazine *La Vie au Grand Air*

BOTTOM RIGHT
John Peers Boland, tennis's first Olympic gold medallist

By 1924 it had become common practice for the International Olympic Committee to pass the running of an event to the national governing body of that sport. Yet the French Tennis Federation was not given the right to stage the tennis, which it would presumably have held at one of the leading tennis clubs in Paris. Instead, the French Olympic Committee staged the tennis at what was described as a piece of waste ground near the main Stade Colombes Olympic stadium. The men's changing room was several hundred metres from the courts, and the women's equivalent was a wooden hut that was locked during play. Some improvements were hastily made, but the tennis players had by now come to expect better from tournaments, and morale in the tennis event plummeted.

The passage of time still doesn't make it easy to understand exactly why tennis was treated so shabbily at the Paris Games, but politics were involved, and perhaps there was some resentment within the IOC that tennis's organisational level was better than its own. The IOC was irritated that the Olympic tennis event was not the pinnacle of the sport's achievements during an Olympic year – let alone during a four-year cycle. Sixteen months earlier, the ILTF had voted to drop the term 'world championship' from references to Wimbledon, but it was still the most prestigious tournament, and the IOC floated the idea that Wimbledon should not be played during Olympic years. This was anathema to the tennis family and further strained relations with the Olympic movement.

Stade Colombes, site of the 1924 Paris Olympic Games. The tennis courts were situated a hundred yards from the stadium and consisted of three tennis courts within one spectator arena, causing noise disturbance during matches.

U. S. TENNIS PLAYERS MAY QUIT OLYMPICS

Myrick Threatens to Withdraw Team Unless "Civilized Facilities" Are Provided.

DISCONTENT IS GENERAL

"The Americans played under protest this afternoon while the French officials began to look about for things which would please the players, and a few towels and several bottles of water quickly made their appearance on the courts."

"The discontent is not confined to the Americans, but is general among most of the various nations assembled at Colombes. Jean Washer of Belgium, after his match against Francis T. Hunter yesterday under a burning sun, with no comfortable, cool spot to retire to in the rest interval, told his friends he would never play another match under such conditions."

PUBLISHED: 17 JULY 1924, *THE NEW YORK TIMES*

VALUE OF OLYMPICS DOUBTED BY FRENCH

Feeling of Uneasiness Follows in Wake of Disturbances Which Marred Games.

PROGRAM MAY BE CURTAILED

Movement is Started to Eliminate Those Sports Which Were the Source of the Most Trouble.

"There was, on Sunday, the curious failure of the crowd at the tennis finals between Miss Wills and Mlle. Vlasto and between Richards and Cochet to appreciate the fine points of the game. Again and again the losing stroke of the American was cheered, while the brilliant winning strokes by both were allowed to pass unnoticed except by a small number of those present who really appreciated the game....Patriotism took the place of an appreciation of the game and drowned the sporting sense."

"It is the memory of the incidents which arose during these events which is causing a feeling of uneasiness here, and the hopes that the games would create a feeling of friendliness among participants seem to have been sadly deceived. There already is begun a movement for the elimination for the future of those events which have this time caused trouble."

PUBLISHED: 23 JULY 1924, *THE NEW YORK TIMES*

Helen Wills (left) defeats Julie Vlasto 6–2 6–2 for the women's gold medal at the 1924 Games. Wills went on to win the doubles as well with Hazel Wightman.

The tragedy of the great fallout was that it happened after one of the most sparkling tennis events ever to grace the modern Olympics. The up-and-coming French generation led by Jean Borotra, René Lacoste and Henri Cochet turned out, alongside one of the leading Americans, Vinnie Richards, and the defending champion Louis Raymond from South Africa. The player of the decade, Bill Tilden, was missing following a somewhat fabricated dispute with the US National Lawn Tennis Association, and Lenglen was missing from the women's event through illness, but Helen Wills, Hazel Wightman and Kitty McKane were still in the lineup. And there were some great matches, even with the continuing chaos (see panel, page 35). Richards won the gold medal, despite letting Cochet come back from two sets down in the final, and Wills won the women's gold, crushing the Frenchwoman Julie 'Diddie' Vlasto, who had beaten McKane in the semis after dropping the first nine games. The last Olympic tennis event to be played for 64 years saw Richards and Marion Jessop win the mixed doubles gold over Wightman and Richard Williams, son of Duane Williams, the man credited with the idea of forming an international tennis federation.

LEFT TO RIGHT
The tennis stars of the era: Henri Cochet of France, American Vinnie Richards and Frenchman Jean Borotra at 1924 Paris. Richards won gold in both singles and doubles, Cochet silver in both, and Borotra the doubles bronze medal.

Members of the American Olympic team hanging out at the 1924 Games. Vinnie Richards is pictured top left in front of Seat 21. USA swept all five gold medals in the tennis event.

Discontent over the 1924 Paris Olympics extends to Great Britain

After the Olympics, the ILTF asked the IOC for discussions on the treatment of tennis. Such was the indignation in the tennis world about not being on equal footing to other Olympic sports that the ILTF put a number of proposals to the IOC. These included giving the ILTF at least one representative on the IOC, allowing the ILTF to cooperate in the technical and material organisation of Olympic tennis events, and rejecting the IOC's calls for Wimbledon (or any official tournament) to be suspended in Olympic years – that in turn effectively rejected the IOC's request for the Olympic tennis event to be regarded as the world championship of lawn tennis. By today's negotiating standards, it was not a peaceful overture.

The IOC was indignant too and rejected all the ILTF's demands. Having gone in so forcefully, the ILTF either had to back down and lose face, or withdraw from the Olympic fold. There was only one option, and tennis disappeared from the Olympic portfolio.

Was it a tragedy? In some ways, yes, because tennis lost its place in the biggest sporting festival in the world and not only had to fight very hard to get back in, but it was also a couple of decades before the Olympics truly returned to the tennis psyche. But some sort of rupture would have happened anyway in the following decades, especially in the 1960s, when tennis embraced professionalism well before the Olympics did.

"After a lengthy discussion, the following resolution was carried unanimously, namely: The International Lawn Tennis Federation, not having obtained satisfaction on all the requirements placed before the International Olympic Committee by the previous meeting (1926), resolves not to take part in the Olympic Games until such time as full satisfaction shall have been obtained."

FROM THE ILTF REPORT OF THE 1927 ANNUAL GENERAL MEETING

ABOVE
The decision as it appeared in the 1927 AGM report. The ILTF had sent two delegates to the 1926 Olympic Congress of Prague with a view to obtaining support of other international sports federations in persuading the IOC to give the ILTF representation on their body. Seventeen of the 18 federations present voted in favour of the ILTF's proposal, but the IOC was indignant. The following year, just prior to the 1928 Amsterdam Olympics, the ILTF held its own 'Official Championships of Holland' in The Hague a few weeks ahead of the Olympics, which attracted big names such as Jean Borotra, Francis Hunter and Cilly Aussem.

THE 1924 OLYMPICS

Although it's hard to work out why the tennis and Olympic families fell out in the 1920s, the tennis event at the Paris games of 1924 certainly testifies to a relationship that had broken down. Among the features of the tennis event were:

- Some courts were never watered despite sweltering heat, so they became dust bowls.

- Photographers wandered at will, even onto the courts during rallies.

- There were reports of young and inexperienced umpires allowing themselves to be sidetracked by critical comments or objections from the stands.

- Vendors were shouting about the refreshments they were selling right by the courts, even when the ball was in play.

The railway station of Colombes under construction for the Olympic Games.

Development of the athletes' Olympic village.

The precursor to tennis's return to the Olympics was a successful demonstration event at the 1984 Los Angeles Games. The total attendance at the Los Angeles Tennis Center was 31,186 for the six days, despite the absence of the world's top players, such as John McEnroe, Jimmy Connors, Martina Navratilova and Chris Evert Lloyd.

TENNIS'S RETURN

ILTF President and IOC member Giorgio de Stefani

It would be wrong to say that tennis didn't figure in the Olympics between 1924 and 1988. It was twice a demonstration sport: in 1968 and in 1984, as a precursor to becoming a full-medal sport in 1988. The timing of 1968 seems odd in retrospect, as that was the year that tennis went open while the Olympics remained limited to amateur athletes. Tennis therefore had effectively barred itself from returning as a full-medal sport, unless it committed to playing only amateurs, which would have meant rejecting almost all the game's big names. However, the organisers in Mexico were very keen to have tennis among the demonstration sports, and the ILTF president Giorgio de Stefani, an IOC member, was strongly in favour. So tennis featured as a demonstration sport in the 1968 Mexico City games.

BELOW

After the 1927 resolution rejecting tennis in the Olympics, the matter came under discussion a further three times. The 1931 AGM was informed that the IOC wanted to include tennis in the 1932 Los Angeles Games but it was decided that unless the IOC was going to agree to the ILTF's four proposals, no steps would be taken. In 1947 discussions of substituting the Olympic Games for either Wimbledon, Forest Hills, Paris and other Official Championships were rejected by 105 votes to 34. And in 1960, representatives of USSR and Hungary proposed the reinstatement again, with 87 votes cast in favour and 138 against. The matter was not broached again until 1964. The below extracts from the ILTF AGM minutes narrate the journey to tennis's inclusion as a demo event in the 1968 Mexico City Games.

8 JULY 1964, VIENNA

The President pointed out that as a necessary first step the Committee of Management recommend that the Federation should apply to the International Olympic Committee for confirmation of recognition, and if this was granted the I.L.T.F. should apply for lawn tennis to be included in the Olympic Games.

Mr L.A. Baker (Mexico) said that the time had come to return lawn tennis to the Olympic Games and he suggested that the I.O.C. should be asked if the game of lawn tennis could be included.

The President asked Dr. de Stefani (a member of the International Olympic Committee) to give his opinion.

Dr. de Stefani (Italy) gave a summary of the reasons why lawn tennis had not been included in the Olympic Games after 1924.

One of the delegates asked if the Olympic Committee would allow the I.L.T.F. to organise lawn tennis events in the Olympic Games.

Dr. de Stefani replied that this would be in accordance with the present policy of the I.O.C. for all sports.

Mr. D. Gossudarev (U.S.S.R.) said the introduction of lawn tennis in the Olympic Games would be a great help to the game of lawn tennis.

A vote by a show of hands was taken. 35 nations were in favour and 5 against the proposal of the Committee of Management. Six nations abstained from voting.

The motion was therefore agreed.

7 JULY 1965, MUNICH

Dr. de Stefani (Italy) reported that the International Lawn Tennis Federation was now recognised by the International Olympic Committee as one of the international federations of the Olympic standard whose sport was not included in the Official Programme.

He said that Rule 30 of the I.O.C. stated that the Programme should include at least 15 of the 2 official sports but two "additional games" could be added if agreed by the organising committee. An approach had been made to the organising committee of the XIX Olympic Games to be held in Mexico City in October 1968 to see if lawn tennis could be added as one of the additional sports, and he hoped that representatives of all federations present would do everything they could towards this end. The Mexican Lawn Tennis Federation were doing their best to help.

In reply to an enquiry, Dr. de Stefani said his personal opinion was that, if sanction was granted, a tournament should be organised to include men's singles and ladies' singles only.

6 JULY 1966, BASLE

The Committee have not only made an approach themselves, but have also encouraged all the Nations to write to the organisers of the Olympic Games in Mexico City in 1968 in the hope that lawn tennis can be included as one of the optional Games. It is understood that a decision will be taken this year and further efforts are being made to press the case for lawn tennis.

The following recommendations of the Committee of Management were approved:

Entries - A maximum of two men and two women from each country.
Events -

Men's singles	- 64 players
Men's doubles	- 16 pairs
Ladies' singles	- 32 players
Ladies' doubles	- 16 pairs
Mixed doubles	- 16 pairs

Organising Committee - The I.L.T.F. to appoint members of the Organising Committee.

12 JULY 1967, MONDORF-LES-BAINS

Mr. F. Guerrero (Mexico) reported that lawn tennis would be included as an optional sport in the Olympic Games.

This was noted with applause.

As President of the Mexican Federation, he thanked the delegates, and especially Dr. de Stefani and Mr. Reay, for their help in bringing this about. The Committee of Management had recommended that his Association should organise the event, and he assured the delegates they would do their best.

The recommendations of the Committee of Management were adopted:

Countries - That all nations affiliated to the I.L.T.F. both Full Members and Associate Members, should be eligible to send players to take part.

Events -

Men's singles	(maximum 2 players from each country)
Ladies' singles	(" 2 " " " ")
Men's doubles	(" 1 pair from each country)
Ladies' doubles	(" 1 " " " ")
Mixed doubles	(" 1 " " " ")

Number of players - That no more than three men and three women may attend from any country.

Expenses - That the travelling expenses are defrayed by the nations taking part. (It is expected that the Organising Committe will provide living accommodation and meals at very reasonable charge.)

The story of tennis's return as a full Olympic sport began in the 1970s, with two crucial figures behind it. The first was David Gray, a British journalist who in 1973 gave up his job as tennis correspondent for *The Guardian* newspaper to become the ILTF's general secretary. The other was Philippe Chatrier, who in 1977 became president of the ILTF.

Chatrier was convinced about the need to develop the sport, and one of his first actions was to set in motion the train of events that led to the establishment of the ITF's development department. He recognised that large sums of government money were given to Olympic sports, so if tennis was to grow in countries where it had barely taken root, he had to get it back in the Olympics.

Gray and Chatrier found a friend in Juan Antonio Samaranch, the Catalan who was president of the International Olympic Committee. A fan of tennis who enjoyed showing people his certificate from having been the top player at Barcelona's Real Club de Tenis in the 1920s, Samaranch could see the benefits of having the sport back in the Olympics. The overtures from the ITF happened to come at the time when Samaranch was trying to find a way of reconciling the IOC's amateur ethos with the need to have the best athletes competing at the Games.

Journalist appointed ILTF secretary

By Rex Bellamy

David Gray, tennis correspondent of *The Guardian*, has been appointed secretary of the International Lawn Tennis Federation, a post that carries with it secretarial responsibilities to the Davis Cup and Federation Cup nations. With the nominee of the Association of Tennis Professionals, he will also serve as joint secretary of the Men's International Professional Tennis Council.

Mr Gray's appointment follows the retirement of Basil Reay. Aged 47, he joined *The Guardian* in 1954 and became tennis correspondent in 1956, combining this task with political and industrial reporting. He has always been more interested than most of his colleagues in the politics of tennis and it is equally in his favour that he is among the handful of tennis writers most respected by the players.

Tennis, he said yesterday, had become part of his way of life and it should not be too difficult to exchange the role of journalist for that of administrator. Reasonably, too, he pointed out that his existing contacts would be useful to him in his new job. He said it was rather like a dramatic critic stepping on stage to play Hamlet. Changing the image, he said he saw himself as a man with an oil can, trying to keep things running smoothly.

He has a three-year contract and will take up his new duties some time in August. His first aim, he said, would be " to look at things from the other side of the fence ". But he made no secret of his interest in the presentation of tournaments, and his hope that the women's game could be brought back into the international fold, as opposed to its present concentration in America.

The power and influence of the ILTF have declined a good deal since the introduction of open competition in 1968. But they still have—and must obviously retain—an important role in acting as a joint representative body for the national associations, in supervising the amateur game, and in serving as best they can as a bridge between amateurs and professionals.

PUBLISHED: 21 MAY 1976, *THE TIMES*

"You are a candidate. You smile. You seek to influence IOC members, NOC members and representatives. You listen to the gossip. Your old friends, the journalists, hearing whispers from decision-making voices, pass on to you hopeful snippets of near-truth. After a time you begin to think that everyone must be growing bored with your obsessive pursuit of a single goal."

DAVID GRAY, *SHADES OF GRAY*

From his impressions of the Olympic Congress in Baden Baden in 1981, where the ITF was due to hear the decision on tennis's bid for reinstatement into the Olympic Games.

Chateau de Vidy, Lausanne, 1980: Monique Berlioux (IOC Director), Philippe Chatrier (ITF President), Juan Antonio Samaranch (IOC President) and Pablo Llorens (ITF Vice President)

"If we can offer an ambitious young player the possibility of representing his country in an Olympic competition, of becoming a national hero and earning a gold medal, then we can hope that he will feel that the financial sacrifices are worthwhile and that any decision to turn professional will be made with maturity of mind and a much greater knowledge of the real problems involved in a life wholly devoted to sport.

In many countries, when funds are allocated the money goes primarily to Olympic sports. If tennis were added to the programme, it would be easier for our national tennis federations to obtain money for new courts and better training programmes. That is something which is more important to our poorer federations than to those which represent developed countries."

PHILIPPE CHATRIER SPEAKING AT AN OLYMPIC PROGRAMME COMMISSION IN 1978

The packed Olympic Park Tennis Center at 1988 Seoul, the scene of tennis's return as a full-medal sport

The first breakthrough came in 1980, when the IOC agreed for tennis to be a demonstration sport in Los Angeles in 1984. Three years later it was decided that the 1984 event would be for under-21 players only, a compromise that actually helped tennis, because even without the world's top names, the event sold out every day. The under-21 players still included such big names as Pat Cash, Stefan Edberg, Jimmy Arias, Steffi Graf, Kathy Horvath and Andrea Jaeger, who were all known as the up-and-coming generation on the professional circuit. The IOC had effectively accepted professional tennis players competing at the Olympics. Edberg and Graf took the golds, albeit commemorative medals rather than full Olympic medals.

As the deal was always that a successful demonstration event in 1984 would lead to full medal status in 1988, the IOC had no hesitation in approving tennis's return after a 64-year absence. In retrospect, the Seoul tennis event in September 1988 was a fairly low-key return. The world's top two players, Ivan Lendl and Mats Wilander, who had just played out a thrilling five-set final at the US Open to determine who would top the year-end rankings, both declined to attend, and Miloslav Mecir took the gold medal, beating Tim Mayotte in the final. Both men went on to rank in the top 10 but were never frontline Grand Slam contenders. The women's event had more glamour, as Steffi Graf went to Seoul as only the third woman to win all four Grand Slam singles events in a calendar year, and thus coined the term 'Golden Slam' by taking the gold, beating Gabriela Sabatini in the final. Sabatini had carried the Argentinean flag in the opening ceremony.

TOP

The 1988 gold-medal-winner Miloslav Mecir meets 90-year-old Jean Borotra, who, along with Kitty Godfree, were special guests in Seoul as medal winners of the last Olympic tennis event in 1924

BOTTOM LEFT

Gabriela Sabatini during the final against Steffi Graf in Seoul. As well as winning the silver medal, the 18-year-old Sabatini was Argentina's flagbearer at the opening ceremony.

BOTTOM RIGHT

Steffi Graf achieves the Golden Slam in 1988 by becoming the first person to win all four Grand Slams and the Olympics in one year. She remains the only player to this day to do so.

Australia's Mark Woodforde and his doubles silver medal at the Sydney Games parade in Adelaide on 5 October 2000. As well as being so successful in their own right, the Games were a breakthrough for tennis as they marked the first-ever sold-out Olympic tennis event, and boasted the strongest-ever men's field.

BECOMING ESTABLISHED

Leander Paes carries the flag for India at the 2000 Sydney opening ceremony

For players who had grown up with tennis outside the Olympics, it took a while before the Olympic tennis event represented more than just a nice break from the regular tour. The first three or four Olympics featured players who were particularly committed to the Games, often for personal reasons. The two singles gold medallists at the 1996 Atlanta games, Andre Agassi and Lindsay Davenport, both had parents who were Olympians, as had Leander Paes, who won the men's singles bronze medal.

But the value of an Olympic medal gradually began to seep through to tennis players. By the time Todd Woodbridge and Mark Woodforde won their doubles gold in Atlanta, they had won six Grand Slam men's doubles titles, including four Wimbledons, but it was the Olympic gold that took their recognition back home in Australia to a new level. Yevgeny Kafelnikov was French Open champion in 1996 and Australian Open champion in 1999, and topped the world rankings for six weeks in 1999, yet nothing ignited the enthusiasm back home in Russia more than his gold at the 2000 Sydney games. And Justine Henin went to the 2004 games in Athens without a great deal of conviction yet was won over by the event and emerged with the gold medal, despite having been 1–5 down to Anastasia Myskina in the last set of their semifinal.

TOP

Mark Woodforde and Tod Woodbridge won gold at 1996 Atlanta, as well as at Sydney four years later

BOTTOM

Atlanta's singles gold medallists Lindsay Davenport and Andre Agassi of USA followed in their parents' footsteps as Olympians

RIGHT

Sydney's singles gold medallist Yevgeny Kafelnikov

Justine Henin's victory in Athens – Belgium's only gold medal in 2004 – reignited her love for the game: "I've never been happy like I was in Athens, just to be on the court. That was probably the key to my success. Hopefully I enjoy my victories more from now on."

TOP LEFT

At a record-breaking London 2012, the Williams sisters became the first players in history to win four Olympic gold medals, with Serena achieving the Golden Slam on the way.

TOP RIGHT

After four failed Grand Slam title attempts, Great Britain's Andy Murray defeats Roger Federer for Olympic gold. Both the men's and women's singles finals were the most-requested live streams on BBC Sport's Olympic website.

BOTTOM

Crowds exceeded 206,000 for the nine-day event, which saw Wimbledon bathed in colour for the first time

The Olympic tennis event arguably reached its peak in 2012, when it was staged at Wimbledon. The IOC president Jacques Rogge had said at the London Games' opening ceremony that the Olympics were 'coming home'. That certainly seemed to apply to tennis, which was staged at Wimbledon in 1908, albeit at Worple Road rather than the Church Road grounds used since 1922. Not only was the Olympic tennis event played at the sport's most prestigious venue, but the singles medal rostrums boasted an aggregate of 37 Grand Slam singles titles, testifying to the quality of the medallists. And the Olympic crowd on Centre Court, which had differed in character from the traditional Wimbledon Centre Court fans, enjoyed the spectacle of a British gold medal, as Andy Murray rode the crest of the wave of an astonishing performance by his country's athletes to crush Roger Federer in the final. Like Elena Dementieva in Beijing four years earlier, Murray had found that embracing the team ethic inherent in the Olympics had enabled him to achieve a gold medal while Grand Slam titles had persistently evaded him.

BRONZE MORE ECSTATIC THAN SILVER

The nature of tennis as a one-against-one sport gives rise to a strange syndrome at Olympic medal ceremonies: the winner of the bronze medal almost always looks happier than the winner of the silver. That's because the ceremony takes place not long after the silver medallist has lost to the gold medallist, whereas – according to the rule since 1996 – the bronze medallist must win a play-off so stands on the podium fresh from a victory. The bronze play-off is also normally played the day before the gold/silver match, so the medallist has an extra day for the achievement to sink in.

- Leander Paes wept tears of joy on the podium in Atlanta, having become the first citizen of India in 44 years to win an Olympic medal in an individual sport. He had lost his semifinal to Andre Agassi, and then lost the first set of the play-off to Fernando Meligeni but fought back to beat the Brazilian 3–6 6–2 6–4 to claim the bronze. For Paes, the joy was not just about the success; it was because both his parents were Olympians (his mother in basketball, his father in hockey), and also because his sporting hero, Muhammad Ali, had lit the Olympic flame at the opening ceremony.

- Look at photos of the men's singles rostrum from Sydney 2000 and you'd think Arnaud di Pasquale had won the gold. He had in fact won the bronze, having beaten a chronically nervous 19-year-old Roger Federer in the bronze-medal play-off. The ceremony took place shortly after a five-set final in which Tommy Haas had twice come back from a set down but ultimately lost to Yevgeny Kafelnikov. The Russian looked satisfied but far from ecstatic, the German was downcast and exhausted, while the Frenchman looked like the cat who'd got the cream.

- In Athens 2004 Mario Ancic and Ivan Ljubicic won the bronze medal in the men's doubles, beating Leander Paes and Mahesh Bhupathi 16–14 in the third set of a four-hour match that finished after one o'clock in the morning in front of 300 die-hard Croatian fans. The two players jumped into each other's arms and threw their shirts to the crowd. On the rostrum, they took their bronze medals alongside the glum-looking silver winners, Nicolas Kiefer and Rainer Schuettler, who had squandered four match points in their defeat to the gold-medal winners, Fernando Gonzalez and Nicolas Massu.

Ivan Ljubicic and Mario Ancic

"This bronze, it shines like a gold" **NOVAK DJOKOVIC, 2008 BEIJING**

Germans Michael Stich and Boris Becker put their differences aside to win the gold medal at 1992 Barcelona.

LEFT Roger Federer's doubles gold-medal win with Stanislas Wawrinka in Beijing made up for his disappointing year **RIGHT** London 2012 celebrated the return of mixed doubles after an 88-year absence and the event was won by Belarusians Max Mirnyi and Victoria Azarenka.

Olympic doubles is arguably the highest-quality doubles tournament in today's world of tennis. Such is the allure of a medal, of any colour, that the event brings out many of the top singles players. Boris Becker and Michael Stich – rivals for German sporting affections and two very different characters – put their differences behind them for the sake of a gold medal in doubles at the 1992 Barcelona games. Roger Federer's gold medal with Stanislas Wawrinka at the 2008 games in Beijing rescued a year that, by his standards, had been very disappointing and proved the springboard for him to win the US Open a few weeks later. Even if a player has an injury niggle, he or she may prioritise the doubles over the singles for a better chance at a medal.

Tennis's links with the ITF were enhanced when the Federation gave its top honour, the Philippe Chatrier Award, to Juan Antonio Samaranch in 2000. The Spaniard was known as an authoritative figure but his willingness to engage with the tennis world to get tennis back into the fold was crucial to the sport's reinstatement (as was his support for Davis Cup). Samaranch had changed the IOC from a financially-troubled institution in 1980 to an organisation that now contributes significant revenue to each of its constituencies. And from that has flowed many benefits, most notably the Olympic funds that have gone to promoting tennis in central and eastern Europe, but also in countries right around the world.

Perhaps one of the best postscripts to tennis's return to the Olympics came in 2006 when Francesco Ricci Bitti became the first ITF president to be elected to the IOC following the reform of 2000, which defined membership categories to national Olympic Committee presidents, international federation presidents and athletes, rather than individual IOC memberships like those of Ricci Bitti's predecessors Philippe Chatrier and Giorgio de Stefani.

Tennis's reinstatement as an Olympic sport was completed in 2012, when the Olympic tennis event returned to Wimbledon and mixed doubles was reinstated after an 88-year absence. Fittingly, the first modern-day champions were Victoria Azarenka and Max Mirnyi from Belarus, two players whose careers have profited from the development money that stemmed from tennis's return to the Olympic fold.

WAS THIS THE SLOWEST COURT EVER?

Since its return to the Olympics in 1988, tennis has been played on a medium-paced hard court with just two exceptions: Barcelona 1992 and London 2012. The clay of the Vall d'Hebron tennis centre in Barcelona was so slow that many wonder whether it was the slowest court ever used for a major tournament.

- Boris Becker, then ranked fifth in the world, beat Christian Ruud of Norway in a four-hour, 50-minute first-round match that featured two tiebreaks in the punishing Catalan sun; he was then beaten by Fabrice Santoro in the next round.

- Goran Ivanisevic certainly earned his silver medal. He won four successive five-set matches, beating Bernado Mota, Paul Haarhuis, Jakob Hlasek and – in the longest one – Fabrice Santoro, against whom Ivanisevic lost the first two sets on tiebreaks before winning the decider 8–6.

- Mary Joe Fernandez needed medical treatment for dehydration after beating Patricia Hy of Canada 12–10 in the final set of a match that saw Fernandez save four match points.

- The men's gold-medal match took five hours and three minutes to complete, Marc Rosset beating Jordi Arrese 8–6 in the fifth after the Spaniard recovered from being two sets down. Rosset had beaten another Spaniard, Emilio Sanchez, in a four-hour quarterfinal, which meant he played for nine hours against Spaniards en route to the gold medal.

ITF President Francesco Ricci Bitti was elected to the International Olympic Committee in 2006.

"'ALL THE WORLD'S A STAGE
AND ALL THE MEN AND WOMEN
MERELY PLAYERS'"

SIR JOHN SMYTH
TENNIS AUTHOR

CHAPTER 03

A MODERN PROFESSIONAL SPORT

THE PROFESSIONALISATION OF TENNIS

IF THERE WAS ONE ISSUE THAT TOOK THE INTERNATIONAL LAWN TENNIS FEDERATION FROM A GLOBAL UMBRELLA ORGANISATION WHOSE MAIN JOB WAS TO LOOK AFTER THE INTERESTS OF ITS NATIONAL ASSOCIATIONS, TO AN ACTIVE PARTY IN THE BURGEONING GLOBAL TENNIS SCENE, IT WAS THE ISSUE OF PROFESSIONALISATION. THE ORIGINAL RULES OF TENNIS HAD MADE IT CLEAR THAT TOP-LEVEL TENNIS WAS FOR AMATEURS, SO THE ADVANCE OF THE CAREER TENNIS PLAYER CHALLENGED THE FUNDAMENTAL ETHOS OF THE GAME, AND BY EXTENSION THE ROLE OF NATIONAL ASSOCIATIONS. ALTHOUGH THE ISSUE WAS RESOLVED WHEN TENNIS WENT 'OPEN' IN 1968, THAT MOVE TRIGGERED A WHOLE RANGE OF COMMERCIAL RIPPLES THAT CHANGED THE FABRIC OF TENNIS AND THE ROLE OF THE HARD-WORKING AND DEVOTED PEOPLE WHO HAD RUN THE SPORT UP TO THEN. THE IMPACT CAN STILL BE FELT TODAY.

'SHAMATEURISM'

The success of tennis in the 1920s gave birth to an issue that was to dog the sport for the next 40 years. Some players who had done very well after investing lots of time and money into perfecting their tennis wanted to earn an income from their playing ability. But tennis was a strictly amateur game, so the only way they could do this was to quit the recognised tennis circuit and play exhibition matches in makeshift venues.

In 1926 the first professional tour began, ushering in an era of split amateur and professional circuits that made it very difficult, if not impossible, to determine the greatest players of all time. Once Bill Tilden had turned professional in 1930, the four major championships (later the Grand Slam tournaments) could no longer claim to be contests involving the greatest tennis players on the planet.

Amateur players had to have jobs alongside tennis. Some were able to use their tennis in 'safe' ways, such as those who ran sports shops or worked for tennis equipment and apparel companies. But other activities were more controversial, such as Bill Tilden's journalism. He wanted to write articles from Wimbledon in the years when he was a competitor, and in 1928 the US Lawn Tennis Association threatened to ban him for allegedly overstepping the boundary between amateur and professional status.

HOPE THAT TILDEN WILL PLAY FADES

Star Refuses to Join Davis Cup Team Unless He Is Permitted to Report Matches.

NO CONCESSION, SAYS WEAR

Declares Amateurism Will Not Be Sacrificed and Player-Writer Rule Will Not Be Waived.

By ALLISON DANZIG.

The hope that William Tilden would be a member of the United States Davis Cup team this year faded considerably yesterday with the disclosure that the American champion has refused to play unless he can wield his pen along with his racquet during the international matches.

Joseph W. Wear, chairman of the Davis Cup committee, informed THE NEW YORK TIMES by telephone from Philadelphia last night that Tilden has issued the ultimatum to Captain Fitz-Eugene Dixon in Paris that the United States Lawn Tennis Association would have to grant him the right to write or his services would not be available. Mr. Wear was in communication with Captain Dixon both by cable and telephone.

PUBLISHED: 9 JULY 1930, *THE NEW YORK TIMES*

As both a journalist and tennis player, American Bill Tilden was one of the first to fall foul of the professional versus amateur controversy. The issue reached a head in 1930, when Tilden refused to compete on the Davis Cup team unless the USLTA waived the restriction to allow him to report on the matches. By the end of 1930, Tilden had turned pro.

Suzanne Lenglen is greeted by promoter Charles C. Pyle (centre) and American footballer "Red" Grange on arrival in New York for her professional tour of the United States. Lenglen was the first woman to turn pro, signing up with Pyle in 1926 for a reported $50,000.

In 1933, the ILTF set up a committee to 'revise the amateur definition'. Extracts from the minutes of the meeting at which the committee reported on its findings give an insight into the attitudes of the time. The committee clearly recognised the growing problem that was to become known as 'shamateurism', but at no stage in the seven-page report did it attempt to understand the reasons why tournament promoters and organisers felt the need to offer attractive expenses to amateurs, thereby creating shamateurism. There was an inherent assumption that only those players willing to decline offers to turn professional and then reject anything more than the most basic of expenses were worthy of representation.

The Committee is unanimous in believing that the question of amateurism is of capital importance to the future of Lawn Tennis and if the bad features of sham amateurism are allowed to spread, our game will sink to a level from which it will be very difficult to raise it up again.

Lawn Tennis is not a sport for professionals. Let it be well understood that when we speak of professionals, we do not refer to the teachers, whose value is recognised by everybody, but to the players who play each other for money and promote tours from which the element of sport is absent; these tours (those conducted by Tilden for instance) are devoid of sporting interest, because the value of the results is nil. If these contests had any attraction or novelty when they began, the public are taking less and less interest in them and with good reason.

The young persons of all countries who go in for Lawn Tennis should be drawn from the pick of the industrious section of the community, from whatever class they may come and nothing should be done to encourage a state of professionalism which can be tolerated in some sports, but not in ours. Our young people should also be protected against the sham amateurism which has developed since the War to such a disquieting extent.

The Committee's object is to affirm the desire of the I.L.T.F. to take action against those so-called amateurs who manage to live at someone else's expense from January 1st to December 31st and who go around the world without putting their hands in their pockets.

Some persons may object that our minds are far away from present-day requirements, that we must progress with the times and not worry about prejudices which are no longer in the fashion. On the contrary we are convinced that the time has come when we must make our choice, either "laisser-faire" and shut our eyes to the deplorable and demoralising practices which actually exist, or take vigorous action and lead Lawn Tennis back to the fold of pure amateurism. There is the dilemma. There is no half-way house.

After the Second World War, a pattern emerged whereby young players would burst onto the scene, win a handful of Grand Slam tournaments, and then accept an offer to join Jack Kramer's professional tour. Those who chose to continue playing the Grand Slams, Davis Cup and other official tournaments had to remain amateur, though from the 1950s it became clear that many amateurs were being given under-the-table payments by tournaments and their national associations to secure their availability for the sport's most prestigious honours. This made a sham out of the idea of players being amateur, and the practice became known as 'shamateurism'. It was an open secret, and by the 1960s some players were becoming increasingly cavalier in revealing how much they were really paid (see panel, opposite).

Until 1968, players who had not turned professional were dependent on their national associations for the ability to play, and some associations put restrictions on players' movements. For example, a number of southern-hemisphere countries wanted their top home players to play in a tournament season that ran from about October to March. Yet those players were often asked to play exhibition matches and special events that would finance their overseas trips to the likes of Roland Garros, Wimbledon and Forest Hills. With air travel less advanced than it is today, nipping home to play in an important home tournament was just not an option. As a result, the US tennis authorities banned their players from playing outside the USA from the end of Wimbledon until after Forest Hills, and the Australian authorities insisted their

players remain home from December until the end of March. New Zealand and South Africa had similar rules.

Matters in Australia reached a head in 1964, when the leading male players felt the end-of-March restriction was too harsh. They formed a players' association that faced off against the Lawn Tennis Association of Australia, led by an 'old school' president, Norman Strange. Faced with the prospect of not having a Davis Cup team, the Australian captain, Harry Hopman, persuaded Roy Emerson and Fred Stolle to make peace with Strange, but was content to let Ken Fletcher, Marty Mulligan and Bob Hewitt break their ties. Fletcher never played Davis Cup again, while Mulligan played for Italy and Hewitt played for South Africa, culminating in a Davis Cup winner's medal in 1974.

THE REALITY OF 'SHAMATEURISM'

The ludicrous situation in which tennis found itself in the mid-1960s was summed up by Derek Penman, the chairman of the British LTA, in his speech to the LTA Council on 14 December 1967:

'We know the so-called amateur players bargain for payments grossly in excess of what they are entitled to but without which they cannot live. We know that tournament committees connive at this, else there would be no players at their tournaments. We feel we owe it not only to ourselves but to our players to release them from this humiliating and hypocritical situation, and that the players should be able to earn openly and honestly the reward their skill entitles them.'

Once Wimbledon had announced it would be allowing professionals, the *Sunday Times* newspaper of London printed a list of what the amateur players had been earning. Players like Mike Sangster, Owen Davidson and Torben Ulrich were reported to be earning between $300 and $400 a week; John Newcombe, Tony Roche and Rafael Osuna were said to be on $700 a week; and Manolo Santana was supposedly on $1,000 a week. The figures were probably on the low side – Santana later admitted he was on $1,500 a week.

Bobby Riggs and Jack Kramer's showdown at Madison Square Garden in 1947 kickstarted a pro tour that Kramer would eventually take over in 1952

"I was a tennis slave.... The contract makes the player the property of the national association. If I go through a rugged tournament such as Wimbledon and say afterwards I am tired and would like a rest, the association says, no, you have commitments to play here and there."

LEW HOAD REFLECTING ON HIS AMATEUR EXPERIENCE AFTER TURNING PRO IN 1957

In his 1948 book *My Story*, Bill Tilden wrote, 'If tennis is to realise its full potential, it must find a solution to the professional/amateur problem which has plagued it for so many years. The sporting public wants to see the best. It doesn't give a hoot whether that best is amateur or professional.' Indeed a year earlier, the All India Lawn Tennis Association had proposed abolishing the distinction between amateurs and professionals at the ILTF's annual meeting in 1947, yet the idea was rejected unanimously. In 1953 the great Australian player and Davis Cup captain Norman Brookes spoke out in favour of open tennis.

By 1960 the momentum seemed unstoppable. There were so many quality players on the professional circuit – Frank Sedgman, Ken McGregor, Pancho Gonzalez, Lew Hoad, Ken Rosewall, Tony Trabert, Alex Olmedo, Pancho Segura and others – that the winners of Wimbledon and the other major titles were clearly not the best in the world, merely the best amateurs. So another motion was put to the 1960 ILTF general meeting suggesting that tennis be made open so prize money could be offered at official tournaments and the professionals would be allowed back. It needed a two-thirds majority and fell five votes short in somewhat farcical circumstances (see panel, below). If that set back the cause, it was further set back when, in early 1962, the US Lawn Tennis Association voted to oppose the principle of open tennis.

EIGHT YEARS TOO EARLY

Tennis could – some say should – have gone open in 1960. A motion was put to the ILTF's general meeting in Paris that tennis should go open, but it was defeated by five votes. Afterwards it emerged that two of the delegates were absent because they were arranging that evening's entertainment on riverboats; another delegate was in the toilet; while another fell asleep and didn't vote. Whether the necessary two-thirds majority could have been assembled if all delegates had been present is not absolutely clear, but it does paint a picture of a sport whose well-meaning lay organisers were at times blissfully unaware of the changing reality of top-level tennis.

The proposal of the Special Committee is as follows:-

That, as an experiment, the eight "Official Lawn Tennis Championships" recognised by the I.L.T.F. be allowed, if so desired by the National Association concerned, to be open to all players, amateur and professional, for the calendar year 1961. Also that the Committee of Management be authorised to sanction up to a maximum of a further five "open" tournaments during that year provided application is made before 1st November 1960.

Australia dominated Davis Cup in the 1950s and 60s, but throughout that winning run they regularly lost some of their best players to the professional tours, like Ken Rosewall and Rod Laver. When open tennis arrived, Tony Roche and John Newcombe (pictured far left) also turned pro, leaving the Australia team very weak. It wasn't until professionals were admitted to Davis Cup in 1973 that Australia was able to recapture the Cup, with its old-time greats Laver, Newcombe, Rosewall and Mal Anderson on board.

Once he had turned pro in 1949, American Pancho Gonzalez was ineligible to compete at the Grand Slams, despite being arguably the greatest player of his time.

Tokyo, 27 September 1954: a welcome fit for heroes by the residents of Tokyo as Jack Kramer arrives with his troupe of professional tennis players to tour Japan

Rod Laver wins the 1967 Wimbledon World Professional Lawn Tennis Championships, a provocative response by the All England Club to the amateur-professional debacle. Aimed to 'show the world the game of lawn tennis at its finest', the tournament revitalised public interest in tennis and instigated the sport becoming open.

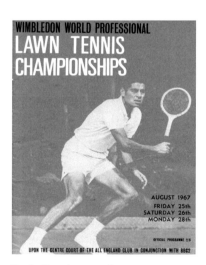

Pancho Gonzalez graces the programme cover for the 1967 Wimbledon pro tournament

It was Wimbledon that finally broke the deadlock. In 1966 Wimbledon's chairman, Herman David, told Brian Cowgill, the BBC Television executive he dealt with over broadcast rights, that he was sick of having 'a second-class champion'. The result was Wimbledon provocatively staging an eight-man professional tournament in August 1967, held in cooperation with the BBC2 channel that was experimenting with colour TV. The tournament was a great success. The eight players were Buchholz, Gimeno, Gonzalez, Hoad, Laver, Rosewall, Sedgman and Segura, and the event culminated in Laver beating Rosewall in a high-quality final.

Two other parallel events took place in 1967 that brought open tennis closer to reality. An emerging professional promoter, World Championship Tennis (WCT), signed up eight top players who became known as 'the handsome eight' (Barthes, Buchholz, Drysdale, Newcombe, Pilic, Ralston, Roche and Taylor). WCT was owned by a Texan oil magnate, Lamar Hunt, whose executive director, Bob Briner, has been quoted as saying, 'We had in one fell swoop taken all the stars out of the game. If anyone was ever going to see them again at Wimbledon and Forest Hills, the ITF had to make an accommodation.' And a second professional promoter, the National Tennis League Group, also announced it had a number of top players signed up. The group was run by entrepreneur George McCall, and the players it had signed were largely from the remnants of the pro tour that Kramer had run since the late 1940s but relinquished control of in the early 1960s (Gimeno, Gonzalez, Hoad, Laver, Olmedo, Rosewall and Segura, plus new signings Emerson and Stolle).

'The Handsome Eight' (clockwise from top left): Pierre Barthes of France, John Newcombe of Australia, Cliff Drysdale of South Africa, Butch Buchholz of USA, Niki Pilic of Yugoslavia, Dennis Ralston of USA, Tony Roche of Australia, and Roger Taylor of Great Britain

Texan billionaire Lamar Hunt (pictured in red) was approached in the 1960s by promoter Dave Dixon to join a new pro tennis venture that became World Championship Tennis. The game's top amateurs in theory were only earning expenses; Hunt was offering contracts upwards $55,000 a year.

The success of Wimbledon's event, and the fact that the players it had featured were all signed up with professional promoters, persuaded the British Lawn Tennis Association (LTA) to back Wimbledon, and in December 1967 the LTA's council voted to abolish the amateur/professional distinction as of April 1968. Although the British said they were willing to 'go it alone' if necessary, the LTA sent two senior board members, Derek Penman and Derek Hardwick (later an ILTF president), on a tour to convince other associations around the world of the need to support open tennis.

In hindsight, it's easy to believe the world was ready for an end to the shamateur era in 1968, and once Wimbledon had made the first move, everything would fall into place. But there was still a lot of support for the amateur game, and the passage from Wimbledon's professional tournament in August 1967 to the first open tournament in April 1968 was a bumpy one.

The LTA's Derek Hardwick (left) and Derek Penman (right), who canvassed the rest of the world on the principle of open tennis, to the disapproval of the ILTF

'Bend or break' tennis ultimatum

By REX BELLAMY,
Tennis Correspondent

"If you won't bend, we'll break you." This, in effect, was the warning issued to the International Lawn Tennis Federation at the weekend by the United States L.T.A. Australia, which on Tuesday said it would follow the I.L.T.F. line, is now reported to be making contingency plans for a breakaway international organization.

Like Britain, the Americans want the I.L.T.F. to grant every country self-determination in two spheres—first, the status (amateur or otherwise) of their own players, and second, the promotion of tournaments open to all. Unlike Britain, America intends to retain a class of players who are "amateur" by definition.

The I.L.T.F. is to meet in Paris on March 23 or 30. Unless it changes its rules and clarifies exactly what it means by the word "amateur", the United States association within 20 days of the Paris meeting will empower their president, Mr. Robert Kelleher, to resign.

This is the most significant move since Britain decided, last December, to hold open tournaments (a view widely approved) and abolish the distinction between amateurs and professionals (a step far in advance of world opinion, though many defended Britain's right to take it). It is obvious that the I.L.T.F. must either bend or break.

If the I.L.T.F. fails to achieve a compromise later in the month, it will no longer be the effective governing body of international tennis.

At the annual meeting of the I.L.T.F. last July, Britain proposed that the international body should sanction experimental open tournaments for two years. The proposal was seconded by Australia and supported by the United States, but it was defeated by 139 votes to 83.

The I.L.T.F. consists of 65 nations wielding 289 votes. A change of rule (which is what the rebels and their sympathizers demand) requires a two-thirds majority of the votes cast. Abstentions mean that there can be no firm estimate of the votes required. But with about 150 votes already assured, sanction for open tournaments seems certain. There is no chance of the I.L.T.F. abolishing the distinction between amateurs and professionals—but unless it concedes self-determination on this issue, they seem likely to forfeit their authority.

Australia, France, Great Britain, and the United States have 12 votes each and are traditionally the great powers of the game. The only difference between Australia's position and that of Britain and America is that the Australians, for the time being, have committed themselves to toeing whatever line the I.L.T.F. selects.

M. Roger Cirotteau, the French L.T.F. president, forecast yesterday that they would adopt a policy similar to Australia's—supporting open tournaments, but against rebellion.

Mr. Bill Edwards, the Australian L.T.A. president, said after the American decision that if the I.L.T.F. rejected the open tennis move, "Australia could easily have another meeting and decide to follow the United States in a breakaway".

Hardly noticed in the furore was west Germany's decision, made on Saturday, to support open tournaments.

U.S. takes tough line, page 11.

PUBLISHED: 5 FEBRUARY 1968, *THE TIMES*

US takes tough line in favour of open tennis

From BUD COLLINS*—Coronado, California, Feb. 4

Bob Kelleher will come out of the West riding "shotgun" in the good old Gary Cooper style. If the International Lawn Tennis Federation will not budge from its hypocritical ways the gun will go off and America will join hands with Britain—and any other country that cares to come along—in making open tennis a reality and establishing a new, more rational league of tennis playing nations.

Robert J. Kelleher, Harvard-trained Los Angeles lawyer and president of the United States Lawn Tennis Association, finds himself armed with an historic "shotgun" resolution as he approaches the extraordinary I.L.T.F. meeting on March 30, probably in Paris. This was the most important piece of legislation passed at the tradition-ending U.S.L.T.A. convention.

The forceful resolution means—although not quite saying it—that Americans will play at Wimbledon, the United States will have open events of its own, and that the U.S.L.T.A. will cut its ties with the I.L.T.F. unless that stodgy, antiquated body reforms and permits self-determination by all nations on the matters of open events and interpretation of amateurism.

Open-minded

The *fin de siècle* setting seemed hardly in keeping for this iconoclastic performance. The U.S.L.T.A. is an organization with a conservative, often reactionary, past whose status quo preservers have been labelled "backward old goats" by President Kelleher. Yet from this Victorian Hotel del Coronado came the unmistakable cry of the 20th century and a demand for ...

Robert Kelleher

dramatic. A white-haired man of 68, he has gone blind since completing his two-year term a year ago. His disappointment in the open-minded conduct of his successor, Kelleher, showed in his remarks.

But the delegates of the 17 sections were as certain in their minds as the men of the British L.T.A. had been in deciding that 1968 must be the year of standing up and acting.

Before Tressel spoke, vice-president Alistair Martin of New York, who is to become president in 1969, exhorted the delegates: "We must develop a more responsive I.L.T.F.: we must legalize open tennis and thus see that shamateurism withers. The tennis world watches us and holds its breath."

The response was prolonged applause. Shortly the delegates gave ...

the same. We will no longer tolerate any other course.'"

The lone dissenter was the middle states (Philadelphia area) association represented by Richard Sorlien who believes that "home rule on opens will produce anarchy and chaos. It is a delusion to believe that opens will help the game. The interest in amateur fixtures will go down."

The word amateur is still cherished by the U.S.L.T.A., even though officials realize they may have to sanction higher payments to amateurs in the interest of honesty. "We want practical and forcible amateur rules ", Kelleher says. "The current ones (28 dollars a day maximum) are not realistic and we realize they are abused."

Little thought was given to emulation of Britain in abolishing distinction between amateurs and professionals and calling everybody just plain players. A resolution to that effect was unanimously voted down. Nor was there an outright statement that Americans would enter Wimbledon come what may. A resolution of that nature was replaced by the "shotgun" resolution.

Pay off

One of its sponsors, Harry Kirsch, of Boston, president of the New England Association, said: "It simply wasn't strong enough to state that we would send our players to Wimbledon. That took care of only one tournament and didn't really attack the problem. We want to stay within the legal framework of the I.L.T.F. if possible.

"We want to change the I.L.T.F. to a reasonable position and so we ...

PUBLISHED: 5 FEBRUARY 1968, *THE TIMES*

Vice-president Alistair Martin of New York, who is to become president [of the USLTA] in 1969, exhorted the delegates: 'We must develop a more responsive I.L.T.F.; we must legalize open tennis and thus see that shamateurism withers. The tennis world watches us and holds its breath'.

Kelleher promises, 'this isn't an empty threat nor is it merely a vote saying we favour opens, such as the vote we took prior to the 1967 I.L.T.F. meeting, when open tennis was again disapproved. Our resolution directs me to say to the I.L.T.F.: you have failed to promulgate or enforce realistic and practical amateur rules. Therefore the time has come to take away from the I.L.T.F. all but small responsibilities. The U.S.L.T.A. wishes to make its own amateur rules and to decide for itself the question of opens and for others to be able to do the same. We will no longer tolerate any other course'.

In February 1968 the USLTA voted for open tennis. It wasn't quite the clear-cut backing its forward-thinking president, Bob Kelleher, had wanted, but it was a resolution that allowed him to say to the ILTF that the Federation had failed to enforce realistic and practical amateur rules, and that unless the ILTF embraced the professionals, the USLTA would leave. The fact that the USA was backing Great Britain – plus hints of support from Sweden and a few other nations – changed the tone of two ILTF meetings held in Paris in February and March 1968. The ILTF effectively knew it could not hold itself together without acceding to open tennis, but it was also aware of the intense support for the amateur game.

The ILTF therefore looked for a compromise and found one that allowed all sides to save face, albeit at the cost of several years of subsequent grief. Players were divided into three categories: 'authorised player', 'contract professional' and 'amateur'. All three could compete in professional tournaments, but amateurs could not accept prize money, while authorised players could pocket prize money at certain designated tournaments, but they would still remain under the control of their national association rather than the promoter of a professional tour. The British hated the categorisation, but they backed down in the interests of a solution that allowed for open tennis without the breakup of the ILTF, and in March 1968 the sport effectively went open.

The first open tournament was held at Bournemouth in Great Britain in April 1968, and the first open Grand Slam event was the 1968 Roland Garros, which could now be termed the French Open (although that is an English-language shorthand – the tournament is still officially 'Les Internationaux de France', literally 'the French internationals'). Ken Rosewall won both events. Mark Cox, the British left-hander, was the first amateur to beat a professional when he defeated Pancho Gonzalez in the second round at Bournemouth.

Later in the year, Arthur Ashe became the first amateur to win a Grand Slam tournament with professionals competing when he beat Tom Okker in the US Open final, but because of that distinction, Okker walked away with $14,000 in prize money while Ashe received just enough to cover expenses (Okker was an authorised player under the Dutch tennis association, while Ashe had chosen to stay amateur so he could continue to play Davis Cup, from which all players who took payments were excluded until 1973).

Ken Rosewall en route to winning the title at the 1968 British Hardcourt Championships in Bournemouth, Great Britain, which was the first open tournament and offered total prize money of £5,490

Arthur Ashe wins the 1968 US Open and earns the kudos of becoming the first amateur to win an open Grand Slam tournament. Runner-up Tom Okker walks away with $14,000 in prize money.

"We knew open tennis was going to be a success, but we didn't know it was going to be a bonanza."

DEREK HARDWICK AFTER ROSEWALL BEAT LAVER IN THE FINAL AT 1968 BOURNEMOUTH

Rod Laver wins the third of his four Grand Slam titles in 1969 that would end up crowning him the only man in history to complete a true Grand Slam (in a calendar year and with everyone eligible to compete). "I didn't find out who were the best players until I turned pro and had my brains beaten out for six months."

In nearly all respects, April 1968 is the start of tennis's modern era. That doesn't mean everything that happened beforehand was unimportant, but it's hard to know how good a player really was before 1968. Would Don Budge have achieved the Grand Slam in 1938 if Fred Perry and Ellsworth Vines had been in the draws? Would Rod Laver have done the same in 1962 if Hoad, Rosewall, Trabert, Gonzalez and company were in the draws? We will never know, but Laver remains the only man to have completed a calendar-year Grand Slam with everyone eligible to compete in all four majors (1969).

And it could all have come much earlier. 'The terrible thing', wrote Jack Kramer in 1979 in *The Game*, 'is that professional tennis should have taken over in the 1930s. There was some genuine agitation for an open game amongst the tennis federations as early as 1930 – had the USLTA been on the ball and worked for open tennis, it might well have become a reality 50 years ago'.

VISIONARIES ON THE RIVE GAUCHE

In light of what happened in the years after 1968, it's interesting to note that in 1960, a young French visionary, Philippe Chatrier, invited Jack Kramer and Jean Borotra to dinner in Paris. At the time, Kramer was still running his professional tour, but his interest in it was waning, while Borotra was the de facto leader of French tennis. Chatrier later told the tennis journalist and historian Richard Evans, 'I wanted to persuade Jean to have Jack come back into the official game and organise a professional department of the ILTF'. The defeat of the 1960 motion to authorise open tennis meant Chatrier's idea was a nonstarter, but it shows that the ideas for professionalising the sport were there long before they were politically acceptable.

"Going open lent respectability to the sport. Now when asked what a person did for a living he or she could say, 'I'm a professional tennis player.' Suddenly it was as valid as being a lawyer or doctor."

DONALD DELL, ADMINISTRATOR, ENTREPRENEUR AND AGENT

A BRAVE NEW WORLD OF PROFESSIONAL POTENTIAL

In theory, the end of the split amateur and professional circuits should have liberated the sport, and in many ways it did. But in practice, it created a new set of problems, not just related to the authorised player compromise. The players may have turned professional, but it took a while for the administration of tennis to do the same.

One of the first outward signs of the brave new world was the 'Grand Prix' circuit of men's tournaments. This was largely the brainchild of Jack Kramer, although he had been working so closely with Donald Dell and Philippe Chatrier that it was really a product of all three. The Grand Prix was based on the idea of a league table or standings, in which every win would bring a player a certain number of points. The top eight would qualify for the year-ending 'Masters', and the top 30 would pick up various bonus payments. This system was put into action in 1970, with Stan Smith winning the first Masters in Tokyo. Its modern-day equivalents are the ATP World Tour Finals for the men and the WTA Championships for the women.

Although it had been Kramer's idea, the Grand Prix was run in association with the ILTF, something that could not be said for the other high-profile professional tours, Lamar Hunt's World Championship Tennis and George McCall's National Tennis League Group (NTL was subsumed into WCT in 1970–71). Hunt's chief administrator, Mike Davies, the former British player who had turned professional in the mid-1960s, signed up more and more top players for the WCT tour, which effectively creamed off most of the big names from the Grand Prix events (but not the Grand Slam tournaments, at least not until WCT scheduled a tournament during the French Open in 1971). A look at the tennis calendar for the years 1968–71 shows a programme of open tournaments run under the ILTF – many of them traditional championships run by the ILTF's member national associations, like the German Open in Hamburg and the Italian Open in Rome – interspersed with tournaments for contract professionals run by WCT and NTL.

Alarmed by the increasing control the promoters had over players and the tennis calendar, the ILTF approved Jack Kramer's idea of the Grand Prix. It was launched, albeit as an 'experimental' Grand Prix in 1970 and ran from April to December with 20 tournaments taking part in six countries. Players competed for a bonus money pool and qualification into the season-ending Masters event, the first of which was won by Stan Smith, who pocketed $15,000.

The directors of World Championship Tennis, from left, Lamar Hunt, Al Hill Jr. and Mike Davies, convene at the 1970 US Open to announce the new WCT Finals for the following season, a rival to the Grand Prix Masters.

Allan Heyman, ILTF president during the early – and tumultuous – years of open tennis

In the new era of open tennis in which no one quite knew where exactly tennis was heading, there was such suspicion surrounding a Texan oil millionaire with bags of money that Hunt was viewed with great scepticism by the ILTF's president, the Danish lawyer Allan Heyman, its long-standing British secretary Basil Reay, and Wimbledon.

By the middle of 1971, Hunt had 32 of the top professionals under contract, and when WCT scheduled a tournament that clashed with the French Open, the frosty relations between WCT and the ILTF came to a head. Worried that the top players were being spirited away from the traditional tournaments that open tennis was supposed to reinvigorate, the ILTF voted to ban WCT's players from all ILTF-sanctioned tournaments, which included the four Grand Slams, as of 1 January 1972. To break the impasse, Hunt and Heyman signed an agreement in April 1972 that would allow the WCT players back. The agreement, which carved up the tennis year between WCT and the traditional tournaments (WCT was given the first four months, after which the ILTF Grand Prix started), probably amounted to an illegal abuse

of monopoly positions, but its most controversial aspect lay in the timing. Heyman insisted it had to be ratified by the ILTF's annual meeting, which took place the week after Wimbledon. Matters were not helped by WCT scheduling a tournament in St. Louis during Wimbledon. The result was that the WCT players were banned from the 1972 Wimbledon, among them John Newcombe, who was unable to defend his men's singles title from 1970 and 1971.

In hindsight, the ILTF-WCT agreement probably gave the players the incentive they needed to form a players' association. Such an association had been under discussion for many years, but a concern that the leading professional promoter and the ILTF were now cooperating sent a fear through locker rooms that the players were vulnerable to being squeezed. The result was the formation of the Association of Tennis Professionals (ATP) in September 1972. The eloquent South African player Cliff Drysdale was its first president, and Jack Kramer agreed to become the first executive director (interestingly on no salary, so he could be as much a 'volunteer' as Heyman in the role of ILTF president).

The success of WCT continued to grow in 1972, reaching its peak at the final in Dallas, Texas, as an audience of 23 million tuned in to see Ken Rosewall beat Rod Laver in an epic five-set match. The match inside the Moody Coliseum is still considered one of the greatest matches in tennis history, and for Laver, his biggest loss.

COMPUTER RANKINGS

One of the first things the Association of Tennis Professionals did was establish computer rankings. Loose rankings had existed up to then, but very much as informal lists reflecting the opinions of leading journalists, in particular the year-end top-10 ranking compiled by Lance Tingay and published in the London *Daily Telegraph*, which was widely accepted as the world rankings. Many national associations had national rankings, but it was impossible to make an objective acceptance list of international players by comparing, for example, the sixth-best player in India with the third best in Brazil.

Before 1973 entry to tournaments had been largely a matter of who the tournament director wanted. Obviously the big names all got in because they helped ticket sales, but the lower-ranked players could often find themselves part of a lottery. There was even anecdotal evidence that some players were denied entry to tournaments because they had allegedly been rude to a tournament director, or an official had taken a dislike to them.

In August 1973 the first rankings were published, making Romania's Ilie Nastase the first official world No. 1. A player's performance at all qualifying tournaments in the previous 52 weeks earned him ranking points, which he kept for a year (thereby enabling a player who did well at one particular tournament to qualify for direct entry the following year, even if his other results were unfavourable). Alterations have been made over the years – notably over which tournaments qualify for ranking points, whether to include all tournaments a player enters or only his best, and how to weight the Grand Slams – but the system in use today is largely the same as it was in 1973. The ATP introduced doubles rankings in March 1976, with South Africa's Bob Hewitt as the first individual doubles No. 1. The women's ranking system was introduced in November 1975, with Chris Evert as the first No. 1.

There are people who feel that the ITF, as the sport's overall governing body, should have control over the ranking systems, and there is some logic in that. In the mid-1970s, Philippe Chatrier accepted that the ITF would respect the ATP and WTA rankings, thereby effectively handing over responsibility for rankings to the two tours, and the ITF today uses the ATP and WTA rankings for Davis Cup and Fed Cup purposes.

Outside the High Court in London, Niki Pilic (far left) – with Cliff Drysdale, Arthur Ashe and Jack Kramer – awaits judgement on the ATP's appeal to lift his ban from the ILTF for refusing to play Davis Cup. The ban was eventually reduced from nine months to one, but by the time the decision was made it would still prevent Pilic from playing Wimbledon.

THE PILIC AFFAIR AND ATP BOYCOTT

Within a year of being founded, the ATP had a battleground on which to demonstrate whether the players were willing to show their teeth. In 1973 the Yugoslav left-hander Niki Pilic was banned from all official tournaments for refusing to play a Davis Cup tie against New Zealand. Pilic said he had indicated he *might* play the tie, while the Yugoslav tennis association, which was run by his uncle, believed the player had *committed* to play. When Pilic and Allan Stone qualified for the World Doubles Finals that same week, he decided to put the doubles ahead of the Davis Cup (Davis Cup carried no prize money at that time, and Pilic was legally contracted to the doubles). He was banned for nine months, a decision that outraged his fellow players.

The role of Heyman was interesting. It is easy with hindsight to portray him as being hopelessly out of touch with the spirit of the times (he had, after all, been vehemently opposed to open tennis in 1967). But he was under pressure from many national associations to ensure that they retained control over tournaments and circuits, and by implication not to let the players get too powerful. As such, Heyman saw the Pilic dispute as a chance to tell the players who was still boss. And by telling people that the players might boycott other tournaments but they would never refuse to play Wimbledon, he steered the battleground to Wimbledon.

Pilic appealed against his nine-month ban and was given permission to play the French Open while his appeal was heard. After hearing Pilic's appeal, the ILTF agreed to reduce his ban from nine months to one, but by the time the decision was made, even a one-month ban would still prevent him from playing at Wimbledon.

Although Pilic was far from being the most popular person in the locker room, the players believed in the principle that he should be able to honour his contract and not have his schedule dictated by national associations. In protest, 81 players opted not to play Wimbledon. Two of them changed their mind at the last minute: Ilie Nastase, who was not a member of the ATP but initially said he would join the boycott, only to then claim that he was under pressure from the Romanian government; and the British No. 1, Roger Taylor, who was under tremendous pressure to support Wimbledon, even though his father, a trade unionist, was encouraging him to boycott. Taylor was given a standing ovation as he entered the Centre Court for his first-round match, but neither he nor Nastase made it to the final. The two finalists, Jan Kodes and Alex Metreveli, were both from Soviet bloc countries who had been ordered by their governments to play. Indeed players from Soviet bloc countries were banned by their governments from joining the ATP.

STARS WILL
BOYCOTT
WIMBLEDON

Judge says Pilic
must not play

WIMBLEDON
WALK-OUT

Minister steps in
as Wimbledon
players quit

June 29, 1973: The media run wild in the aftermath of the player boycott on day four of Wimbledon.

Making headlines: Pilic's absence from Wimbledon sparks 81 players to boycott the event in protest and the Minister of Sport to intervene.

Wimbledon's tournament referee Mike Gibson in the stands of Centre Court with the revised list of male competitors.

Heyman's calculation that the players wouldn't boycott Wimbledon proved a miscalculation. Drysdale and Kramer had conducted themselves with considerable diplomacy, showing respect for Wimbledon and clothing all public statements in a sense of sorrow rather than anger. They had also said all along that they wanted the dispute to go to independent arbitration, and Heyman's refusal to accept this fuels the theory that the Dane believed fighting the players over Wimbledon was an area in which the ILTF – and by extension the national associations – could win. Although Wimbledon had carried on, it was diminished by the boycott. A year earlier the WCT professionals had barely been missed as Stan Smith and Ilie Nastase played out a glorious five-set Wimbledon final; Kodes's three-set win over Metreveli in the 1973 final paled in comparison.

Even though the direct results of the boycott took a while to filter through, the players had won. National associations had effectively lost the power to tell their players when and where they could play. After Wimbledon, the ILTF set up a Grand Prix Committee, which gave the players their first representation alongside the ILTF. In September 1974 this mutated into the Men's International Professional Tennis Council (MIPTC). This was a body set up to run the men's tour, with a board consisting of an equal split between the ILTF and the ATP.

Chairman of the All England Club Herman David, who had thrust the concept of open tennis on the ILTF, faces the media in light of the player boycott

In the aftermath of the boycott, the ATP lost one of its board members, the former British player and Davis Cup captain John Barrett (right), whose links to the British tennis establishment made him potentially a bridge between the two sides.

VOTING ON THE COUNCIL

- After the Wimbledon boycott of 1973, the ILTF established a Grand Prix Committee made up of seven members: three representatives each from the ILTF and the ATP, plus the ILTF's president as chairman.

- The first Men's International Professional Tennis Council (MIPTC) that started in September 1974 had the same seven members, but with the ILTF president having no voting rights (except a casting vote).

- In January 1976 the Council was expanded to nine with the addition of three representatives of tournaments, but with the chairman elected from among the nine (it was the ILTF president, Philippe Chatrier, until 1985).

If the traditionalists were having to stomach a revolution in professional tennis in the years after 1968, the arrival of World Team Tennis (WTT) in 1974 took the development of the sport a lot further – in some respects too far for some of the revolutionaries.

WTT began in 1974. The four-month, US-based league season featured teams that were franchised in major American cities and hired some of the top names to represent them. Because its season ran from May to September, it clashed with some of the major traditional tournaments (though it always stopped for Wimbledon and the US Open), and thus prevented some players from playing the French Open. WTT was initially banned by the ILTF, and Jack Kramer felt betrayed by the leading ATP players who signed up for WTT, including its first president, Cliff Drysdale. There is a certain irony here, in that the players had boycotted Wimbledon for the right to determine their own schedules, but Kramer was calling on his old friend Chatrier to get the ILTF to ban players who chose to play WTT.

The ILTF and USLTA eventually sanctioned WTT, but the Italian and French associations went ahead independently and banned certain WTT players from the 1974 Italian and French Opens. One of them was Jimmy Connors, who sued the ATP for restraint of trade, a move that added intrigue to the 1975 Wimbledon final given that Connors was playing against the ATP president, Arthur Ashe.

Billie Jean King and Fred Stolle, original members of WTT's Philadelphia Freedoms

By January 1976 the board gained three more members, as representatives of tournaments were added. The boycott had led to the men's tour being in the hands of an international, independent and democratic body in which the ILTF, players and tournaments were all represented, albeit one which took seven years to get its own administrator (from 1974 to 1981, these duties were carried out by the ITF's secretary and an ATP official, working as joint secretaries, until the North Carolina lawyer Marshall Happer was appointed the Council's administrator in 1981). The players enjoyed a further victory, as the MIPTC conceded that the ATP would continue to run the computer-ranking list that determined entry into tournaments, an innovation the ATP had introduced in 1973 (see panel, page 65).

Marshall Happer, administrator of the Men's International Professional Tennis Council, which was effectively the ruling body of the men's game from 1974 to 1989

David Gray (left) became general secretary of the ILTF in 1976 with Philippe Chatrier (right) joining as president the following year. They fought to regain the IOC's trust in the ILTF after the federation was removed as a recognised organisation for 'opening the gates to professional players'.

The early years of open tennis also galvanised the ILTF into modernising itself, and it was fortunate to have a president elected in 1976 who had the vision to take the Federation into the modern era. Philippe Chatrier had come up through the French Tennis Federation (FFT), of which he had been vice-president from 1968 to 1972, and president since 1972. He effectively became the first professional president of the ILTF, although he never took a salary from the Federation because he maintained his position (and income) from the FFT.

Chatrier's vision had three main pillars: 1) He could see that the traditional tournaments would only survive if they were run along modern, businesslike lines, so he needed to professionalise the ILTF as a route to professionalising the national associations.

2) He saw the need to bring Davis Cup officially into the ILTF fold, with centralised rights and sponsorship deals for both it and the Federation Cup.

3) He wanted tennis back in the Olympics in order to release various sources of worldwide funding that would allow the game to grow around the world.

Chatrier was assisted for the first half of his presidency by David Gray, a former British tennis journalist who succeeded the long-serving Basil Reay as secretary (Gray had the title 'general secretary', essentially the equivalent of chief operating officer in today's business language) and who shared

Chatrier's vision. The most visible sign of the Chatrier/Gray regime was the dropping of the word 'Lawn' from the ILTF name to create today's ITF, but that was cosmetic compared to the behind-the-scenes structural and constitutional changes the two men were making. These included the reform of Davis Cup to reduce the burden on players and the creation of new ITF departments for professional tennis and development.

Another crucial ITF figure was Chatrier's predecessor as president, Derek Hardwick, who was one of the ITF's three representatives on the MIPTC until his death in 1987. Hardwick was held in great esteem by the players, having shown his willingness over several years to fight their cause.

"When open tennis came about, the game was about to experience the biggest growth in its history, and for a governing body like the ITF we had to choose our options, either to modernise our organisation or to disappear, simple as that. So as soon as resources became available, we hired people, highly qualified professional people, to perform in various departments duties that were long overdue."

PHILIPPE CHATRIER SPEAKING IN 1988 ON THE 75TH ANNIVERSARY OF THE ITF

The ITF took over management of Davis Cup from the Davis Cup Nations in 1979 which necessitated the establishment of official departments for marketing and men's tennis. Davis Cup sponsorship from NEC in 1981 enabled Chatrier to hire professional staff to oversee the professional game.

The Pro Council's tripartite arrangement began to cause cracks in the day-to-day running of the sport. In 1982 Bjorn Borg (left) pleaded for a lighter Grand Prix load, which was refused by the Council, and subsequently led to his retirement from tennis. Ivan Lendl (right) received special dispensation to play a reduced number of Grand Prix events in 1987 after claiming to be overworked, which ruffled other players' feathers.

PLAYER POWER

Yet there was a final stage of the professional revolution that came in the late 1980s, which Chatrier's reforms were unable to prevent. The MIPTC (by now shortened to 'MTC' or 'Pro Council') was a tripartite arrangement of the ITF, the players and the tournaments. But in the late 1980s the three parties were becoming increasingly antagonistic, despite the steady growth of professional tennis. There were disputes between the tournament directors and the players, notably a frustration among tournaments that the players were playing too many exhibition matches, and the tournaments and the players felt the ITF was holding back progress by frequently rejecting new commercial opportunities to grow pro tennis.

The first sign of trouble came in 1985, when the ATP decided to challenge Philippe Chatrier's position as chairman of the Pro Council. Until then, Chatrier had been elected usually on a 5-to-4 vote. The ATP put its executive director, Mike Davies, up against Chatrier, and Davies was elected by a 5-to-4 vote. Within a month, Davies had been fired by the ATP (ironically, he was signed up shortly after to work for the ITF), and the former South African player Ray Moore became the Pro Council's new chairman. While he continued to work with the Council, Moore and another ex-player, Harold Solomon, began pursuing the idea of the players running their own tour.

Former South African player Ray Moore was on the ATP Board of Directors and became president in 1983–85, before being elected as chairman of the Pro Council in 1986.

The end of 1989 was always going to be a crunch time, because a number of contracts were expiring. The food multinational Nabisco, which in 1985 had taken over from Volvo as the Grand Prix's sponsor, let it be known in early 1988 that it would not extend its sponsorship after 1989. The Pro Council's contract with WCT ended after 1989, and the Council had a contract to fund aspects of the ATP's activities that also expired at the end of 1989. With Moore far from convinced about the value of the Council, and the ATP having appointed Hamilton Jordan, US president Jimmy Carter's former chief of staff, as its executive director, the players were clearly preparing for their own tour. The Council's cause was further harmed by the untimely deaths of two of its leading supporters: the ITF's Derek Hardwick from cancer in 1987 and the ATP's Ron Bookman in a freak cycling accident in 1988.

Hamilton Jordan moved from the White House into the role of executive director of the ATP just as tennis reached the height of its political era.

Hamilton Jordan details plans for the new ATP Tour in the car park of Flushing Meadows, and Wimbledon chairman Buzzer Haddingham defends his support of the idea to the media. The ATP paper *Tennis at the Crossroads* laid out the frustrations players had with their lack of power under the current system.

The process in which the Association of Tennis Professionals took over the running of the men's tour – and at the same time transformed itself from a players' union into a tour body under the name 'ATP Tour' – had a spectacular defining moment. In September 1988 the US Tennis Association declined to make the US Open's interview room available for an ATP press conference to answer questions about *Tennis at the Crossroads*, a provocative paper that highlighted the problems the ATP saw and aired for the first time the option of the players running their own tour and issuing a

set of conditions to the ITF (see panel, opposite). So instead, Jordan called a press conference in the car park outside Flushing Meadows, and with Mats Wilander, Yannick Noah, Tim Mayotte and Brad Gilbert behind him, he was able to convey the message that the traditional tournaments weren't working with the players.

Despite the dramatic launch of *Tennis at the Crossroads*, there was still time for the Pro Council to be salvaged. The four Grand Slams reacted by saying that if the ATP was not happy with the Council, the Council could

continue to run men's tennis under the ITF's auspices without ATP voting rights. A few weeks later, the Council's administrator, Marshall Happer, worked out a compromise whereby the ATP would have equal voting rights with the tournaments on tour matters, but the ITF would have equal voting rights with the players on Grand Slam matters. But this was effectively scuppered when the Wimbledon chairman, Buzzer Haddingham, told the ATP a few days later that Wimbledon would not oppose the ATP running its own tour, as long as the majors were given their desired slots.

One of the most dramatic off-court images in the history of tennis was the announcement by the ATP's executive director, Hamilton Jordan, flanked by a handful of leading players, that the ATP was considering abandoning the Pro Council and running its own tour. The announcement was made in the car park at Flushing Meadows, but the lead-up and follow-up to the parking lot press conference has been largely forgotten.

27 Aug 1988

The ATP delivers its *Tennis at the Crossroads* to the Pro Council at 9 a.m. The paper effectively incorporates an ultimatum to the ITF:

'Mr [Ray] Moore stated that the Player Representatives and the ATP would not continue to participate and support the MTC in 1990 and the future under the current structure and that continuation would be agreed only if:

(i) the Grand Slams agreed to pool their television rights; and

(ii) the ITF Representatives withdrew as voting members of the MTC with the ITF permitted as observers at MTC meetings; and

(iii) the MTC was restricted to consist of four ATP Representatives, three Tournament Representatives and two Independent Business Men.'

29 Aug 1988

The presidents of the four Grand Slam tournaments issue a joint statement saying, 'If the present structure of the Men's Tennis Council (MTC) is no longer acceptable to ATP's management, then the undersigned representatives of Wimbledon, the US Open, the French Championships, and the Australian Open will ask the International Tennis Federation, the governing body of tennis for the past 75 years, to form a new structure to carry on the worldwide work for the game.'

30 Aug 1988

The ATP issues a press release concluding, 'Because our suggestions for reform were rejected out of hand by the Grand Slams and were never seriously considered, we do not expect the current system to address the problems facing our sport and we will begin to make plans for a tour in 1990.' Later that day it requests permission from the USTA to hold a press conference to answer questions in the main interview room at Flushing Meadows. The USTA declines.

31 Aug 1988

The USTA notifies the ATP that it will, after all, allow the main interview room to be used for the ATP conference, but the ATP rejects the change of decision, saying it has made alternative arrangements. Hamilton Jordan – supported by Mats Wilander, Yannick Noah, Tim Mayotte and Brad Gilbert – stage a press conference in the parking lot outside Flushing Meadows.

4 Oct 1988

MTC administrator Marshall Happer proposes restructuring the Council to be run by two operating committees: one with equal representation between the ATP and ITF to oversee Grand Slam issues, the other with equal representation between the ATP and the tournaments to oversee tour issues.

13 Oct 1988

Representatives of the ATP have a private meeting with Buzzer Haddingham, the chairman of Wimbledon, who tells them that Wimbledon would not oppose the ATP running its own tour, as long as the majors were given their desired slots. This effectively undermines the Grand Slams' statement of 29 August. Emboldened by Haddingham's assurance, the ATP rejects Happer's compromise proposal and announces it will run its own tour at the start of 1990.

With the players having backed the idea of an ATP-run tour (85 of the top 100 supported the idea), and similar support coming from the tournament directors – including many of the traditional tournaments that had supported the ITF over World Team Tennis in the 1970s – the ATP took the plunge. Just a few weeks after the press conference in the parking lot, the ATP announced that from 1 January 1990 the players would take over the running of the men's circuit, dovetailing its schedule with the Grand Slams and the Davis Cup. It was, in effect, a move to throw the ITF's three representatives off the Pro Council, because the new ATP Tour board was made up of three players and three tournament directors. This effectively ended the raison d'être of the Pro Council, which Happer liquidated at the end of 1989.

The ATP Tour was created in the form of the American PGA, so the ATP as a players' association or union was dissolved and folded into a new entity known as the ATP Tour Inc, comprised of the non-Grand Slam tournaments and the players. The ATP Player Council took over the functions of the old ATP, but very much as an advisory body to the ATP Tour board. The Grand Slam tournaments, which had been part of the Grand Prix run by the Pro Council, were not formally part of the ATP Tour and therefore not bound by its rules. Since there would no longer be a Council, the four majors and the ITF formed the Grand Slam Committee to administer the rules and Code of Conduct for the Grand Slams, and also to act as a forum for other matters of mutual interest among the majors.

The antagonism ushered in a cold war between the ATP, the Grand Slams and the ITF, of which the most outward manifestation was the presence in the calendar of two year-ending finales: the ATP Tour World Championships (initially in Frankfurt, later in Hannover) and the Grand Slam Cup (in Munich) run by the ITF on behalf of the four major tournaments which provided $6 million in prize money and $2 million to the ITF for the development of the worldwide game. Relations thawed in the late 1990s when the ITF, Grand Slams and ATP came together in a combined year-end event called the Tennis Masters Cup, which was run by the ATP under its format but with involvement from the ITF.

The schism brought some serious concerns among the traditionalists that having the players and non-major tournaments running their own tour would be a recipe for chaos, especially in areas like officiating (the players would effectively be hiring the umpires). That has proved less of an issue than areas such as tournament ownership and appearance fees and guarantees.

The Grand Slam Committee faces the media at the first-ever Grand Slam Cup in Munich in 1990, the ITF's season-ending championships run on behalf of the four majors. The committee was established following liquidation of the Pro Council at the end of 1989 and retained links with the ITF and the Grand Slams, which had decided to remain independent from the ATP Tour.

In practical terms, the tour has worked fairly well, with the ATP (it dropped the 'Tour' in 2000 but is still effectively the ATP Tour and not the old Association of Tennis Professionals) becoming more of a multinational corporate administrator of men's tennis than the global cooperative many had feared the tour would become.

The question that remains from the demise of the Pro Council is whether the ITF as the game's overall governing body should really have no participation in the day-to-day running of the men's tour, and whether having separate governing bodies for the sport and the men's (and women's) tour is good for the overall growth and health of the game, as opposed to specific interests. In addition, one could argue that the ATP had more to gain from retaining the Pro Council, which had control over the Grand Slams, for at the end it had six supporters among the nine Council members, a body it replaced with one on which it had three supporters out of six members and no involvement with the Grand Slams.

If one of the ATP's stated aims was to narrow the gap between its top tier of tournaments and the Grand Slams, the opposite seems to have happened. The gap in turnover between the four majors and today's Masters-1000 tournaments is now vastly greater than it was in 1990; players hardly ever miss a major (other than through injury) while they do occasionally miss a Masters event, and sports editors generally gear their tennis coverage around the four Slams, with the rest treated as merely 'the tour' or 'warm-up events'. It is hard to escape the conclusion that the ATP breakaway has led to the Grand Slams becoming further removed from the everyday tour than would have been the case if the Men's Tennis Council had continued after 1989.

WHAT DID THE COUNCIL EVER DO FOR US?

The Men's International Professional Tennis Council is sometimes dismissed as a bit of a failure, or at least an in-between stage in tennis's development from the end of the amateur era to the point where the players could run their own tour. But the 15 years of the Council saw a number of successes. Indeed Philippe Chatrier was proud of the MIPTC concept and often spoke about the Council's deviation from the normal 'management v union' model with collective bargaining agreements to a joint participation in the management of professional tennis by all of the constituencies involved.

Among the MTC's accomplishments during its existence (1974–89) were:

- Streamlining the world calendar and administration of the circuit

- Promotion of the Grand Prix and sponsorship of it (by Pepsi Cola, Commercial Union, Colgate Palmolive, Volvo and Nabisco)

- Promotion of the year-end Masters in New York

- Development and enforcement of the professional player's Code of Conduct

- Development of professional standards for tennis officiating and the introduction of professional touring officials

- Introduction of drug testing

- Introduction and development of the player pension fund

Today, the ITF sanctions and works closely with each tournament through its presence on the Grand Slam Committee, providing administrative, officiating and media support.

THE PROFESSIONALISATION OF WOMEN'S TENNIS

Gladys Heldman, founder of *World Tennis* magazine and women's tennis pioneer

The professionalisation of women's tennis took a different form and a different timeline. There had never been split amateur and professional circuits in women's tennis, largely because there had never been any entrepreneurs willing to sign up female players for a professional tour. When the National Tennis League Group began signing up players in 1967, it contracted a handful of women, among them Billie Jean King, Rosie Casals and Ann Jones, but that was as far as women's pro tennis went until 1968. Yet two years after open tennis was established, the revolution that created the modern Women's Tennis Association (WTA) took place.

With professional tennis arriving in 1968, female players began to earn money. But tournaments offered women less prize money than men. That was largely accepted, especially in an era where most men's matches were the best of five sets, while all women's matches were the best of three. In addition, the purely commercial promoters (as opposed to traditional tournaments that had started to offer prize money) recognised that the women didn't sell as many tickets as the men. But the discrepancy started to eat away at the composure of some of the leading women players, and a constellation of circumstances created the perfect storm in September 1970.

When Ken Rosewall won the 1970 US Open, he pocketed $20,000 in prize money. By contrast, the women's singles winner, Margaret Court, who was completing the Grand Slam, took home just $7,500. Two weeks later, Jack Kramer's Pacific Southwest tournament was offering the men's champion $12,500 and the women's champ just $1,500. Incensed at what they saw as a severe undervaluing of women's tennis, Billie Jean King and her doubles partner, Rosie Casals, approached Gladys Heldman, the publisher of *World Tennis* magazine and champion of women's rights, and sought her support. Heldman complained to Jack Kramer, the tournament director of the Pacific Southwest, and said the women players might boycott his tournament if he didn't redress the balance somewhat. Kramer replied that a boycott would suit him fine, as he could increase the men's prize money by topping it up with what he had budgeted to pay the women.

Virginia Wade walked away with just an expenses cheque after winning the first open tournament in Bournemouth as an amateur. The tournament had begun under a dark cloud after several women pros had boycotted due to the disproportionate prize money for men and women, a discrepancy which by 1970 had vastly increased.

From left: Francoise Durr, Ann Jones, Rosie Casals and Billie Jean King became the National Tennis League's first female pros in 1968.

Gladys Heldman and her rebel women with their $1 contracts: standing from left, Valerie Ziegenfuss, Billie Jean King, Nancy Richey and Peaches Bartkowicz. Seated from left, Judy Dalton, Kerry Melville-Reid, Rosie Casals, Heldman and Kristy Pigeon.

Joe Cullman, chief executive of tobacco company Philip Morris, provided the prize money to launch the Virginia Slims circuit.

Faced with this situation, Heldman hastily staged a tournament in Houston for the same September week as Kramer's event in Los Angeles. She raised $5,000 in prize money by getting a long-standing contact, Joe Cullman, the chief executive of the Philip Morris group of companies, to sponsor it. Philip Morris had just launched a new brand of cigarettes called Virginia Slims aimed specifically at women, and Heldman's call to Cullman was the start of a quarter-century relationship between women's tennis and Virginia Slims that only ended with the widespread ban on tobacco sponsorship in 1989.

But Heldman had a problem. Kramer understandably objected to a rival tournament, and as his tournament was part of the Grand Prix circuit, he effectively invoked the power of the ILTF to deny Heldman's event the sanction it needed. At the last minute, Heldman was granted a licence to run an amateur tournament, but as she was committed to paying prize money, that would have meant a return to under-the-table payments from the shamateur era. Her only way out was to have a purely professional tournament, thereby removing the need to get official approval. So she signed up eight of the leading players for a token $1 fee and announced that the Virginia Slims of Houston tournament would be the first in a women's tour to have the same status as WCT, even if the players were getting a fraction of the money the male WCT professionals were pocketing.

Heldman's efforts could have been a flop if no one had come to watch the women players. But being part of a mission to establish women's tennis, the players, led by the eloquent Billie Jean King, were keen to make it work and took up every opportunity they could to publicise their circuit. In her years as US Fed Cup captain, King never missed an opportunity to tell the generation of Chris Evert, Martina Navratilova, Monica Seles, Jennifer Capriati, Lindsay Davenport and the Williams sisters that their riches stemmed from the pioneering work done by King and her generation, and that failure to help promote the sport when the opportunity presented itself was a betrayal of the legacy they had inherited.

The Women's Tennis Association (WTA) was founded in 1973 and earned an instant success with the US Open agreeing to equal prize money for women and men. The women's tour introduced rankings in March 1975 at the start of the Virginia Slims circuit, and in 1994, the WTA divided itself into the WTA Players Association and the Women's Tennis Council, the latter starting following an initiative from the ITF president, Philippe Chatrier. (Until the creation of the WTC, all women's circuit sponsorship agreements were signed by the WTA and the ITF.)

The WTA (for a while the Women's International Tennis Association or WITA) never had a rupture with the ITF the way the men did in 1988–89, but it did take over the running of its own tour in 1995, albeit with closer cooperation with the ITF than the men had had (today, the ITF has a representative on the WTA board). The mechanism was a merger of the WTA Players Association and the Women's Tennis Council to form the WTA Tour. The word 'Tour' was dropped in 2010 on the 40th anniversary of Heldman's revolution. The Grand Slams remain part of the WTA and contribute financially to it; this contrasts with the ATP, to which the Grand Slams contribute nothing despite the ATP having pushed hard in 1988 for a pooling of Grand Slam television revenues.

As well as renowned fashion designer for the female tennis stars, former player Ted Tinling acted as spokesperson for the Virginia Slims circuit, the first women's pro tour. He publicised its slogan 'You've come a long way baby' on tennis attire (modelled here with Rosie Casals).

"*Virginia Slims was one of the game's pioneering ventures. It showed, to the surprise of many who were promoting tennis at the start of the decade, that women could draw large crowds and attract the same kind of sponsorship as the men in the United States. With their flair for publicity, their energy and enthusiasm, Virginia Slims won converts everywhere. Among those converts were, it has to be said, the leaders of the ITF, who had been sceptical and chauvinistic at the start but finished admirers.*"

PHILIPPE CHATRIER

"YOU CANNOT BE SERIOUS,
THAT BALL WAS ON THE LINE!"

JOHN MCENROE
THE 'SUPERBRAT'

CHAPTER 04

PLAYING BY THE RULES

THE ITF'S ROLE ON RULES AND ENFORCING THEM

ESTABLISHING A UNIFORM SET OF INTERNATIONAL RULES
WAS ONE OF THE MAIN REASONS FOR FOUNDING THE ITF 100 YEARS AGO
AND REMAINS A CORE PURPOSE OF THE FEDERATION TODAY.
YET DESPITE THE DRAMATIC CHANGES IN TENNIS OVER RECENT DECADES,
THE RULES OF THE SPORT HAVE STAYED REMARKABLY CONSTANT.
THE DIMENSIONS OF THE COURT HAVE REMAINED UNCHANGED
SINCE 1877, AND THE ONLY ADJUSTMENTS TO THE RULES THAT AFFECT
ALL PLAYERS – FROM THOSE PLAYING IN PUBLIC PARKS TO TOURING
PROFESSIONALS – ARE THE FOOT-FAULT RULE THAT CHANGED IN
1908 AND 1961, AND CHANGES TO SCORING, NOTABLY THE
INTRODUCTION OF THE TIEBREAK IN 1970.

A UNIFIED SET OF RULES

It seems strange in retrospect that the International Lawn Tennis Federation took a decade to establish a unified set of Rules of Tennis. If one of the central purposes of the Federation was to ensure the game would continue to grow with certain uniform standards that would make it recognisable in all parts of the world, forming a uniform set of rules would be a logical role for the ITLF. Yet the oldest-established national associations were suspicious about handing over power for rule changes to an international body, and indeed one of the reasons the United States Lawn Tennis Association didn't join the ILTF until 1923 was scepticism about control of the rules.

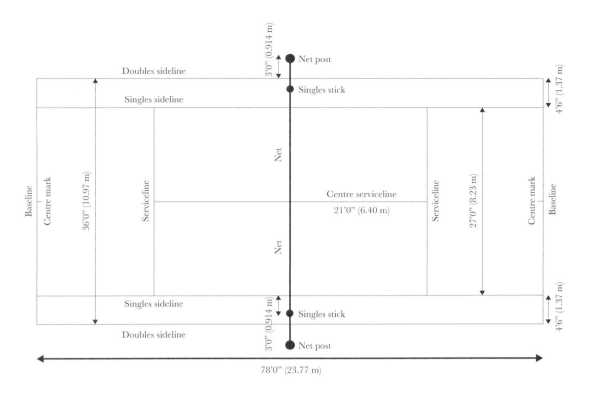

Net post
3'0" (0.914 m)

Doubles sideline

Singles stick

Singles sideline

4'6" (1.37 m)

Net

Baseline
Centre mark
36'0" (10.97 m)
Serviceline

Centre serviceline
21'0" (6.40 m)

Serviceline
27'0" (8.23 m)
Centre mark
Baseline

Net

Singles sideline

4'6" (1.37 m)

3'0" (0.914 m)
Singles stick

Doubles sideline

Net post

78'0" (23.77 m)

Dimensions of a tennis court have remained unchanged since 1877. Lawn tennis entrepreneur Walter Clopton Wingfield used the hourglass-shaped court (narrower at the net with wider baselines) as a feature of his patented lawn tennis kit, before the All England Club tournament committee standardised the rectangular court used today.

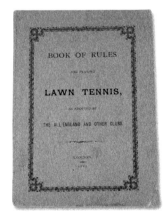

PLAN TO HARMONIZE LAWN TENNIS RULES

International Federation Invites All Nations to Participate in a Conference.

MEETING CALLED IN PARIS

Executive Committee of U. S. L. T. A. Voting on Proposition to Send Representatives.

"The official rules of the various nations are practically identical, but it will be the object of the conference to eliminate certain minor differences in the various codes. Absolute uniformity is the goal, inasmuch as tennis is now played in every continent and, in the case of the Davis Cup contest, has enlisted the participation of so many nations that any possible chances for misunderstanding concerning the rules is regarded as especially undesirable"

PUBLISHED: 14 MAY 1922, *THE NEW YORK TIMES*

Matters such as the discrepancy between the British and American classification on size and weight of a ball, the foot-fault rule, and use of spiked shoes were on the agenda for the first meeting on rules in 1922.

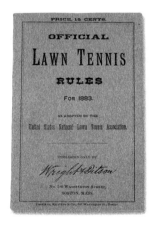

Nations and clubs adopted and printed their own rules until the ILTF became the governor of rules in 1924 and published the first official Rules of Tennis.

White tennis balls in use at Wimbledon in the 1980s. In 1972 the ITF allowed yellow balls into the Rules of Tennis after research proved they had better visibility on television.

The ILTF's first decade was characterised by efforts to end the wrangling that was preventing the Federation from having the final say on rules. The deadlock was broken in 1922, when the ILTF's Advisory Committee (the committee that effectively ran the Federation) set up an International Rules Board made up of representatives from 13 countries. It drew up a set of draft 'Official ILTF Rules of Tennis', which were sent to national associations for comment. They were approved at the ILTF's annual meeting in Paris on 16 March 1923 and came into effect on 1 January 1924.

Since then, remarkably little has changed. The foot-fault rule was changed in 1961, thereby allowing players much greater power on their serves (see panel, right). Yellow balls were allowed in 1972 for better visibility on television; Wimbledon was the last top-level tournament to use white balls up to 1985. Rules have been rephrased to address certain developments, the best example being the change in official tennis documentation in the late 1960s that listed court and net dimensions in both imperial and metric; the dimensions themselves didn't change, and the round numbers on the imperial side testify to the origins of the sport among countries that use feet and inches rather than metres and centimetres.

CHANGES TO THE FOOT-FAULT RULE

Tennis must have a foot-fault rule or a player would be able to serve from on top of the net. The rule changed twice in the 20th century, in 1908 and 1961.

In the years leading up to 1908, a trend was growing for servers to steal a march on getting to the net by starting their service motion from the very back of the court, running up to the baseline and serving the ball as part of a motion that continued towards the net (similar to a cricketer bowling the ball at the end of a run-up, or a javelin thrower running before launching the spear). This was thought to give the net rushers an unfair advantage, so the rule was changed to require servers to have at least one foot on the ground when the serve was struck.

In 1961 that requirement was repealed. It didn't lead to a return of run-up serves, but it did pave the way for more powerful serves, as players were then able to launch themselves into the air and hit the ball at a much higher point, as long as they didn't land either foot on or inside the baseline before hitting the ball.

Today most players know whether they're liable to commit foot-faults or not based on their personal service motion, hence the shock and indignation among those who don't normally foot-fault when they are called for an infringement. That doesn't excuse the kind of rant Serena Williams issued to a line umpire who foot-faulted her during the 2009 US Open semifinals. As Williams had had an earlier warning and lost the match on a point penalty, the incident is arguably the highest-profile case of a foot-fault in the history of tennis.

A foot-fault can also be called across the centre line or from a position beyond the sideline, although these infringements are rare.

Electronic line-calling systems were introduced into professional tennis in 2006; the Hopman Cup was the first event to implement such a system. Under the rules, a player is allowed unlimited challenges to line calls but with a maximum quota of three unsuccessful appeals per set (plus an additional appeal in the tiebreak).

TRY THIS ON THE PRACTICE COURT

There have been various suggestions for rule changes over the years. One that never came before the ITF was the idea that left-handers should begin their service games from the left court (traditionally the 'advantage' court) rather than the right (deuce) court. This tackled the perennial perception that left-handers have an advantage over right-handers because they can use an away-swinging serve in the ad court where most of the big points are played.

Another suggestion, which made it into a proposal paper and is known as a '50–40 scoring system', was that servers had to win four points to win a game, while receivers only had to win three. So at 3–2 to the server, it would effectively be sudden death. The paper's co-authors say this system reflects the balance of strength between the players, but it does assume an advantage to the server so may be less appropriate on slower surfaces.

In the late 1990s there were fears that the big servers were spoiling the sport by killing off rallies in favour of aces and three-stroke serve-volley points. In order to reduce the power of the serve, someone suggested putting an extra line beyond the baseline, behind which the server would have to serve. The idea never caught on.

Two developments in the 2000s reflected changes in society and technology. Once the ITF's technical department was satisfied about the accuracy of the Hawk-Eye electronic review system, the rules were altered to allow for electronic review where Hawk-Eye was installed (or any other technology that met minimum standards of accuracy). And when the credibility of matches was called into question by a handful of betting scandals, changes were made to prevent players from betting on matches.

Other rules have been altered to tackle specific issues, such as the 'spaghetti stringing' controversy in the late 1970s (see page 220), and the latest change is the 2012 stipulation that official tournaments for children under 10 must be played with specific balls for juniors. The professional player's Code of Conduct was introduced in 1975, so when a chair umpire calls 'code violation', it is this Code of Conduct that has been violated.

The 70–68 final set of John Isner and Nicolas Mahut's first-round match at 2010 Wimbledon sparked debate about the implementation of the final set tiebreak rule at all events. The match stretched over three days, and the final set lasted 8 hours 11 minutes alone. The Australian Open, Roland Garros, Wimbledon, Olympics, Davis Cup and Fed Cup are the only events not to use a final set tiebreak.

Founder of the tiebreak, James Van Alen

There are subtle differences in rules between tour bodies, Grand Slam tournaments and Davis Cup. Players at Grand Slam events are allowed 20 seconds between points, whereas on the ATP circuit they are allowed 25. The ATP and US Open reserve the right (and use it) to extend the 60-second break at changes-of-ends if a television-rights holder wants a longer commercial break. And since 2000 professional tennis has had a sit-down break after a completed set but no sit-down after the first game of a set, a convention that is rarely observed at club level.

Perhaps the most significant changes have been to the scoring system. By far the biggest was the tiebreak, which was introduced at the US Open in 1970 (see panel, opposite). This has led to variations in scoring, notably tiebreaks in final sets, and the relatively new 'match tiebreak' that replaces a final set and requires a person or pair to reach 10 points with a lead of at least two, rather than the standard seven points. In 2006 the ATP introduced a 'no advantage' rule for its tour doubles events, which has led to a more predictable length of matches (at deuce, the two pairs play a 'sudden death' point, with the receivers deciding from which side the servers will serve). The ITF experimented with 'short sets' in the 1990s, which effectively amounted to traditional sets but starting at 2–2; yet while this is still legal, it has failed to catch on outside certain junior tournaments.

The man credited with inventing the 'set of points' that we know as the tiebreak was James van Alen, the same man who founded the International Tennis Hall of Fame in Newport, Rhode Island. He came up with a handful of variations, of which his preferred one was the 'nine-point tiebreak': if the score reached 4–4, both players had set point (or match point if appropriate).

The US Open was the first prominent tournament to adopt the tiebreak, imposing it for the 1970 championships at 6–6 in all sets (even final sets). With the 'sudden death' situation at 4–4, the US Tennis Association used the slogan on its 1970 advertising material 'You are cordially invited to sudden death in the afternoon at Forest Hills'. But the nine-point tiebreak didn't catch on, and in

1975 the US Open switched to the 'first to seven with a lead of two' format that is used today.

Wimbledon introduced the tiebreak in 1971, albeit the 'first to seven' breaker and at 8–8, not 6–6. By the late 1970s the tennis world had settled on 6–6, and Wimbledon adopted this in 1979. Davis Cup was the last high-level tennis event to introduce the tiebreak in 1989.

Many tennis historians believe the tiebreak didn't fully arrive in tennis consciousness until 1980, when Bjorn Borg and John McEnroe played an 18–16 breaker in the fourth set of the Wimbledon final. Borg had seven championship points, having already had two at 5–4 in that set, and McEnroe had seven set points, the last of which he converted. But Borg served superbly in the final set and won it 8–6.

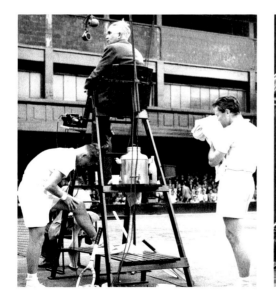

Before seats were introduced for change of ends in the early 1970s, players would towel-down standing up, have a brief refreshment and quickly return to the court. It was the advent of television commercial breaks that instigated the two-minute set break rule.

The infamous 1979 US Open match between Ilie Nastase and John McEnroe, where chair umpire Frank Hammond (left) defaulted Nastase for stalling tactics, which created pandemonium among the raucous night crowd inside the stadium. The decision ended up backfiring on Hammond, who was replaced in the chair.

OFFICIATING

When tennis went open in 1968, it created a gulf between the professionals who played the game and the amateurs – sometimes volunteers – who administered it. And that administration extended to officiating. When the Men's International Professional Tennis Council was founded in 1974, a group of supervisors was formed to bring officiating up to the required standard. But for the first decade, those in umpire's chairs were still largely enthusiasts earning a little pocket money doing something they enjoyed a lot more than their day job. The discrepancy was highlighted in two incidents that took place in 1979 and 1981.

In the first week of the 1979 US Open, John McEnroe and Ilie Nastase were drawn to play each other in a dream night match. The match was hyped by the local media, and a raucous crowd turned up to watch both tennis and temper tantrums. When Nastase pushed his delaying tactics too far, he was penalised by the chair umpire, Frank Hammond. When Nastase persisted, Hammond docked him a point, then a game, and eventually defaulted him. Nastase was a multimillionaire, while Hammond was a lay official earning a small match fee. Hammond's interpretation of the rules was correct, and he was backed by the referee, Mike Blanchard. But when the US Tennis Association feared there would be a riot because of the match's premature conclusion, the tournament director, Bill Talbert, ordered the contest to resume with Blanchard in the umpire's chair. These days, there is nothing to stop a top player from being defaulted for bad behaviour, but professional chair umpires who see the players several times a year generally have a feel for the subtleties that would prevent a player from getting close to being defaulted.

Players Beware!
Point Penalty in Effect

By PARTON KEESE

Tennis fans at the United States Open may not realize it yet, but a "bombshell" is ready to go off sometime during the tournament. For the first time in Forest Hills history, a player, without hitting a ball, can lose a point, a game, a set and even a match entirely at the discretion of an umpire.

For the last seven years, the United States Tennis Association has had a system of point penalties designed to curb delaying tactics, profanity, acts of obscenity and abuse of officials. Until this year, it could not use it except in junior tournaments or events totaling less than $17,500 in prize money.

Suddenly, the door has been opened. "Last year's mess involving Nastase at the Open, I think, was responsible for the I.M.P.T.C. [International Men's Professional Tennis Council] deciding to invoke these penalties against misbehavior," said W.E. (Slew) Hester Jr., president of the U.S.T.A.

"They gave permission for 10 international tournaments to experiment with the point system, and, counting the U.S. clay courts at Indianapolis, this is only the second time it's being used for a Grand Prix tourney in this country."

PUBLISHED: 1 SEPTEMBER 1977, *THE NEW YORK TIMES*

The point penalties system was introduced in the 1970s and was trialled by the USTA in junior and scholastic tournaments. The system got the green light by the MIPTC in 1976 and was enforced for the first time at a Grand Slam at the 1977 US Open. The Code of Conduct is not part of the Rules of Tennis; each tournament has its own code of conduct regulation.

TECHNICALLY ILLEGAL

The Rules of Tennis allow for a certain amount of flexibility in interpreting rules. For example, a chair umpire is encouraged not to give players a time violation without first tipping them off that they are close to getting an official warning. And a couple of things that have become commonplace are still not officially part of the rules, and are thus technically illegal. For example, mid-match coaching is not allowed, other than in team events. Therefore, the WTA's current experiment that allows players to call a designated coach once per set is just that: an experiment. The experiment is approved by the ITF, but at some stage the WTA will have to submit a report with a recommendation for mid-match coaching to be admitted under the Rules.

"All umpires are urged to remember: THE OBJECTIVE IS TO DETER, NOT PUNISH"

FROM THE 1977 AGM PAPER ON THE POINT PENALTIES SYSTEM

In 1981 Edward James was in the chair for the first round match at Wimbledon between McEnroe and Tom Gullikson. Early in the second set, McEnroe lost his temper after a dubious line call, screaming 'You cannot be serious! That ball was on the line, chalk flew up' and went on to call James 'the pits of the world'. James gave McEnroe a point penalty, and he received a second one after an expletive was directed at the referee Fred Hoyles. James and Hoyles were enforcing the rules against a background of McEnroe being an international star, while James was a servant to the game, earning a match fee for doing something he loved. McEnroe went on to win Wimbledon that year.

Up until the mid-1980s, referees and umpires were amateurs who volunteered their services in addition to their day jobs. Today, officiating is a professional career with an established certification programme.

Issue and Debate

The Tennis Officiating Muddle

By NEIL AMDUR

After the $400,000 Grand Prix Masters tennis tournament at Madison Square Garden, controversy continues over officiating and the behavior of top-ranking professional players.

"Not a match goes by when there is not a squabble," Jimmy Connors said of the officiating problems. Four calls were corrected or overruled during his semifinal loss to Vitas Gerulaitis. In the Connors-Bjorn Borg match, Joe Beerman, a linesman, described the verbal abuse he had received from Connors as "the worst in 20 years in the game."

A few weeks ago John Sadri, an American, was fined $250 two times for obscene gestures, foul language and other incidents during the Australian open. In London recently Ilie Nastase, the flamboyant Rumanian, again provoked problems for officials during a match in a world doubles tournament.

"He should have been kicked off the court after the first set," Harry Targett, the chief umpire, said of Nastase's behavior. "The trouble is the authority of umpires has been whittled away over the years, and until it is restored this sort of behavior will continue."

On-court outbursts could be prevented if referees and umpires had greater authority, tournament officials stress.

Referees and umpires already have too much power in pro tennis and are too inconsistent, Connors and other players lament.

Should a central agency be set up to govern officiating at tennis tournaments?

The Background

Tennis is the only major sport in which many referees and umpires remain unsalaried volunteers. (Umpires include chair umpires and line umpires, who are commonly called linesmen). At the Masters, Ray Benton, the tournament director, negotiated a new contract with the Eastern Tennis Umpires Association for the 20 matches during the five-day event. The fee was $3,800, with a full complement of 12 officials for each match.

At last summer's United States Open, which offered $563,000 in prize money, the 170 officials were paid $27.50 a day for each day worked during the tournament. However, the traditional reimbusement at many tournaments remains a free meal, drink chits or match tickets.

"I umpired for 20 years and never received a penny of expense money until I went to the U.S. Open," said Robert N. Rockwell of Bloomington, Minn., chair-

man of the umpires committee for the United States Tennis Association.

Rockwell said that 1,700 umpires had been certified by the association in the last 10 years. He listed the various grades of umpires as follows: sectional line and chair umpires, U.S.T.A. line and chair umpires, and stadium chair and professional chair umpires.

Some umpires, such as Frank Hammond of New York and Mike Blanchard of Phoenix, who officiated the controversial John McEnroe-Nastase match at the Open last summer, and Blanchard's wife, Flo, travel regularly on the men's and women's tours. Others are semipros who can afford to travel but would like reimbursement, Rockwell noted. The third and largest group of umpires are the amateur volunteers who work at the sectional and local level for love of the game.

"How do you structure something like this?" Rockwell said. "It's very difficult."

PUBLISHED: 1 SEPTEMBER 1977,
THE NEW YORK TIMES

The professional vs amateur officiating debacle made the headlines of 'Issue and Debate' in *The New York Times*. The full article discussed the arguments for and against the existence of an established governing body of officiating.

There are two categories of on-court offence that can prompt an official to default a player mid-match. Some offences are limited to a match, such as a succession of code violations, while others fall into a category of serious offences that can lead to further penalties, such as suspensions from official matches. The offence of 'aggravated behaviour' is considered serious. This normally involves a form of anger-fuelled violence or unprofessional conduct that may be out of character for the player but is nonetheless dangerous for officials or spectators. The following players have fallen foul of the aggravated behaviour rule:

Thomas Muster – In 1990 the Austrian was in the process of a remarkable comeback from a career-threatening knee injury. He was committed to a tournament in Prague but said an injury prevented him from playing, so he was ordered to play or face a fine. He told the organisers he would go out for his match against Claudio Pistolesi and retire hurt after one point, which is exactly what he did, constituting an offence of aggravated behaviour. The ATP fined him $25,000 and suspended him for 10 weeks, but both were reduced on appeal. (The official record of the match notes Pistolesi as having won '1–0 ret' but in fact he won '0–0 ret', which may be too esoteric for tennis computers to handle.)

Jeff Tarango – The incident in which Jeff Tarango fell foul of the French chair umpire Bruno Rebeuh at Wimbledon in 1995 is known in tennis folklore for the language Tarango used, and for Tarango's wife, Bernadette, later assaulting Rebeuh. But Tarango's offence was to walk off court without the permission of the officials – the moment he did that, he was guilty of aggravated behaviour and liable to instant default.

Tim Henman – Henman, a generally mild-mannered if fiercely determined player, could claim to be a shade unlucky: when he belted a loose ball in anger, there happened to be a very fast ball girl running across the net at the time. The incident occurred in the fourth set of a doubles match at Wimbledon in 1995, when Henman and Jeremy Bates were playing Henrik Holm and – ironically, given his fate in the singles – Jeff Tarango. The ball struck the girl full on the cheek, and as it had been hit in anger, the referee Alan Mills had no choice but to default the British pair.

Gustavo Kuerten – Bruno Rebeuh also disqualified the otherwise mild-mannered Gustavo Kuerten at the 1998 French Open. Kuerten and fellow Brazilian Fernando Meligeni had just lost a first-set tiebreak against Jonas Bjorkman and Patrick Rafter when he threw his racket towards his chair from the service line. Whether he aimed at his chair or the umpire's chair (the Brazilians were angry at some controversial line calls Rebeuh had awarded against them) is not clear, but the racket hit the ground and rebounded to strike the shoulder of a fan sitting in the first row. Kuerten apologised and said he hoped the incident would make him 'a more mature guy'.

David Nalbandian – The mercurial Argentinean was defaulted midway through a tour final for kicking an advertising hoarding that splintered, injuring a line umpire. The match was the final of the ATP tournament at London's Queen's Club in June 2012, an event that had suffered horrendous luck with injury withdrawals and awful weather. Just as the final between Nalbandian and Marin Cilic was getting interesting, midway through the second set Nalbandian kicked the board in front of the baseline judge after losing a point. Had the board not broken, Nalbandian might have been warned but would not have been defaulted. Had it splintered but not caused any injury, he would probably have got away with it. But the fact that the line umpire suffered a bloody and painful gash to his shin constituted the offence of aggravated behaviour that meant the authorities had no choice but to instantly default Nalbandian.

Roger Federer has never been defaulted despite some tempestuous matches in his junior and early professional days. But tour officials did have to have a quiet word with him about the force with which he hit balls to ball persons. Because he was used to dealing with balls coming at him at speeds well over 200 km/h, he had got into the habit of hitting balls to ball kids at speeds that not all of them could handle. He has since reduced the power of such deliveries.

Tim Henman apologises with flowers

It was only in the mid-1980s that the first touring professional chair umpires came along. The MIPTC – by then shortened to the MTC or 'Pro Council' – hired an American (Richard Kaufman) and an Englishman (Jeremy Shales) to become their first professional touring chair umpires. When the ATP broke away from the Pro Council to found its own tour in 1990, both the ATP and the ITF set up their own officiating departments. On the women's tour, the WTA initially used the ITF's officials but in the 1990s set up its own officiating department, later appointing its own supervisors in the 2000s. In 1997 the three bodies and the Grand Slams came together to form a joint certification scheme for officials.

These days, all chair umpires are freelance, except for a couple of long-serving officials from the days of salaried appointments. Most are associated more with one tour body but will generally work for all three (ITF, ATP and WTA). Chair umpires are graded in five bands: green, white, bronze, silver and gold. Any chair umpire officiating in a main-court singles match in the second week of a Grand Slam tournament is likely to have gold status.

UNRAVELLING THE MISOGYNY

For years it was considered totally acceptable for male chair umpires to officiate in women's matches, but female officials never officiated in men's matches. The ITF began to change this in the 1990s, when Jane Tabor (later Jane Harvey) umpired some Davis Cup matches, and the Grand Slam tournaments began scheduling female chair umpires for men's matches. In 2005 Sandra de Jenken, a slight, unassuming but tough young Frenchwoman from Nice who had an authority about her that referees and supervisors felt would be respected by male players, became the first female chair umpire to officiate at a Davis Cup final.

Sandra de Jenken at the 2005 Davis Cup final

LEFT Certification is administered through the ITF **RIGHT** Carlos Ramos, member of the ITF/Grand Slam team of Officials, teaching an ITF Level 1 (Green Badge) Officiating School in Tangier, Morocco in October 2011. The ITF provides comprehensive training across four levels of officiating.

Ken Farrar, the ITF's first Administrator of Officiating, keeping Brad Gilbert and David Wheaton apart at the 1990 Grand Slam Cup. Philippe Chatrier had approached Farrar in 1988 to upgrade and professionalise officiating, and Farrar was reponsible for implementing the ITF Officials Classification/Certification Programme and ITF Officiating Schools Programme.

The MIPTC's first professional touring chair umpires: left, Richard Kaufman and right, Jeremy Shales

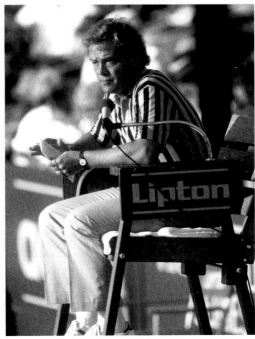

There's a school of thought that believes the scope for gaining an advantage through drugs is limited in tennis, especially compared to sports like running, cycling and swimming, where physical strength, power and stamina play a much bigger role than in a sport like tennis, where technique, tactics and the performance of opponents are central to the outcome. There may be some truth in that, yet the ITF has been eager to keep tennis 'clean', by keeping all drugs that could give players an unfair advantage, and be harmful to their health, out of the sport. Anti-doping rules don't just affect the players – officials and so-called 'support personnel' are also subject to testing.

Anti-doping testing began in the 1980s but initially only for recreational drugs. The ITF had to agree to adopt the International Olympic Committee's anti-doping rules as a condition of tennis returning to Olympics as a full-medal sport in 1988, and the rules were part of tennis's first drug testing programme in 1986, which was drawn up by the Men's Tennis Council and thus involved the ITF, the ATP, the Grand Slams and tour tournaments. Despite steroids having been used illegally in other sports at that time, the banned substances in tennis were initially only heroin, cocaine and amphetamines, but from the late 1980s, the focus shifted more to performance-enhancing drugs, albeit with recreational drugs still banned.

The aim of today's Tennis Anti-Doping Programme is to protect the health of the player as well as to ensure equal and fair competition across the board. An anti-doping rule violation is not just about detecting the presence of a prohibited substance, players can also be found guilty for possession or aiding and abetting.

NO HIDING PLACE, EVEN FOR TOP NAMES

Some people are cynical about efforts to keep tennis clean, but the Tennis Anti-Doping Programme has the support of the top players, and some high-profile players have been caught in the anti-doping net:

Greg Rusedski

• Mats Wilander, the former world No. 1, along with the Czech player Karel Novacek, was found to have evidence of cocaine in his system during an anti-doping test at the 1995 French Open. Wilander claimed his sample had been mishandled and issued legal proceedings against the ITF but later withdrew them and accepted a three-month ban.

• Bohdan Ulihrach, Greg Rusedski and six unnamed players tested positive for nandrolone, which they claimed came from electrolyte tablets administered by ATP trainers. Ulihrach was the first in 2002 and Rusedski tested positive in 2003 but claimed his case was identical to that of Ulihrach and the other six. Although all could have been banned for two years because of the strict liability rule (see panel, page 100), the likelihood that the illegal substances emanated from contaminated tablets handed out by people whom players were entitled to trust led an ATP anti-doping tribunal to exonerate them.

Mariano Puerta

• Mariano Puerta's run to the 2005 French Open final appeared to be a triumph for a player who had previously served a nine-month ban for having taken clenbuterol (he claimed it was to treat asthma, which helped him get his original two-year ban reduced to nine months). But shortly after losing to Rafael Nadal, Puerta was found guilty of a second offence, which carried a 10-year ban (which at the age of 26 would effectively end his career). Puerta said the traces of etilefrine, a cardiac stimulant, in his system could only have come from having drunk from the same glass as his wife, who was taking etilefrine, on the day of the final. Puerta's ban was reduced to nine months, and he returned to the tour, though his second comeback was much less successful than his first.

Sesil Karatancheva

• Bulgaria had a quarterfinalist at the 2005 French Open, but Sesil Karatancheva tested positive, both in Paris and at a tour event a few weeks later, for nandrolone. She claimed she was pregnant at the time, but one of her samples was tested for pregnancy hormones and found to be negative. She served a two-year ban and shortly after returning opted to play for Kazakhstan.

• It seemed a joke to some, but a lengthy investigation established that the 23-year-old Frenchman Richard Gasquet, found guilty of having cocaine in his blood in Miami in 2009, could only have gotten it by kissing a woman in a night club. Gasquet went to the trouble of having a hair sample analysed to prove his innocence, and an investigation established that kissing 'Pamela' in the small hours of the morning was the most likely cause of the cocaine in Gasquet's system. His one-year ban was reduced to two and a half months, which was the length of his suspension at the time the case was decided.

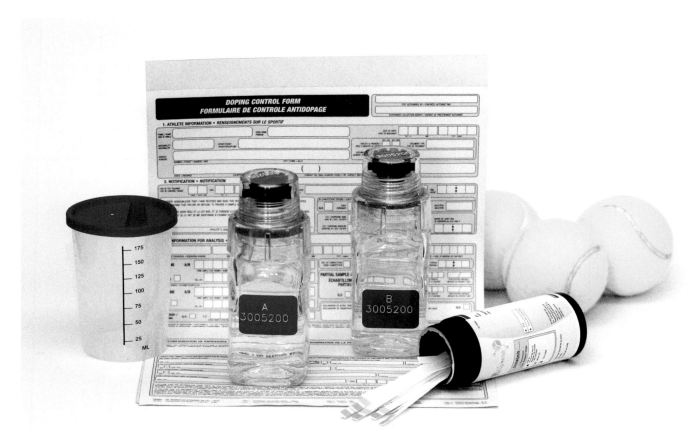

Drug-testing equipment used by the Doping Control Officer. The ITF currently contracts International Doping Tests and Management, one of the biggest independent testing organisations in the world, to provide its testing services. Players and their support personnel are all subject to 'no-advance notice' testing.

In addition to the ITF, the ATP and WTA were also active in anti-doping, and in the early 1990s each of the three bodies pursued its own approach, reflecting a period of frosty relations, especially between the ITF and ATP following the formation of the ATP Tour in 1990. But in 1993 the three came together to adopt a unified Tennis Anti-Doping Programme. Its aim was two-fold: to ensure equal and fair competition on court, and to protect the health of professional tennis players. Apart from agreeing to a set of fixed standards at all top-level tournaments, the programme also included a strong educational component and guidelines for the independent administration of testing. In many respects, tennis's anti-doping programme became a model for other sports, but setting an example could never do the job of a global, non-sport-specific anti-doping authority, and in November 1999, the World Anti-Doping Agency (WADA) was founded. Its aim was to

establish a code of practice that would effectively unify the standards and efforts of all sports across the world to keep harmful and unfair drugs out of sport. The first WADA code was adopted by all international federations representing Olympic summer sports by the 2004 Athens games, and by all IOC member nations by the Turin winter Olympics of 2006. The ITF played a major role in the foundation and development of WADA, notably through the role of its president Francesco Ricci Bitti, who is a member of the WADA Foundation Board, the supreme authority of WADA.

The Tennis Anti-Doping Programme has been beefed up in recent years. In 2004 the ITF began an out-of-competition testing programme, and in 2006 it took over the management, administration and enforcement of anti-doping at ATP sanctioned tournaments, including Challenger events. A year later, it took over the same role at all the leading WTA-sanctioned events.

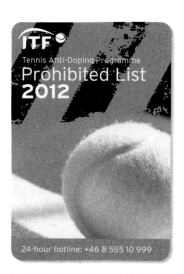

The TADP wallet card listing prohibited substances and a guide to testing

WORLD ANTI-DOPING AGENCY
play true

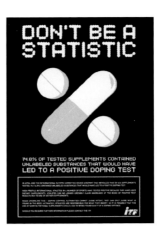

ABOVE

Early anti-doping posters

LEFT

While WADA operates as an arbiter of consistency across the world of anti-doping, the Court of Arbitration for Sport (CAS) is the check and balance that allows any lack of justice – real or perceived – to be appealed. Guillermo Canas is one example of an offender to have appealed his penalty to CAS and succeeded in having his suspension reduced. Canas was initially banned for two years following a positive doping test for a diuretic; the medication was supplied to him by tournament staff, but he failed to take responsibility for checking its contents.

DRUG TESTING (ITF, ATP, WTA) 1996–2011

Year	Tests	Doping Violations	Violations/Test (%)
1996	743	3	0.4
1997	853	1	0.1
1998	963	1	0.1
1999	1,073	0	0.0
2000	1,178	2	0.2
2001	1,240	1	0.1
2002	1,429	0	0.0
2003	2,028	1	0.0
2004	1,650	3	0.2
2005	1,807	10	0.6
2006	1,963	3	0.2
2007	2,028	8	0.4
2008	2,018	3	0.1
2009	2,128	4	0.2
2010	2,075	3	0.1
2011	2,150	3	0.1

The original 2004 WADA code had an optional 'whereabouts' rule, which asked players to say where they would be every day during the 'off season' in November and December, in order to allow for random out-of-competition testing. In 2009 the 'whereabouts' regulations were made compulsory and tightened to be fully compliant with the newly introduced revision of the WADA code. Players are now required to give the full address at which they will spend every night of the year – three months at a time, in advance – including nominating an hour between six in the morning and eleven at night when they can be tested if required. Failure to be available for testing counts as a 'missed test', while failure to submit whereabouts information counts as a 'filing failure'. Any combination of three filing failures or missed tests may result in an anti-doping rule violation. Players who have committed three such whereabouts violations are subject to a ban from tennis of between 12 and 24 months. (A 'standard' anti-doping rule violation – if evidence of a prohibited substance is found in a urine sample – carries anything from a warning to a ban for four years.)

If a player has an illness or condition that requires use of a medication containing a substance on the WADA Prohibited List, a Therapeutic Use Exemption (TUE) must be obtained, which permits the use of that substance, in strict accordance with the stated dosage, ingestion route and frequency.

STRICT LIABILITY

A feature of the Tennis Anti-Doping Programme is that a player is responsible for anything in his or her body, irrespective of how it gets there. This is known as 'strict liability'.

This has seemed very harsh on players who have been given food supplements in good faith that turn out to be contaminated, but if players could pass on the fault to a third party (whether a person supplying a supplement or spiking a drink, or an item of medication that had a banned substance in it), then any anti-doping appeal would rest on a judge or jury to determine 'intent', which is impossible and thus could easily render the whole system unworkable.

Having said that, the 'no significant fault or negligence' provision of the WADA code does allow a player who is found to have a banned substance in his/her sample to claim a lack of intent to enhance performance. This is normally done by players who accept their guilt but are trying to keep their punishment to a minimum, perhaps by claiming there was a banned substance not listed on the label of a medication. Mariano Puerta and Richard Gasquet are among the players who have successfully had punishments reduced by showing they have acted in good faith (see panel page 97), but no player has had a ban rescinded.

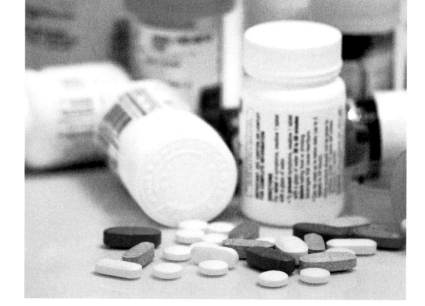

One means by which players are educated on the Tennis Anti-Doping Programme is through a series of cartoons produced by the ITF, which provide information on the relevant parts of the testing process within a lighthearted narrative.

If the whereabouts rule seems pretty draconian for the players, well, that's what the players themselves thought when they were first presented with it. At a stormy meeting of the ATP Player Council in January 2009, a succession of players expressed a level of indignation that experienced observers said was pretty much unprecedented. But at the end of a very long discussion, Roger Federer, the still relatively new president of the Council, said that while the indignation was understandable, everyone wanted a clean sport, and this was the price they would have to pay. The players have since accepted the whereabouts rule as part of their reality.

The ITF contracts an outside company to carry out drug testing at tournaments. The company currently with the contract is IDTM (International Doping Tests and Management), one of the biggest independent testing organisations in the world, which works with WADA in a number of sports. Anti-doping is a responsibility looked after by the ITF's Science and Technical department rather than its Rules department.

The more a player plays, the more he or she is likely to be tested. Top players can expect to be tested more than 10 times a year.

"It would be naive to think that there isn't a risk of systematic doping. Which is why we've got a wide-ranging programme in place. Ideally, you would test every player every day. Clearly, there aren't enough resources to do that, so you have to find ways to make the programme as efficient and as effective as possible, which is why every one of our tests is 'no advance notice' so it's a surprise to the player when someone turns up to test them.

DR. STUART MILLER, DIRECTOR OF SCIENCE & TECHNICAL

TIU TENNIS INTEGRITY UNIT

Callum	Tanya	Karl	Sebastian
Received a two year ban from Tennis	Is enjoying a successful career	Received a lifetime ban from Tennis	Is under active police investigation

The Tennis Integrity Protection Programme is an online interactive educational video designed to raise players' awareness of corrupt approaches. It also tells them what they must do if they receive such an approach. All of the scenarios in the video are based on real-life incidences. Players are alerted to complete the programme every time they log on to a tournament player zone.

BETTING ON MATCHES

As an individual sport, tennis is vulnerable to allegations of match fixing. With large sums of money potentially made and lost betting on the outcome and other aspects of tennis matches, there is the possibility for financial gain for players willing to deliberately lose a match, even though such an incentive directly contradicts the competitive instinct that gets a player to the top.

Following a series of high-profile cases of mysterious betting patterns on matches that produced a surprising result, the ITF, ATP, WTA and Grand Slam Committee commissioned two former British policemen, Jeff Rees and Ben Gunn, to carry out an assessment of the risks and challenges that could undermine the integrity of competition in tennis. In May 2008 the two men presented their Environmental Review of Integrity in Professional Tennis, which made several

recommendations, including those for new rules and refinements to create a uniform programme applicable across all four regulatory bodies. The rules came into effect on 1 January 2009, and since that time any player entering a professional tournament is assumed to have agreed to the Uniform Tennis Anti-Corruption Programme, which is effectively an integrity code.

In order to enforce the Uniform Tennis Anti-Corruption Programme, a Tennis Integrity Unit was formed in September 2008, which became operational in January 2009. The Unit is currently headed by Rees and is housed in the ITF's London headquarters, but all four tennis bodies (ITF, ATP, WTA and the four Grand Slams) contribute to its costs.

The Uniform Tennis Anti-Corruption Programme effectively tightened the rules

on betting-related corruption, although the first penalties for betting on matches pre-date the formation of the Tennis Integrity Unit. The first player to be suspended after his involvement in a betting scandal was Alessio di Mauro, who was banned for nine months following an investigation by the ATP.

Since the formation of the Tennis Integrity Unit, the highest-profile cases have been those of the Austrian Daniel Koellerer and the Serb David Savic. Both were accused of 'contriving or attempting to contrive the outcome of an event', which is legal jargon for match fixing. Each man was found guilty of three violations of the Uniform Tennis Anti-Corruption Programme, banned for life and fined US$100,000. Both cases were the subject of appeals to the Court for Arbitration in Sport (CAS) but the life bans were upheld.

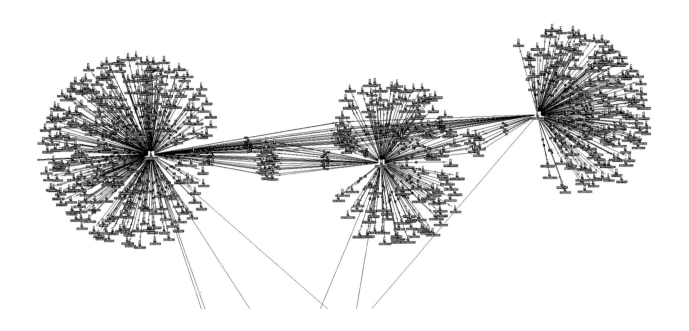

Sophisticated analysis of telephone call data is one of the techniques used by the TIU to investigate suspicious betting patterns, which they are alerted to by betting companies

Players found guilty under the Uniform Tennis Anti-Corruption Programme: from left to right, Daniel Koellerer, Alessio di Mauro and David Savic

"DON'T KEEP THE CUP TOO LONG,
IT'S MEANT TO TRAVEL!"

DWIGHT DAVIS
DAVIS CUP FOUNDER

CHAPTER 05

A GLITTERING PRIZE

DAVIS CUP BY BNP PARIBAS

THROUGHOUT ITS 100-YEAR HISTORY, THE ITF HAS RUN NUMEROUS EVENTS,
LIKE THE MEN'S PROFESSIONAL CIRCUIT UP TO 1990, VARIOUS FUTURES
TOURNAMENT PROGRAMMES TODAY, AND MOST NOTABLY THE TWO
LEADING TEAM COMPETITIONS, DAVIS CUP AND FED CUP.
THESE DAYS, THE JEWEL IN THE CROWN IS WITHOUT QUESTION
DAVIS CUP BY BNP PARIBAS.

GROWTH AND STAGNATION

Because Davis Cup predates the ITF's foundation by 13 years, it's easy to think that it has been at the centre of ITF activity since the start. But the ITF has only been responsible for Davis Cup since 1979. For its first 79 years, the competition was run by a parallel committee called the Davis Cup Nations. Its secretariat shared an office with the ITF, and the ITF was involved in aspects of the Davis Cup's existence, but the Davis Cup Nations had its own separate annual meeting, and the competition's rules were owned by the US Tennis Association, as the trophy had been given by an American, Dwight Davis.

The first Davis Cup tie took place at the Longwood Cricket Club in Boston on 8 August 1900, with Davis himself hitting the second ball: he played in the first match, but as he received serve in the opening game, the first shot was hit by his British opponent, Earnest Black. Soon word was spreading about a great team competition, and other nations wanted to participate. The French and Belgians entered in 1904, with Belgium reaching the final, and soon a combined Australia and New Zealand team under the name Australasia was playing and winning the cup.

MEETING OF DAVIS CUP NATIONS
At the Offices of the Lawn Tennis Association
TUESDAY, JUNE 28th, 1932.

Back Row.	F. H. Woodward, M.B.E. (New Zealand)	C. J. Thompson. (South Africa)	L. Chessex. (Switzerland)	N. N. Ladefoged. (Denmark)	N. J. Ahlund. (Sweden)	H. A. Schelli. (Secretary, L.T.A.)	C. Fagerstrøm. (Norway)	B. de Kehrling. (Hungary)	Dr. H. Albrecht. (Austria)	A. Broese van Groenou. (Holland)	J. Gerke. (Czechoslovakia)

Middle Row.	I. A. Baker. (U.S.A.)	V. Landau. (Monaco)	A. Beckett. (Ireland)	Hon. Cecil Campbell. (Egypt)	T. B. Barker, C.B.E. (South Africa)	R. H. Yondale. (Australia)	E. Millington-Drake. (Argentine)	Dr. K. Lindener. (Germany)	H. H. Monckton. (Great Britain)	Sir A. Crosfield, Bart. (Greece)	Sir Samuel O'Donnell. (India)	J. Zwager. (Dutch East Indies)	S. Miyagichi. (Japan)	H. C. Malloe. Asst. Secretary L.T.A.

Front Row.	R. J. McNair. (Great Britain)	C. S. Almond. (Ireland)	J. S. Cushman. (U.S.A.)	Chevalier P. de Borman. (Belgium)	M. Rances. (France)	Hon. Dwight F. Davis. (U.S.A.)	The Rt. Hon. Lord Viscount D'Abernon, P.C., G.C.B., G.C.M.G. President, L.T.A. (Chairman)	P. Gillou. (France)	Dr. H. O. Behrens. (Germany)	Marquis Pagano di Melito. (Italy)	J. Clemenger. (Australia)	Colonel B. O. Roe. (India)

Thirty-seven representatives from 25 countries convene for a Davis Cup Nations committee meeting in 1932 at 28 Essex Street, London, headquarters of the Lawn Tennis Association. The Davis Cup Nations ran the competition from 1900 to 1979, when the ITF took over.

Del Monte, California, 1899: from left, Dwight Davis, Beals Wright, George Wright (father of Beals), Holcombe Ward and Malcolm Whitman on the trip during which the Davis Cup idea was born. Davis, Ward and Whitman made up the original 1900 US team.

The competition didn't take on a truly global quality until 1921, when Belgium, Czechoslovakia, Spain, India, Denmark, Japan, Canada and others joined the traditional nations to provide a global spectacle with some shock results, notably India beating the French in France, and Japan reaching the final. The French were developing a great team built around four players who became known as the tennis Musketeers: Jacques Brugnon, Jean Borotra, Henri Cochet and Rene Lacoste. Their win over the Americans in 1927 earned France the right to host the 1928 final, and they used that as a reason to build a new stadium and tennis centre that was given the name of a French aviator, Roland Garros, who had fallen in the last days of the First World War.

Despite the increasing number of participating nations, until 1974 only four countries – the four Grand Slam

TOP

Stade Roland Garros is named after the French aviator and First World War fighter pilot who regularly played at the tennis centre in the 1920s.

BOTTOM

Construction of Stade Roland Garros for France's first home Davis Cup Final in 1928

French Musketeer Henri Cochet wins the fifth and final rubber of the 1931 final versus Great Britain, staged at Roland Garros. France first entered the competition in 1904 and, thanks to the Four Musketeers, was unbeatable between 1927 and 1932.

hosts – won the Davis Cup. The Musketeers won the trophy for France from 1927 to 1932, the British had their golden era in the mid-1930s thanks to Fred Perry's dominance, the USA dominated the late 1940s, and the Australians under their inspirational captain Harry Hopman won the Cup 15 times in the 1950s and 1960s.

But the Davis Cup's format was working against the emerging tennis nations. The challenge-round system, by which the champions went straight into the following year's final, meant some great European teams made it to the latter stages thanks to their clay-court prowess but were then thwarted on grass by the USA or, more often, Australia. A few weeks before he died in 1945, Dwight Davis told Australia's Norman Brookes, 'Don't keep the Cup too long, it's meant to travel'. But it didn't travel beyond its four original homes until two years after the challenge round was abolished in 1972.

Australia – pictured here winning the title in 1952 – was the dominant nation of the 1950s and 60s under the captaincy of Harry Hopman.

DAVIS CUP IS MORE IMPORTANT THAN WIMBLEDON!

One of the most remarkable stories from the Davis Cup's history – which seems unthinkable today – came in 1931, when a player was ordered by his Davis Cup captain to forfeit the Wimbledon final so he'd be fit for Davis Cup.

The player was Frank Shields, whose granddaughter, Brooke Shields, was briefly married to Andre Agassi, and the captain was Sam Hardy. Shields turned an ankle playing Jean Borotra in the Wimbledon semifinals but he still managed to win, setting up an all-American final against Sidney Wood. But with the USA due to play Great Britain in what was effectively the Davis Cup semifinal the following week, Hardy ordered Shields not to play, making Wood the only player ever to win Wimbledon on a walkover.

The gamble partly worked and partly failed. Shields beat Fred Perry on the opening day, but he lost the live fifth rubber to Bunny Austin, as the USA failed to reach the Davis Cup challenge round for the first time in 12 years.

Sidney Wood at 1931 Wimbledon

Protests Flare Anew as So. Africa Is Reinstated by Davis Cup Leaders

Special to The New York Times

LONDON, Jan. 14—South Africa, barred from the Davis Cup tennis competition for the last two years, was readmitted today and organizations opposed to the country's policy of racial segregation (apartheid) announced immediately that demonstrations would be mounted at matches involving the South Africans.

Basil Reay, secretary of the Davis Cup Nations' Committee, ascribed the lifting of the ban to "some change in South African political climate, at least sufficient in the view of the committee to enable them to play."

The move followed a decision by the South African Government to allow mixed-race trials for the Federation Cup, the women's equivalent of the Davis Cup, which will be played in Johannesburg in March. The trials for South Africa's team are authorized to be played only on private courts and watched only by national selectors and tennis officials.

The allusion to the improvement in political climate evoked a bitter response from a spokesman for the Anti-Apartheid Movement in Britain.

"It is regrettable," he said, "that the Davis Cup authority should have chosen to be de-

Davis Cup Draw
SECTION A
Preliminary Round
Israel vs. Iran.
First Round
*Rumania vs. Switzerland; Israel or Iran vs. Egypt; *Italy vs. Austria; Netherlands vs. Norway; *Yugoslavia vs. Poland; Finland vs. Denmark; *Soviet Union vs. Hungary; Lebanon vs. Morocco.
Section B
First Round
Luxembourg vs. Monaco; Portugal vs. *South Africa; France vs. Britain; Bulgaria vs. Spain; Ireland vs. Turkey; Greece vs. *West Germany; Sweden vs. New Zealand; Belgium vs. *Czechoslovakia.
*Seeded nation.
Preliminary round to be completed by March 31, first round by May 8, quarter-finals by May 22, semifinals by June 19 and final by July 24.

ceived by minor gestures on the part of the South Africans."

When South Africa played against Britain at Bristol, Eng-

land, in 1969, the matches were twice interrupted by demonstrators.

South Africa was barred in 1970 and 1971 because it was feared its participation would disrupt the competition. In 1969, Czechoslovakia and Poland protested South Africa's policy of apartheid by withdrawing when they were about to meet the South African team. South Africa and Czechoslovakia are in the same section in this year's European Zone play.

Rhodesia's entry for 1972 was rejected for the second successive year. According to

Continued on Page 24, Column 6

PUBLISHED: 15 JANUARY 1922, *THE NEW YORK TIMES*

TOP LEFT

Stan Smith and Ion Tiriac during the heated 1972 USA v Romania final in Bucharest. The tie was already hit with discord before play even started after the Americans were forced to concede home advantage to Romania as a political statement, despite being drawn to host.

TOP RIGHT

US captain Tony Trabert instructs court maintenance staff to clear up the court after protesters threw oil as part of anti-apartheid demonstrations at the 1977 USA v South Africa tie in Arizona.

LEFT

After a two-year Davis Cup ban, South Africa was readmitted on 14 January 1972 following a decision, albeit divided, by the Davis Cup Nations Committee.

POLITICS AND PROFESSIONALISM

With the challenge round eliminated from the start of the 1972 competition, Davis Cup opened the door for more nations to win the biggest team prize in tennis. But with greater prestige came a new problem: politics increasingly played a part in Davis Cup and almost killed it at one point.

Under the new format – whereby all ties were drawn home or away by lot – USA should have been at home for the 1972 final. The Americans had played Romania in North Carolina in their last meeting, so following pressure from the US State Department, they conceded home advantage to Romania. That led to one of the most embittered Davis Cup finals ever, in which the USA just about edged out Ion Tiriac and Ilie Nastase, but not without a number of incidents that left some very bad feelings between the two nations.

The 1974 final was lost to politics, with India refusing to travel to South Africa. With various nations refusing to play other nations (see panel, opposite), matters reached a head in 1976 when the American, British and French tennis associations threatened to pull out of the following year's Davis Cup. That risked killing the competition completely, so in July 1976, the president of the Spanish association, Pablo Llorens, successfully persuaded nations that 1977 be viewed as a 'neutral year' in which the situation could be reviewed. On the whole, this diplomatic initiative worked and the boycotts died down. There were still isolated incidents though – one of which saw the racket-wielding US captain Tony Trabert chase down two anti-apartheid demonstrators who invaded the court during a USA-South Africa tie in Tucson, Arizona – but the political crisis had been largely averted.

Davis Cup's success as an event for nations has made it a tempting target for governments to use as a vehicle for protest. In the 1970s a dozen or more teams refused to play against South Africa, several refused to play against Chile, Morocco refused to play against Algeria, and Kenya refused to play against New Zealand because New Zealand's rugby team had played South Africa. Politics has invaded individual ties too, as the following examples testify.

USA v Germany, Wimbledon, 1937

Playing for the right to challenge a weakened British team in the final, USA and Germany were 2–2 after four rubbers, leaving Gottfried von Cramm, the elegant German aristocrat, facing the powerful American Don Budge in the fifth rubber. It's reported that just before the two players went on court, the locker room attendant told von Cramm he had a long-distance phone call from the German chancellor Adolf Hitler. Hitler was still sore from Jesse Owens's four gold medals at the Berlin Olympics the previous year and allegedly made clear to von Cramm the need to beat the Americans for the sake of national prestige. Much doubt has been cast on the story, but von Cramm was certainly under pressure to deliver Germany's first passage to a Challenge Round. Von Cramm took the first two sets, but Budge fought back to take the third and fourth. Von Cramm led 4–1 in the fifth, but again Budge fought back, broke to lead 7–6 and won the match on his sixth match point. The Americans went on to beat Great Britain in the final, while von Cramm was arrested the following year on dubious homosexuality charges.

Czechoslovakia v Soviet Union, Prague, 1971

It was just three years since Soviet tanks had rolled into Prague to crush the 'Prague Spring', and Czechoslovakia and the Soviet Union were playing each other in the Czech capital. The Soviet team was led by the mild-mannered Alex Metreveli, who became public enemy number one that weekend: all his winners were booed, people laughed when he slipped on the damp clay and suburban trains running along an elevated stretch of track by the court frequently slowed down so drivers and passengers could contribute their indignation. The Czechoslovaks' top player, Jan Kodes, who had just defended his French Open title, was beaten by Metreveli in five sets in the opening rubber. Frantisek Pala made it 1–1 but there was no way the home side was going to win if it lost the doubles. When Kodes and the giant Jan Kukal trailed Metreveli and Sergei Likhachev by two sets to one, things were looking ominous, but the Czech pair came back to win in five. On the final day, a tiring Kodes summoned enough strength to beat Vladimir Korotkov in the third, to signal a victory that meant so much more for the winning nation than it ever should have in purely sporting terms.

South Africa v India, Johannesburg, 1974

The 1974 Davis Cup final is the only one not to be played. South Africa had a formidable team of Cliff Drysdale, Ray Moore, Bob Maud and the doubles pairing of Bob Hewitt and Frew McMillan, who posted an incredible 18 consecutive wins on South American clay. But they never got to play the third round of American Zone South against Argentina, who became the sixth nation to refuse to play South Africa because of its racial-segregation policy. Three rounds on, South Africa reached the final with an emphatic win over Italy in Johannesburg and was due to play India. India's players were braced for their government to order them not to play, but the Indian tennis association was apparently the first to decide and announce that India would decline to face South Africa and therefore concede the Cup.

U.S. Withdraws; Britain, France Quit '77 Davis Cup

By Barry Lorge
Special to The Washington Post

LONDON, July 1—The United States resigned today from the Davis Cup Nations and Great Britain and France withdrew their 1977 entries in a move that may sound the death knell of the Davis Cup as a major international competition.

The withdrawal of the three influential countries came at the annual general meeting of the Davis Cup Nations, the body that administers the premier international team competition in ten-

nis. It followed rejection of a U.S.-led resolution calling for a rules change to suspend nations that enter the Davis Cup and then default for political reasons.

The U.S., Great Britain and France are three of only six nations that have won since Dwight Davis Jr. of St. Louis put the sterling silver cup, originally called the "International Lawn Tennis Challenge Trophy," into play in 1900.

The U.S. defeated Great Britain, the only challenger, that first year in Boston, and has won the cup 24 times,

more than any other nation. Britain has won nine times, and France six.

The only other countries to win are Australia (23 times), South Africa (by default, in 1974) and Sweden in 1975.

The rules-change proposal, which was originated by the U.S. Tennis Association and strongly backed by the British and French associations, would have imposed suspensions on any country that refused to play another because of political considerations. The first offense would have drawn a one-year suspension and a second of-

fense within a five-year period a three-year suspension.

The resolution fell three votes short of the two-thirds majority needed for passage. The vote was 32-21 in favor, but 35 votes were required for adoption. A second, slightly modified resolution, failed by the same vote.

The Davis Cup has been plagued by disruptive forfeits the last two years. In 1974, the Indian government prevented its team from playing South Africa in the Cup final.

The last two years Mexico has eliminated the United States, then de-

faulted to South Africa in the next round. The Mexican government, in refusing to let its team play, has cited a United Nations ruling on sporting contacts with South Africa.

But when USTA officials outlined their plan in February to withdraw from the Davis Cup unless the rules were changed, they emphasized that the problem goes beyond South Africa and opposition to its apartheid racial policies.

"If it was just problem with South Africa I'm sure it could be worked out," Joseph Carrico, chairman of the

U.S. Davis Cup Committee, reiterated today. "What has appalled us is the refusal by some countries to play others simply because they don't like their government or politics."

The Soviet Union, for example, said repeatedly that it would not play Chile because of its opposition to the ruling military junta in Santiago. Similar attitudes have been expressed by other countries.

Chile has already won the American Zone in 1976, and is awaiting a challenger from the European Zone in the

See DAVIS, D4, Col. 5

PUBLISHED: 2 JULY 1976, *THE WASHINGTON POST*

Davis Cup politics reached a head in 1976 and nearly killed the competition. USA resigned from the Davis Cup Nations and Great Britain and France withdrew their entries for the 1977 competition following rejection of the US-led suggested rule change suspending nations who default Davis Cup ties for political reasons. USA said 'they could not afford to have their leading competition controlled by powers outside the National Associations'.

The ITF officially took ownership of the Davis Cup competition in 1979, and today its event operations, communications and commercial departments work closely with national associations and stakeholders to deliver around 90 ties in 70 countries per year.

Meanwhile, Davis Cup was also facing internal challenges from a rapidly professionalising tennis world. In retrospect, the period 1979–81 was arguably the most significant in the Cup's history, as two things happened that saved the competition.

First, the Davis Cup Nations asked the ITF to take responsibility for the competition. The initiative is thought to have come from Philippe Chatrier, who believed that, with the professionalisation of tennis, the best way to cement the strength of the Davis Cup was to have it run by the organisation that represented every tennis nation. The Davis Cup Nations agreed and in 1979 formally asked the ITF to take over the ownership and running of the competition. The effect was not dramatic, as the ITF had been closely involved in the running of the Davis Cup anyway, but on matters where a vote was required, the ITF used its weighted voting system, as opposed to the 'one nation, one vote' system that had been used until then.

The second was a change of format that came into effect in 1981. Under the format adopted in 1971, teams that reached the final had to play five, six or sometimes seven ties in a year, which was acting as a disincentive for the leading players to turn out for their countries. So under a new model devised by both the ITF's general secretary David Gray and former president Derek Hardwick, a 16-nation World Group was established, which cut the number of ties a team would play in a year to a maximum of four. This also limited the number of teams that could win the Cup in a given year to 16, but a comparison of the Davis Cup commitments of players before and after 1981 shows how much it relieved the pressure on the successful nations. The World Group model still exists today, and while there have been a handful of suggestions about the schedule and whether the two finalists should get byes into the following year's quarterfinal round, it has largely worked very well.

A comparison of the maximum number of matches a player could contest under the three Davis Cup formats:

Challenge Round (1900–1971) – 1 year, 3 matches
USA were defending champions in 1969–71 and under the challenge round format automatically received a bye into the final of those years, meaning a player like Stan Smith would only have to play once a year. Players from the opposing team regularly had to play 15 matches or more in a year to reach the final.

Final Round (1972–1980) – 1 year, 18 matches
With the introduction of the Final Round, all nations had to play multiple rounds to reach the final. In 1975 Bjorn Borg played six ties and 17 matches in one year for Sweden to win the trophy, having competed in the Europe preliminary round, quarterfinal, semifinal, and final; the Interzonal semifinal; and the final.

World Group (1981–present) – 1 year, 12 matches
The 16-nation World Group cut the maximum number of ties for a nation to four, which meant 12 matches maximum for a player per year. John McEnroe would regularly play all four rounds for USA in the years they reached the final, but nowadays most nations end up playing just two ties a year.

THE DAVIS CUP STRUCTURE

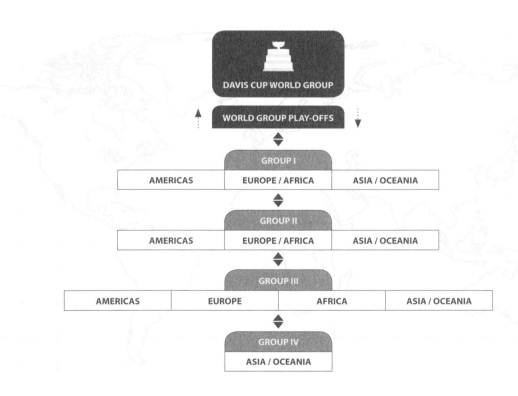

The introduction of the World Group offered greater variety of competition. Under the previous system, nations would find themselves regularly competing against the same opponents. The worldwide format also meant that the best teams had more chance of reaching the final, rather than meeting at an early zonal stage. Promotion and relegation were also a spur to perform.

Yet it was always going to take more than a format change to bring Davis Cup into the modern era – it needed a standard bearer and found one in the form of a most unlikely personality.

John McEnroe had burst onto the scene by reaching the Wimbledon semifinals as an 18-year-old in 1977. His volatile temper made him many enemies, especially among tennis traditionalists, but his sublime talent meant he couldn't be ignored. When he was selected to play for the USA in the 1978 Davis Cup, he took to it with a relish that would last his entire playing career. Not only was he always willing to play for his country, but he regularly wore his USA Davis Cup team tracksuit at tournaments around the world, including the Grand Slams. With Davis Cup looking for credibility, the biggest name in tennis was not only willing to play but to advertise the fact. Hence there's a school of thought that says McEnroe might even have saved Davis Cup – he certainly gave it a massive boost at a time when it could have been very vulnerable.

TOP AND BOTTOM
John McEnroe's Davis Cup debut in 1978 couldn't have come at a better time for the competition. He would compete in every one of USA's 21 ties from the 1978 Final through to the 1984 Final.

NEC was title sponsor of Davis Cup from 1981 to 2001, prior to the ITF signing with BNP Paribas. The agreement with the French bank currently stands through 2016.

Davis Cup's first sponsorship deal in 1981 with the Japanese company NEC had wider implications for the ITF. Until then, the Federation's funding had come largely from membership subscriptions, but the income from Davis Cup sponsorship allowed the governing body of the game to build up a decent-sized staff, knowing it wouldn't be totally dependent on income from national associations.

The deal with NEC lasted until the end of 2001, and the ITF was able to have a seamless transition to the French bank BNP Paribas, which sponsors Davis Cup to this day. The original Banque Nationale de Paris (BNP) had been involved with the French Open since 1973, and after merging with the Paribas bank in the 1990s, it was looking for profile-raising sponsorship opportunities and decided to sponsor

another tennis competition. After visiting a couple of venues and chatting with players, the bank opted to sponsor Davis Cup. It has since sponsored Fed Cup and various other team and individual events. These days, the revenue from BNP Paribas and Davis Cup's other international sponsors and partners makes up about 50 percent of the ITF's operational income.

Rafael Nadal's regular participation in Davis Cup has been a big boost for the event in Spain, with increased attendance figures and TV coverage, and added sponsor interest.

Novak Djokovic credits his success in 2011 with the 'freedom' gained from Serbia's historic Davis Cup title win in 2010. He was instrumental in the nation's breakout from the Europe/Africa zone.

Davis Cup has also been central to the return of tennis to the Olympics since 1988. In order to be eligible for nomination to the Olympics, a tennis player must be 'in good standing with his national association'. He must also have made himself available for selection for at least one Davis Cup tie in two of the four years of an Olympic cycle, of which at least one has to be in the year before or during an Olympics. (Similar rules apply to Fed Cup.) The existing Davis Cup format has survived for 32 years. It has not been immune from criticism, and its clash with the American sports' concept of concentrating their matches in short but intensive seasons has prompted numerous suggestions for an alternative format for the competition, many of them emanating from the USA. The fact that dissatisfaction with Davis Cup has generally been concentrated in North America indicates that most parts of the world are happy with it, but with tennis becoming physically more demanding of the top players and thus adding to scheduling pressures, there is a risk that references to a problem with Davis Cup's schedule becomes the problem itself.

Interestingly, even the players who are most critical about Davis Cup schedule value the competition. Novak Djokovic credits his amazing 2011 year with the 'freedom' gained by Serbia winning the Davis Cup in 2010. Andy Murray has said he wants the Davis Cup to thrive but just wants a schedule that's a little more friendly to the top players. And Rafael Nadal has confided to friends that his irritation with Davis Cup is at least partly due to having to decline the call of his country when a tie doesn't fit with his very punishing tournament schedule.

A 'world cup of tennis' concept to rival Davis Cup was mooted in 2010. But fans responded in support of Davis Cup at the Spain v Switzerland first round tie in Logrono.

THE FOUR PILLARS OF DAVIS CUP

There are four distinguishing features, or 'pillars', of the modern Davis Cup that are central to its existence:

- **Home and away** – The home and away system, with enthusiastic local supporters and vocal visitors, creates the unique atmosphere that characterises Davis Cup.

- **Nomination by national association** – To play for their country, players must be in good standing with their national association, which in turn feeds a sense of responsibility for the growth of the sport in their nation.

- **Following the rules of tennis** – The ITF is the guardian of the rules of tennis and takes this role seriously. It follows then that Davis Cup has resisted the temptation to experiment with rule changes, other than in the lowest zones, in order to protect the integrity of the competition.

- **Annual** – Because the tennis calendar is annual, the ITF believes Davis Cup should also be played annually for many reasons, including scheduling, promotion and revenue generation for the ITF and Davis Cup nations.

"How many times in my career have I played a tennis match in a packed stadium, regardless of which country I was in at the time? How many times in a competition have I seen the fans involved from the very first point to the very last? How many times in your life have you seen tears in the eyes of a player as well as in those of the spectators, who have just witnessed a pure moment of intense emotion? Not very often! There's only one competition in the world that can create that magic – and it's Davis Cup."

GUY FORGET, FORMER DAVIS CUP PLAYER AND CAPTAIN FOR FRANCE

In 2009 the ITF published the results of a survey into the economic value of Davis Cup. It was commissioned at a time when a number of suggestions were being made for alternative formats, some of which contained an implicit assumption that Davis Cup was not performing well economically. Among the findings of the survey were:

- Davis Cup generates an annual economic impact of $184 million. The economic impact is measured through the financial effects of tourism and other industries in nations hosting a tie.

- The economic impact for a Davis Cup final is a minimum of $6 million and was up to $37 million for the 2009 final, thanks to the large capacity of Barcelona's Palau Sant Jordi stadium and the participation of Rafael Nadal. The average semifinal generates $5.5 million, and the average tie in the World Group and Zone Groups I and II is $2.25 million.

- The competition generates around $53 million in commercial income for the ITF and participating nations each year.

- Davis Cup offers greater value for money than events like the Olympics or the soccer World Cup, because it doesn't require new infrastructure but can instead use existing facilities or create temporary structures. Successful nations can also take Davis Cup ties from city to city, thereby promoting tennis in places that may not usually see top-level players.

Such findings don't necessarily stop discussion about alternative models for Davis Cup, but they do set economic and financial benchmarks by which other suggestions need to be measured.

"Davis Cup is a missionary competition, designed to spread interest in the game as widely as possible."

PHILIPPE CHATRIER

Some of the biggest stories in Davis Cup come from those less prominent nations. In 2007, Luis Horna became front-page news when he won Peru their first ever place in the World Group in front of 3,200 fans at the Rinconada Country Club in Lima.

Juan Margets, ITF executive vice president and chairman of the Davis Cup Committee

In the mid-2000s the ITF consulted with the players about their preferred weeks for Davis Cup ties; 17 of the top 20 players signed a letter saying they would prefer the weeks following Grand Slam tournaments. As a result, the current Davis Cup weeks are largely the players' stated preference, yet what works for the majority of players may not work for the marquee names at the top, who play many more matches in a year than those lower down the rankings.

The ITF is always open to suggestions for improving the format, but many alternatives put forward don't fully take into account the broad role of Davis Cup. The ITF's president, Francesco Ricci Bitti, says, 'Commercially, the ideal view of a top tennis event would be to have the world's top eight marketable names competing in a big city, with a lucrative television contract. Looked at from the perspective of entertainment and making money, this view is not wrong. But this is not Davis Cup, it's something else. It can probably get more money, but we

have more responsibilities. Many of the commercial suggestions we have received betray some difficulties understanding the value the competition can bring around the world, especially in countries without top players'.

The chairman of the Davis Cup Committee, Juan Margets, says the key to the future of Davis Cup is strongly intertwined with the future of the tour. 'The Grand Slam tournaments will always have the main place in the calendar', he says, 'and we need to ensure that the rest of the tour is sustainable. We need to keep talking with the ATP and other interests on the tour, but the players need to keep talking with the tour too. And we have to avoid assuming an event has a problem just because a couple of players choose not to play it. If a top player refuses to play a tournament or two, that doesn't mean those tournaments are in crisis, so just because a couple of players decide that Davis Cup doesn't fit in with their schedule in a certain year, it doesn't mean Davis Cup necessarily has a problem'.

DESPITE THE DAVIS CUP'S LONG HISTORY, GENUINE FINALS HAVE ONLY BEEN PLAYED SINCE 1972 — BEFORE THEN IT WAS A CHALLENGE ROUND INVOLVING THE WINNER FROM THE PREVIOUS YEAR AND THE WINNER OF A GLOBAL QUALIFYING COMPETITION. IN THE SUBSEQUENT 40 YEARS, THERE HAVE BEEN SOME EPIC FINALS.

1984, Sweden v USA

This should have been a superb contest, with the USA parading the near-invincible world No. 1 John McEnroe, world No. 2 Jimmy Connors and in doubles McEnroe and Peter Fleming, who hadn't lost in 14 rubbers. But the Swedish team of Mats Wilander (ranked 4), Anders Jarryd (6), Henrik Sundstrom (7) and Stefan Edberg (20) were the champions by Saturday night. Connors went into meltdown against the unflappable Wilander and ended up shaking the umpire's chair in fury, Sundstrom beat McEnroe, and Edberg had a dream day as he and Jarryd beat Fleming and McEnroe in the doubles. Connors never played Davis Cup again, and McEnroe was – somewhat harshly – banned for two years for general irascibility.

1991, France v USA

Perhaps the most emotional final ever, it became iconic for the conga dance led by France's captain Yannick Noah after the French had sealed its first title in 59 years. Noah gambled on the match-rusty Henri Leconte in the final; Leconte beat Davis Cup debutant Pete Sampras on the opening day, then teamed with Guy Forget to win the doubles, and an inspired Forget beat Sampras to give France a 3–1 lead. In the crowd was Jean Borotra, a survivor of France's previous title in 1932; amid the celebrations, he said to Noah, 'Thank you, I don't know how much longer I could have waited'. Borotra died just over two years later.

1995, Russia v USA

This was known as the 'Sampras final' thanks to Pete Sampras's heroics, which he felt were never truly recognised at home. He was emotionally fragile knowing his coach Tim Gullikson had an inoperable brain tumour, but Sampras battled for five sets against Chesnokov on slow clay to give the Americans the first point, before collapsing at the end and needing to be carried from the court with bad cramps. He was fit enough to partner Todd Martin for a superb straight-sets victory over Yevgeny Kafelnikov and Andrei Olhovskiy in the doubles. And he had enough left in the tank to beat a nervous Kafelnikov in the fourth rubber to see the USA to a third title in six years.

1996, Sweden v France

An unprepossessing venue in Malmo hosted one of the most dramatic final days in Davis Cup history, which was not only the curtain on Stefan Edberg's career, but ended with France becoming the first nation to win the Cup having been match point down in the fifth rubber. France began the final day 2–1 up, and when Cedric Pioline led Thomas Enqvist by two sets, it looked clear-cut for the visitors. But Enqvist came back to win 9–7 in the fifth, leaving the final in the hands of Arnaud Boetsch and Nicklas Kulti, the Swede replacing Edberg who had been injured on the opening day. At 7–6 in the final set, Kulti had three match points, but Boetsch ran out the winner 10–8.

2002, France v Russia

Russia's first Davis Cup title came in dramatic circumstances on indoor clay in Paris. Entering the final day 2–1 down after a quality five-set doubles had gone to France, Marat Safin played a superb match to beat Sebastien Grosjean in straight sets. But Russia's talisman Yevgeny Kafelnikov was injured, so the fifth rubber fell to two 20-year-olds, Paul-Henri Mathieu and Mikhail Youzhny. Mathieu took the first two sets, but Youzhny broke early in the third to start a remarkable comeback. Mathieu was two points from victory at 5–4 in the fourth, but Youzhny won in five to become the first man to win a decisive Davis Cup final rubber from two sets down.

2004, Spain v USA

Spain's second home final saw the biggest-ever crowd for an official tennis match. Hosting an American team led by Andy Roddick and the Bryan twins, Spain built a temporary court at one end of Seville's Olympic Stadium, creating 27,200 seats for the final. Carlos Moya was the Spanish team leader, but the home team's second player was uncertain after Juan Carlos Ferrero had lost form, so the Spanish selection committee gambled on an 18-year-old Rafael Nadal. When Nadal beat Roddick in the second singles, there was no way back for the Americans, and Moya sealed the title he was desperate for by beating Roddick in three tight sets in the fourth rubber.

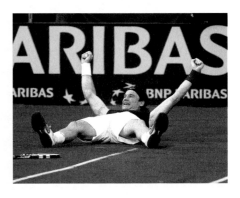

2005, Slovak Republic v Croatia

The breakup of the Soviet Union and Yugoslavia created several new states in central and eastern Europe, many of whom spawned a hungry generation of players, and two of these emerging nations met in the 2005 final. The Slovak Republic had built a brand-new tennis centre in Bratislava, little knowing they would soon host a Davis Cup final. Croatia had been led that year by Ivan Ljubicic, who was having the best year of his career and was unbeaten in nine live rubbers ahead of the final. His doubles victory with Mario Ancic over Dominik Hrbaty and Michal Mertinak was his 11th and the crucial win of the weekend. Hrbaty then played the match of his life to beat Ljubicic in five sets in the fourth rubber, but with Slovakia's second player Karol Beck sidelined having failed a doping test, Ancic had little difficulty beating the inexperienced Mertinak in the fifth rubber to give Croatia the Cup.

"IT REALLY WAS AN EQUALISER,
IN THE SENSE THAT WE WERE
A PART OF SOMETHING,
WE WEREN'T THE STARS."

CHRIS EVERT
USA'S MOST SUCCESSFUL FED CUP PLAYER

CHAPTER 06

A DAVIS CUP FOR WOMEN

FED CUP BY BNP PARIBAS

FED CUP — ORIGINALLY THE FEDERATION CUP — WAS FOUNDED
TO CELEBRATE THE ILTF'S 50TH ANNIVERSARY IN 1963,
SO THE ITF'S CENTENARY IS ALSO FED CUP'S 50TH BIRTHDAY.
ALTHOUGH THE FED CUP HAS SEEN A NUMBER OF CHANGES IN
ITS FIRST HALF-CENTURY, ITS HISTORY CAN BE BROKEN DOWN INTO
TWO PERIODS: 1963-94, AND 1995 TO THE PRESENT,
AS 1995 WAS A YEAR OF MAJOR STRUCTURAL CHANGES
THAT WERE ALSO ACCOMPANIED BY A CHANGE IN NAME.

FORTY-FOUR YEARS IN THE MAKING

In many ways, Fed Cup should have begun about four decades before it actually did. In 1919 Hazel Hotchkiss Wightman, who had been the USA's leading female player in the years before the First World War and had a powerful reputation for sportsmanship, proposed to the ILTF that a competition similar to Davis Cup ought to be started, for women. The all-male committee of the Federation rejected the idea because 'there was not enough interest, nor were there enough top players to justify the expense of a women's team championship'.

Not to be deterred, Wightman directed her energies to starting a new competition the way Davis Cup had started – as a two-nation team event between the best female players of Great Britain and the USA, which became known as the Wightman Cup. This competition lasted from 1923 until 1989, when the relative disparity of strength between the best the British had to offer and the top American female players made the event meaningless. By then Fed Cup was already in existence, but in the 40 years between the starts of the Wightman and Fed Cups, many nations, Australia in particular, applied to join the Wightman Cup, yet it remained a purely British-American event. In its dying days, there were attempts to revive the Wightman Cup as a Europe v USA match, along the lines of golf's Ryder Cup (which also started out as a British-American contest but broadened to include the whole of Europe). But that was rejected, and the Wightman Cup disappeared.

The 1946 American Wightman Cup team set off for Wimbledon, London. From left to right: Captain Hazel Hotchkiss Wightman, Pauline Betz, Margaret Osborne, Doris Hart, Louise Brough, Patricia Todd, and Kay Winthrop. The women's team tournament between USA and Great Britain ran from 1923 until 1989 and was the prequel to today's Fed Cup.

Deeside, Wales, 1974: Virginia Wade was a member of Great Britain's Wightman Cup team for over 20 years and competed in the Federation Cup at the same time in 1967–83. She remains Britain's most successful Fed Cup player to this day.

The Fed Cup trophy was specially handmade in London in 1962 upon donations from ITF member nations amounting to £300.

Nell Hopman joined Hazel Hotchkiss Wightman's campaign for a Davis Cup for women

Hazel Wightman, aided and abetted by Nell Hopman, the wife of the Australian Davis Cup captain Harry Hopman and also a quality player in her own right, lobbied for a women's Davis Cup, but the idea was rejected based on the argument that women didn't have enough drawing power. After marrying into the wealthy DuPont family, the American player Margaret Osborne also proposed an international women's team competition in the 1950s, but that too failed. The breakthrough came in the early 1960s, when Mary Hare, a British citizen living in America who had played Wightman Cup in the 1930s, suggested making the Wightman Cup into a Davis Cup for women. She wrote more than 100 letters to players, administrators and other interested parties throughout the world asking for their support.

As a result of the numerous positive messages she received, Hare, who was the sister of the future ILTF president Derek Hardwick, put a proposal to the Federation in 1962 to hold a team competition for women, played over one week in a single venue to keep costs as low as possible. With the ITLF thinking about how it could celebrate its silver jubilee in 1963, the idea fell on fertile ground, and the first Federation Cup was held at London's Queen's Club in June 1963.

Lawn Tennis

THE LAWN TENNIS ASSOCIATION (Patron: Her Majesty The Queen)

FEDERATION CUP

The Ladies International Team Competition

held under the auspices of the **INTERNATIONAL LAWN TENNIS FEDERATION**

THE QUEEN'S CLUB · 17th-20th June, 1963

INAUGURAL MEETING

ORGANISING COMMITTEE
J. Eaton Griffith, C.M.G., O.B.E. (Chairman)
E. R. Avory, B. A. Barnett, H. T. Baxter, Mrs. W. L. Blakstad, W. S. Kellogg, Lt.-Colonel A. D. C. Macaulay, O.B.E., Dr. R. J. Sandys
Referee - E. Ulrich
S. B. Reay, O.B.E. (Secretary L.T.A.) R. J. Ritchie (Secretary The Queen's Club)

THE LADIES INTERNATIONAL
TEAM COMPETITION

FEDERATION CUP

To commemorate their 50th Anniversary, The International Lawn Tennis Federation have instituted this new competition and have presented a Challenge Bowl to be played for each year.

The Lawn Tennis Association of any country which is a full member of the Federation is eligible to enter, and the idea is that the Competition should be played on the 'knock-out' principle at one centre within one week in a different country each year. In this Anniversary Year—1963 being also the 75th Anniversary of the L.T.A.—the honour of staging the first Competition has been granted to Great Britain.

Each country may enter a team composed of a maximum of three and a minimum of two ladies, and each rubber will consist of two singles and one double. Unlike the Davis Cup, the winner will be required to play through the following year, and the captains will not be allowed to sit on the court.

The idea of playing all rounds at one centre within one week is analogous to 'County Week' in Great Britain, and is designed to avoid the amount of travelling required for the Davis Cup.

The programme for the inaugural Federation Cup, in which 16 nations took part: Australia, Austria, Belgium, Canada, Czechoslovakia, Denmark, France, Germany, Great Britain, Hungary, Italy, Netherlands, Norway, South Africa, Switzerland and USA

In fairness, the first Federation Cup event was not a great success. By taking place alongside the Queen's Club's pre-Wimbledon tournament, many crucial matches were played on outside courts, and rain meant that the final had to be played indoors. But it did feature two of the leading players of the era, Margaret Smith (later Court) and Billie Jean Moffitt (later King), as well as two other Grand Slam champions, Darlene Hard and Lesley Turner (later Bowrey). Victory came down to a deciding doubles, in which the Americans Hard and Moffitt beat Australians Smith and Turner 3–6 13–11 6–3 after saving three match points.

The idea had been to take the competition to various places, and in this respect it was an outstanding success.

The first seven venues were London, Philadelphia, Melbourne, Turin, Berlin, Paris and Athens, and even when countries began hosting the competition for the second time, it was in cities far removed from the first, such as Freiburg in 1970, Perth in 1971 and Naples in 1974.

But by then the Cup was struggling to keep its status in a rapidly professionalising world. In 1970 Gladys Heldman began her Virginia Slims circuit that finally earned female players some commercial clout, and with that came the attitude that players would represent their country only if there was reasonable financial reward. So it was with some relief that the ILTF signed up Colgate-Palmolive in 1976 on a $200,000 sponsorship package.

A FIVER A DAY

The first five Federation Cup competitions took place while tennis was still a strictly amateur sport. Players were expected to pay for the pride of representing their country, but they were given five British pounds a day 'for expenses' as long as their team was still in the tournament. In today's values, that would be about 70 pounds or 110 US dollars.

ILTF president Giorgio de Stefani presents the trophy to the winners of the first-ever Federation Cup, USA's Billie Jean Moffatt, Carol Caldwell and Darlene Hard. USA would go on to dominate Fed Cup, winning again in 1966–67 and 1969, seven consecutive titles in 1976–1982, and another six in 1986, 1989–90, 1996 and 1999–2000.

ON THE FLOOR WITH DELIGHT

The first Federation Cup final was dogged by bad weather. It started outdoors on grass, but rain soon brought it indoors onto the wooden covered courts at London's Queen's Club. While the court was similarly fast and low-bouncing, getting any spectators in was a major task, as the only seating available was on half a dozen benches placed courtside. As the second set of the doubles grew in excitement, the bleachers seating became too much for the US captain, William Scripps Kellogg. Seated on the end of one bench, 'Mr Kellogg' (as he was known to his players) got so excited he slipped off his seat and ended in an undignified heap on the floor. (All in a good cause, as the Americans saved three match points, won the second set, and won the first Fed Cup 6–3 in the third.)

Perth, 1971: Despite losing some of its best players to Gladys Heldman's Virgina Slims circuit, Australia wins the Federation Cup for the second consecutive year thanks to the efforts of Lesley Hunt, Margaret Court and Evonne Goolagong.

In 1977 the 15th Federation Cup saw the event return to Great Britain, and to a slot the week before Wimbledon. But instead of having to be a support act for the men's tournament at London's Queen's Club, the traditional women's tournament at Eastbourne was cancelled for a year to make way for a festival of team tennis that featured the very best in the world. Among the names turning out for their countries were Billie Jean King, Chris Evert, Virginia Wade, Sue Barker Francoise Durr, Betty Stove, Kerry Reid and even Maria Bueno, who at 37 was building up to a comeback at the following week's centenary Wimbledon. In a repeat of the 1963 final, the Americans beat the Australians in the final to claim their sixth title.

Fed Cup has generally escaped becoming the political football that Davis Cup became in the 1970s, but the 1980s did see two incidents that caused the ITF to tread very carefully. In 1982, the 19-year-old Chinese player Hu Na used the Federation Cup week in Santa Clara, California, to disappear and later apply for political asylum in the USA. Her move led to a diplomatic crisis between the USA and China, but that blew over. Ultimately Hu may have got her timing wrong – she defected because she was frustrated at the lack of opportunities the Chinese authorities gave her to play professional tennis outside China, but within a couple of years other Chinese players were allowed to train in America. Hu retired at 29 having never been ranked higher than 50.

The other event came in 1986, when Czechoslovakia was allowed to host the competition on the condition that Martina Navratilova was allowed back to her homeland for the first time since she had defected more than ten years earlier (see panel, opposite).

Devonshire Park, Eastbourne, 1977: Federation Cup returns to British soil for the third time and serves as a warm-up for Wimbledon, attracting all the big names.

Federation Cup enjoyed arguably its most emotional moment in 1986, when it paved the way for Martina Navratilova to return to her native Czechoslovakia 11 years after she had dramatically defected to the USA as an 18-year-old.

In 1983 the Czechoslovak tennis association applied for the right to stage the 1986 Federation Cup. The ITF agreed, on the condition that there were no obstacles put in the way of any eligible player. Although it was a broadly phrased condition, this was done with Navratilova in mind. Since her defection at the 1975 US Open, she had been fearful of landing in Soviet-controlled territory, so much so that she never even took flights that flew over Soviet airspace. This was Navratilova's chance to return home safely.

She not only won the Cup for her adopted nation, but more important, she was triumphantly received by the crowds. No matter that she was playing on an outside court seating 800 for her first-round match while lesser-known players from the Soviet Union and Bulgaria played on the main court (under a sign proclaiming 'Sport helps peaceful understanding among nations'). The crowds strained their necks from the top rows of nearby courts to see her, and on

the elevated rail track that ran behind the courts, an engine kept going back and forth so its driver could witness the great homecoming. After winning her match, Navratilova was mobbed for autographs, including by the line judges.

She even hit the winning shot, beating her successor as home heroine, Hana Mandlikova, in the crucial rubber of the final. The moment the point was over, the Czechoslovak premier rose and left without acknowledging either winner or loser – Navratilova's popularity back home had been a nightmare for the government.

Martina Navratilova's return to Czechoslovakia provided an emotional backdrop to the final in Prague in 1986. "There were people hanging from trees, literally," recalled Navratilova. "When the announcer was instructed not to say my name and just call me 'the player from the United States', people started going crazy and whistling. Finally he said my name but it made a much bigger deal than it actually was."

Nottingham, 1991: Over 75,000 spectators attended the nine-day 'tennis festival' which was a hive of activity and included celebrity appearances, a commercial village, an exhibition court and activities for children. The event ended with Spain winning its first of five Fed Cup titles. Due to the overwhelming numbers in Nottingham, the Fed Cup format was to change for 1992 to include regional qualifying events leading up to a finals week for the top 32 nations.

REFORMATTING THE FORMAT

The format of 16 teams playing a knockout competition, each contest made up of two singles and a doubles, lasted for 32 years. As tennis grew and the demand from new nations to participate in Federation Cup grew with it, qualifying groups were introduced. The 16-nation knockout format reached its peak in 1991 when a record 56 nations gathered in Nottingham, Great Britain. The week ended with Spain lifting its first title, as Arantxa Sanchez Vicario and Conchita Martinez won a deciding doubles against Americans Gigi

Fernandez and Zina Garrison. (Princess Diana also put in an appearance at the opening ceremony to add a touch of royal glamour to the competition.)

Yet the competition still rated below the Davis Cup in player and public recognition, and it was becoming an expensive event for both the ITF and host nations. The Japanese electronics giant NEC had joined as title sponsor in 1980 (a partnership that continued through 1994) but additional sponsorship was becoming difficult to secure. So a decision was made to allocate the

competition to Frankfurt for three years (1992–94), in an attempt to create a permanent annual niche and build up repeat public support and sponsor interest. The first year was a great success, as Steffi Graf led the Germans to their second title, but when Germany lost early in 1993, spectator interest plummeted. The disappointing attempt to revitalise the competition in Frankfurt coupled with the growing number of nations entering the competition – 73 by 1994 – necessitated a rethinking of the format and it happened in 1995.

The 1987 competition in Vancouver was significant for being the first Federation Cup to impact Olympic qualification. With tennis back in the Olympic Games for Seoul 1988, players faced specific qualification criteria which included committing to one's country in Federation Cup. The game's top names travelled to Vancouver and culminated in Steffi Graf's West Germany winning its first title on its fifth appearance in a final, over the American combination of Chris Evert and Pam Shriver.

LEFT The success of Federation Cup in Frankfurt was heavily reliant upon the results of Steffi Graf and the West German team, which meant the competition was on vulnerable ground from the start. **RIGHT** With a change in format in 1995 came the reinstatement of a title sponsor the following year, the Czech KB Bank.

Having seen the great success that Davis Cup enjoys from the home-and-away format, the ITF changed Federation Cup to allow for most ties to involve a home team. The format has been adjusted several times since 1995, including a period when four teams played semifinals and a final in one venue during a single week. But since 2005 the format has been strictly home-and-away, with an eight-nation World Group and a second set of eight nations making up World Group II.

The name was also changed from Federation Cup to Fed Cup – a decision made by the ITF's marketing staff, who felt it would be a lot easier to brand the competition and attract sponsorship with a shorter name. There were suggestions that it should become the Evert Cup or the King Cup, in recognition of the contributions made by Chris Evert and Billie Jean King.

King herself was strongly in favour of resurrecting the name Wightman Cup, because she felt Hazel Wightman had done more than anyone else to sow the seeds of a women's team competition, but Fed Cup was chosen and remains the name to this day.

"I have so much to thank the Fed Cup for. Every time our team went outside the U.S. we learned something and we made new friends. It may be a team tennis competition, but it's also been a fantastic learning experience."

BILLIE JEAN KING, US PLAYER AND FED CUP CAPTAIN

THE BEST-EVER FED CUP MATCH?

The women's team competition has seen plenty of dramatic matches, but few more so than Kimiko Date's 1996 win over the then world No. 1, Steffi Graf, in Tokyo's Ariake Stadium in front of 10,000 people. It was a top-notch German team headed by Graf and Anke Huber, but Japan won thanks to the heroics of Date, who needed just under three and a half hours to beat Graf 12–10 in the final set to give Japan a 2–1 lead. And the win counted for something, for while Huber then beat Naoko Sawamatsu to take the quarterfinal into a live doubles, Japan won the doubles. Graf and Huber won the first set against Kyoko Nagatsuka and Ai Sugiyama, but the Japanese came back to win 6–3 in the third for one of the most spectacular victories in the competition's history.

THE BEST-EVER FED CUP FINAL?

It would be hard to better the 2005 final at Roland Garros, featuring the champions of the previous two years, France and Russia. With Anastasia Myskina taking the first set of the fourth rubber off Mary Pierce, Russia was just one set away from defending its title, but Pierce bounced back to win her greatest match at Roland Garros and level the final at 2–2. So France gambled on Pierce and Amelie Mauresmo in the final against Russia's Elena Dementieva and Dinara Safina. The Russians won the first set, but the French stormed back to take the second. With daylight fading, thoughts turned to an unscheduled third day, but the Russians eked out the final set in the last vestiges of the mid-September Sunday to win their second title.

Like any annual competition, Fed Cup has good years and not-so-good years, but the early 2000s saw a run of landmarks. In 2001 Belgium added its name to the list of winners, in what proved the only triumph for the country's golden generation of Kim Clijsters and Justine Henin. In 2003 France finally got its two star players, Amelie Mauresmo and Mary Pierce, together as France took only its second title in Moscow. A year later, the Russians led by Anastasia Myskina claimed their first title, also in Moscow, while in 2005 France and Russia played out one of the most dramatic finals of recent years at Roland Garros, Russia winning the final doubles on a 6–3 final set to conclude a day of three three-setters just as darkness

threatened to take the final into a third day (see panel, page 135).

The late 2000s were Italy's period of dominance, as its captain, Corrado Barazzutti, was able to pick an admirably consistent four players: Francesca Schiavone, Flavia Pennetta, Sara Errani and Roberta Vinci. Italy first won the Cup in 2006 against Belgium, a shade anticlimactically when Justine Henin retired hurt in the final set of the fifth rubber, unleashing passionate celebrations among the Italians in Charleroi. Italy reached four finals in five years, winning three of them. The current decade has seen the re-emergence of the Czechs, who in 2011 won their first title since Czechoslovakia's fifth title in 1988.

Few teams demonstrate the Fed Cup ethic like the Italians, who were crowned champions in 2006, 2009 and 2010 under the captaincy of Corrado Barazzutti. Francesca Schiavone, Roberta Vinci, Sara Errani and Flavia Pennetta are all long-serving members of the Italian Fed Cup team.

Arantxa Sanchez Vicario contested 16 seasons of Fed Cup, helped Spain win five titles, and became captain in 2012.

Approaching its 50th anniversary, Fed Cup is nearing 100 nations. It is a fully modern competition with its own website, FedCup.com, that, like the Davis Cup's website, exists in both English and Spanish. The competition still attracts the leading players, especially those keen to play in the Olympic tennis events, as Olympic eligibility rules require players to have made themselves available for Fed Cup selection in multiple years leading up to a summer Olympiad. Although Fed Cup does not enjoy the same levels of popularity as its twin, Davis Cup, it still provides moments of remarkable passion and national pride in some great tennis venues that might never otherwise see top-level tennis.

It also has a team of unofficial ambassadors, players like Billie Jean King, Arantxa Sanchez Vicario, Mary Joe Fernandez, Barbara Rittner and Amelie Mauresmo, who are keen to instill into new generations the passion they enjoyed as players.

LEFT Barbara Rittner is the matriarch of the German Fed Cup team and as the federation's national coach concentrates much of her time on nurturing junior players.
RIGHT Mary Joe Fernandez led USA to the finals in her first two years as captain in 2009–10.

"THERE ARE THOSE WHO BELIEVE
THAT THE GREATEST TENNIS TALENT
WHO EVER LIVED WILL NEVER PICK
UP A RACKET BECAUSE HE OR SHE LIVES
IN SOME PLACE LIKE INNER-CITY
DETROIT OR CHICAGO. IF YOU COULD
GET THE RACKET INTO THE HANDS OF
SOME OF THOSE KIDS THEY MIGHT MAKE
ME LOOK LIKE A CLUB PLAYER."

ANDRE AGASSI
TENNIS GREAT AND PHILANTHROPIST

CHAPTER 07

GROWING THE GAME

THE WORK OF THE ITF DEVELOPMENT DEPARTMENT

IN 1986 THE ITF GAVE A $1,000 TRAVEL GRANT TO A SENEGALESE TENNIS PLAYER NAMED YAYA DOUMBIA. IT WAS TO ALLOW HIM TO PLAY A SERIES OF SATELLITE TOURNAMENTS IN FINLAND. HE HAD TO PICK UP THE MONEY IN PARIS, EN ROUTE FOR FINLAND, AND WAS IN SUCH A RUSH TO GET HIS PLANE THAT HE LEFT HIS RACKETS IN THE CAR. EVENTUALLY THEY CAUGHT UP WITH HIM, AND HE EARNED ENOUGH POINTS TO ENTER QUALIFYING TOURNAMENTS ON THE FULL TOUR. IN 1988, RANKED 453, HE WON THE TOURNAMENT IN LYON, BECOMING AT THE TIME THE LOWEST-RANKED PLAYER EVER TO WIN A FULL-TOUR EVENT. THAT YEAR HE REACHED 74 IN THE RANKINGS, AND DURING A CAREER THAT ENDED IN 2000, POSTED A WIN AGAINST IVAN LENDL AND WON A SECOND TOURNAMENT IN BORDEAUX AS A QUALIFIER IN 1995.

THE TALE OF AN AFRICAN WHO STARTED OUT WITH A TRAVEL GRANT OF $1,000 IN HIS POCKET AND WENT ON TO WIN A TOUR TITLE IS A COLOURFUL ONE, AND NOT ALL THE TRAVEL GRANTS ADMINISTERED BY THE ITF HAVE BROUGHT SUCH SUCCESS. BUT DOUMBIA'S STORY IS A SHINING EXAMPLE OF WHAT A SMALL AMOUNT OF MONEY CAREFULLY SPENT CAN DO TO LAUNCH A PLAYER'S CAREER. SUCCESSFUL CAREERS CAN IN TURN INSPIRE OTHER PLAYERS AND CAUSE A VIRTUOUS CIRCLE THAT CAN HELP GROW THE GAME. THAT'S WHY A CORNERSTONE OF THE ITF'S WORK OVER THE PAST QUARTER CENTURY HAS BEEN IN DEVELOPING AND EXPANDING THE SPORT OF TENNIS.

A 'DEVELOPMENT' DEPARTMENT

Before the mid-1970s, development work in tennis had been patchy and suffered from a lack of funds. The ITF's work on development began in 1976 – with something of a wake-up call. At the 1975 ILTF annual general meeting, representatives of African nations were discussing how high the ceiling needed to be to use an indoor arena for Davis Cup ties. As this discussion went on and on, a Senegalese delegate intervened to say that this was a fascinating debate, but did anyone in fact have a supply of balls and rackets they could give to his country, and ideally some advice on how to play tennis?

Tennis EN FRANCE

GRAND PRIX
DE LYON

BLACK MIC-MAC...

Déconcertant, pour ne pas dire plus, le déroulement
du deuxième Grand Prix de Lyon. D'abord avec la chute
de toutes les têtes de série, seul Yannick Noah tenant
son jusqu'en demi-finales ; un samedi à dominante
sombre, puisque trois des quatre joueurs étaient
noirs. Ensuite avec la présence de deux « qua-
lifiés », Eduardo Masso et Yaya Doumbia,
qui devaient se livrer un duel exceptionnel
d'intensité et de chaleur. Enfin avec une
finale noire, la deuxième de l'histoire
du Grand Prix, à l'issue de laquelle Yaya
Doumbia devenait le premier Sénégalais
à inscrire son nom au palmarès du Grand
Prix, un honneur que n'avait jamais
connu un joueur classé aussi loin (453e)
dans la hiérarchie. Après une finale aussi
attendue et classique que celle ayant opposé
l'année précédente Noah et Nyström, Lyon ne
pouvait imaginer version plus diamétralement originale...

De nos envoyés spéciaux Bruno Cuaz
et Christophe Guibbaud.

...ou l'irrésistible ascension de Yaya Doumbia

TOP
Senegalese tennis player Yaya
Doumbia, the ITF development
department's first success story,
makes the front cover of French
Tennis Magazine after winning
1988 Lyon

BOTTOM
Zimbabwe, 1997: One of the
early ITF School Tennis Initiative
programmes, aimed at introducing
the sport to as many primary
school children as possible every
year worldwide. In some parts of
Africa, the absence of equipment
can require creative solutions.

Gil de Kermandec, the French Tennis Federation's first Director of Coaching, conducting an interview at an early West African Junior Championships in Abidjan, Cote d'Ivoire. The WAJC was born out of de Kermadec's report on ways to develop tennis in underdeveloped countries.

The WAJC trophy, 'Trophee Air Afrique'

That awoke in Philippe Chatrier, who by then intended to become the next ILTF president, a recognition that the game's governing body had to be proactive in encouraging the expansion of tennis into new parts of the world. So in 1976 he sent his longstanding associate Gil de Kermadec on a tour of a number of African countries. De Kermadec returned with a report outlining the problems and suggesting what the ILTF could do if it was serious about developing the game, starting in West Africa. Among his recommendations was the idea that money should be provided to assist with equipment, which was expensive and very scarce. In addition, he said courses should be offered to improve the level of coaching, educational material must be available for all, and a small junior competition should be created as an incentive to young players.

The result was the West African Junior Championships, which took place for the first time in late 1977 with four nations participating (today it has more than 300 players from 35 nations). But it wasn't just a stand-alone tournament: it was the culmination of a coaching tour conducted by the American Steve Devereux, who offered coaching clinics and seminars in Nigeria, Togo, Ghana, Cameroon and Senegal. A sign of the amount of work needing to be done was that there weren't enough players in the under-18 category, so a 20-and-under event was held. The event benefited from the logistical support of Air Afrique, an African airline owned jointly by around a dozen governments, which supported the West African Junior Championships by providing greatly discounted tickets for competitors coming from nations served by the airline.

EQUIPMENT

A yearly allowance to every nation involved in the programme, consisting of:

a) Rackets

About fifty rackets would enable serious work to be undertaken. If, hopefully, no more than ten rackets a year were lost or broken, the steady increase in federal equipment would go along with the progression of work.

These rackets should be roughly distributed as follows:

- Children's rackets, 60%: Rackets of this type, short and light, are nowhere to be found in Africa. Training schools for gifted children could not do without them.

- Average quality rackets, 30%: They would be used by confirmed hopes. It is to be noted that such players, when they exist at all, do not own a racket; whenever they train, they are lent rackets which differ each time in weight, balance and tension.

- Good quality rackets, 10%: Intended for the top national players. Most of them have only got one racket of their own or, if they have two, they do not have the same specifications.

b) Gut

An equal number of stringings would enable the rackets to be made best use of. Proposed distribution:

- Cheap nylon (30%): To mend or restring children's or junior players' rackets.

- Good quality nylon (70%): Natural gut does not seem suited for tropical or equatorial climates.

c) Balls

Any balls would be welcome, since even the top players train with used, and often worn out, balls. Whenever it is possible to choose, low pressure yellow balls should be selected, as their characteristics best fit the climate and lighting.

PLAYERS' GRANTS

a) Team grants

These grants would be designed to enable the best national junior team within each qualifying zone to enter several championships in Europe, both to prepare for matches in their eliminating zone, and to go on improving after the contest.

b) Individual grants

They would be reserved for the best players belonging to teams which had not qualified for lack of equal standard partners.

It seems that African national Federations, provided they receive I.L.T.F backing, could induce every foreign firm exploiting or developing the country's natural resources to contribute the funds necessary to meet the cost of transportation and living expenses of one or two national players.

COMPETITIONS

There are no junior competitions in Africa. This is due to the fact that players are often regarded as "juniors" up to the age of thirty, or even later.

Proposing international junior team competitions to African Federations would have the following beneficial results:

- It would make them aware of the necessity of preparing some children to competition.
- They might hope to achieve quick success (it is obvious a junior player requires less time than an adult to reach international standards.)
- It would infuse new life and competitiveness within each Federation and among them all.

They would involve players within definite zones, for distances are huge in Africa, and as the only means of communication available is air transport, travelling is very expensive.

They would necessarily have to spread beyond the limits of the African Continent, so that the best teams might play opponents who could show them where they stood on the international standard scale.

COACH GRANTS

Few African coaches have been given any actual teacher's training. Although it is possible that many of them cannot be expected to take in, digest and apply such principles, it seems however crucial to get those who seem most likely to progress acquainted with these notions.

To achieve substantial results these coaches should be given the opportunity of coming over to train with European or American colleagues both in the technical field (their individual proficiency) and in pedagogy.

These coaches would be selected within each national federation according to criteria to be determined by the I.L.T.F and they would be posted as assistant coaches in tennis camps, clubs or schools what would accept them. A degree, given by the I.L.T.F or by the Federation accepting them should confirm this training so as to put them in a better position when they came back to their country.

TEACHING MATERIAL

Let us finally mention, as a reminder, how useful it would be to circulate written material and films all over Africa.

a) Written material

Liberally illustrated texts, abounding in explicit drawings (many coaches are still illiterate), designed to recall the basic principles of technique, tactics and pedagogy.

b) Films

Filmed reports of important events (main championships, Davis Cup etc) intended to introduce young players to example of high standard playing which they are not likely to meet until they have left their country.

Doug MacCurdy, who became the ITF's first director of development, conducting a coaches' course in Ghana in 1978

Gil de Kermadec and Doug MacCurdy at the inaugural ITF Worldwide Coaches Workshop in 1982, in Delray Beach, Florida

De Kermadec's report became the blueprint for the ITF's development department, even though it took until 1984 for the department to be formally founded. Up to 1984 the ITF's efforts to grow the game were overseen by a development committee, which was dissolved in 1984 to make way for a head of development and five development advisers from various parts of the world. Among the pioneering figures who served on the committee were Enrique Morea, Eve Kraft, Eiichi Kawatei, Alvaro Pena and Alhaji Adejumo.

In the eight years between de Kermadec's mission to Africa and the start of a formal ITF development department, the ITF hired the American coach and talent development consultant Doug MacCurdy for about four months a year, giving him the title 'chief coach'. At the time,

MacCurdy was also administrator of international projects for the USTA. He undertook a number of assignments in Africa starting in 1978, and then turned his attention to South America, Central America and Asia. In 1984 he became the ITF's first director of development, a position he held until 1998 (for three years in the 1990s he was also the Federation's general manager). Since 1998 the development director has been Dave Miley, a tennis coach from Ireland. The other leading figure in development during this time was a Swede, Leif Dahlgren, who was the ITF's development administrator in the late 1980s. The 29-year period since the development department was started has seen massive growth in ITF membership from developing countries, partly as a result of tennis returning to the Olympics.

Cosmetics company Avon was a sponsor of the West African Tour in 1980.

TOP LEFT AND RIGHT
The ITF School Tennis Initiative travels to Bhutan in 1997; here, schoolchildren work on their coordination skills with mini tennis equipment. By 1997, over 60 countries were participating in the programme and the target of getting 350,000 children playing mini tennis around the world had been achieved.

BOTTOM
Leif Dahlgren was one of the pioneers of making the game easy to learn for beginners, and was also a leader in methods of coaching which are cornerstones of coaches' education today.

The Grand Slam Development Fund, established in 1986, provides a way of growing competitive tennis worldwide and gives opportunities to talented junior players from developing countries to compete at an international level. Approximately 40 percent of the annual fund goes to ITF touring teams, like the 2010 ITF/Grand Slam 18 & under team in Europe, pictured here at the ITF headquarters.

THE FUNDING OF
DEVELOPMENT WORK

In 1985 Wimbledon made the first of what it pledged would be an annual donation of £100,000 to help the ITF's efforts to develop the sport of tennis. It was backed up a year later by annual $100,000 grants from the US and French Opens, and the initiative became known as the Grand Slam Trust Fund, later the Grand Slam Development Fund (GSDF), with the mission 'to increase competitive opportunities worldwide'. The Australian Open made its first contribution of $40,000 after moving to its new home at Flinders Park (now Melbourne Park) in 1989. This boosted funding for growing the game, particularly by providing travel grants for young, talented players to compete internationally, and by offering tournament grants for competitive events in parts of the world where the professional game is still fairly underdeveloped. The ITF has administered the GSDF programme on behalf of the Grand Slams since the start.

A tour typically starts with a training camp followed by a series of ITF junior tournaments.

IOC president, Jacques Rogge, visiting the ITF training centre in Burundi in September 2011 shortly after its opening. Rogge met players who will be recommended by the ITF for support from the Olympic Scholarship Programme, which is an Olympic Solidarity initiative established to help talented athletes prepare for future Games.

Funding for development was further enhanced by the Grand Slam Cup. The $2 million for development that came from the tournament replaced the annual grants from the four Slams, which by 1990 aggregated around $400,000. So the increase in development funding was roughly fivefold.

Throughout the late 1980s and 1990s, the ITF continued to contribute development money from its own annual budget, and when tennis returned to the Olympics in 1988, the sport qualified for development income from the Olympic Solidarity funds (worth around $500,000 in 2011). When the Grand Slam Cup ended, the Grand Slams agreed to give their share of the profits from the jointly owned year-ending Tennis Masters Cup (that replaced the ATP Tour World Championships from 2000 to 2008) to development funding. The four Slams also agreed to reinstate their additional contributions. But with the demise of the Tennis Masters Cup and the re-emergence of the ATP World Tour Finals in 2009, development funding has had to be reassessed, and while the total budget the ITF has to work with has remained reasonably constant, some questions remain about where substantial funding for development will come from in the future.

The Grand Slam Cup, the jointly owned ITF and Grand Slam end-of-season championships which ran from 1990 to 1999, was sponsored to the tune of $8 million a year by the Texas computer company Compaq, of which $2 million went to the Grand Slam Development Fund.

WHERE DOES THE MONEY COME FROM....
AND WHERE DOES IT GO?

In 2011 the ITF development department had $4.64 million available for its work. This came from three primary sources:

• ITF budget: $2.34 million
• Grand Slam Development Fund: $1.84 million
• Olympic Solidarity: $460,000

Grand Slam Development Fund money must be used for competition-related purposes, which means tournament grants, junior teams, junior circuits, facility grants and travel grants.

The ITF's money goes to all aspects of development, including development officers, training centres and camps, equipment, coach education, travel grants and various junior initiatives, notably the Junior Tennis Initiative, which assists national associations with their 14-and-under tennis development and high-performance programme.

More than one-third of the total money goes to Africa, with Asia next, at 19 percent of total funding. Development funding has so far provided free equipment to 110 national associations, in the form of 7,778 rackets, 14,989 mini-tennis bats, 22,690 cans of balls, 990 mini-tennis nets, 1,640 200-metre reels of strings and 7,904 coaching books.

One source of funding rarely appreciated by tennis fans is code-violation fines. When a player is fined for breaching the players' code of conduct, the fine goes into development funds. Over $100,000 comes from this source each year.

FROM TOP The 2006 ITF China touring team, the result of a year-long project to establish player development programmes in China ahead of the Beijing Olympics; the Chinese team on tour in Paris; introducing mini tennis in Tonga; donating equipment to national associations is just one element to the Grand Slam Development Fund; developing a national coaching structure in Calcutta, India, with the help of tennis pro Leander Paes

CLOCKWISE FROM TOP Tunisian Ons Jabeur received a GSDF travel grant in 2011 to enter a series of tournaments in Europe and ended up winning junior Roland Garros; a Pacific/Oceania touring team at Melbourne Park on a tour of Australia; development officer Suresh Menon teaching coaching techniques at the Asian Coaches Conference; kids at the ITF training centre in Johannesburg, South Africa in 1997; the GSDF contributed towards the construction of the National Training Centre in Cambodia.

One of the early initiatives of the ITF development department – funded largely by money from the four Grand Slam tournaments – was the establishment of touring teams. These are made up of groups of promising young players from developing tennis nations who have the potential to go on to play Davis Cup and Fed Cup, and possibly to make it onto the full professional tour, but would be unlikely to do so without a helping hand.

The first touring team came from South America and was put together in 1987. Players under 18 years of age were grouped with coaches on a ratio of one coach to about four players and brought to tournaments where they could play competitive matches against top juniors from some of the world's most successful tennis nations. In the following years, teams from Africa and Asia were funded, and further teams from these three continents were added at under-14 and under-16 levels; the top squad of players at the under-18 level then became an all-nations rather than continent-based team. To qualify for the under-18 team, players have to have the kind of ITF junior ranking that would get them direct entry into the junior Grand Slams and other major junior tournaments. These days, around 160 players a year from some 60 countries are given places on touring teams. The team environment complements other assistance, such as travel grants, access to practice facilities and training centres, and entry to tournaments.

A number of players have graduated from the touring team programme to the full professional tour. Two names that stand out are Gustavo Kuerten and Victoria Azarenka, both of whom reached the top of the rankings, but other graduates from touring teams include Marcos Baghdatis, Mahesh Bhupathi, Cara Black, Kateryna Bondarenko, Catalina Castano, Eleni Daniilidou, Luis Horna, Li Na, Nicolas Massu, Leander Paes, Aisam Qureshi, Paradorn Srichaphan and Viktor Troicki.

The success of the touring teams owes much to the former Colombian player Ivan Molina, a French Open mixed doubles champion with Martina Navratilova, who shepherded the first touring team back in 1987 and has been the leading ITF team coach for the past quarter century.

Victoria Azarenka and Kateryna Bondarenko (both right) during training week when they were members of the International 18 & under ITF/Grand Slam team in Europe in 2004. Azarenka has gone on to rank No. 1 in the world, and Bondarenko is a Grand Slam doubles champion.

Members of the 1993 South American 18 & under team in Europe included Nicolas Lapentti (back row, left) and Gustavo Kuerten (front row, left). An ITF coach not only assumes the role of instructor, but also that of parent, teacher and psychologist.

ITF coach Ivan Molina with Romanians Horia Tecau and Florin Mergea, after they defended their boys' doubles title at 2003 Wimbledon. The players were both on touring teams under the guidance of Molina.

TENNIS AS A VEHICLE TO A BETTER LIFE

Eric Hagenimana is from Rwanda. He lost both parents in the Rwandan genocide of 1994 when he was 12 years old. He didn't go to school for a year and a half, but he played tennis. Eric was entered by his federation in the ITF's under-14 tournament in East Africa, in which he did so well that the ITF development officer attending the event offered him a place at the ITF's training centre in South Africa, where he spent four years. He reached the top 100 in the junior world rankings, the top 700 on the ATP, and represented Rwanda in the Davis Cup. He now coaches in France.

Hassan Ndayishimiye from Burundi played in East African tournaments and did well as a 13-year-old, so was offered a place at the ITF training centre in South Africa, where he improved his tennis but also kept up with his education. In 2011 he entered the qualifying tournament for the Wimbledon boys singles thanks to a wildcard requested by the ITF, qualified for the main draw, and became the first player from Burundi to win a round at any Grand Slam tournament.

Sonam Yangchen is a girl from Bhutan whose talent was identified by the ITF's Asian development officer Suresh Menon. She improved to the point where she was given a grant from the Grand Slam Development Fund to play internationally. She went on to earn a scholarship to an American university. She is now a member of parliament in Bhutan and uses her influence to promote tennis among young people in that country.

One of the most important cogs in the ITF development machinery – one that is often unseen and therefore equally often unappreciated – is the regional development officer, the eyes and ears of the development programme. The officer's role is to advise and assist national associations on their tennis activities, conduct coaches education courses and player training, coordinate regional competitions, identify talented players, and generally monitor activities funded by the ITF and GSDF across the globe.

The Federation launched the concept of development officers responsible for a particular group of countries in 1991, when Angus MacAuley was appointed development officer for East Africa based in Nairobi, Kenya. In 1992 Frank Couraud and Gustavo Granitto became development officers in Central America and the Caribbean, and Dan O'Connell was appointed to look after development in Pacific-Oceania from a base in Fiji. Today the ITF has ten development officers: three in Africa, two in Asia, two in Central America and the Caribbean, and one each in South America, Pacific-Oceania and Europe. In 2011 the ten visited more than 110 different countries, each spending an average of 20 weeks on the road.

The ITF also runs four residential training centres: three in Africa (South Africa, Senegal and Burundi) and one in Pacific Oceania (Fiji). These centres offer the 60-or-so youngsters who are based there a blend of schoolwork, general fitness and tennis practice, as well as free time and the chance to learn tennis-related skills such as stringing rackets. Dermot Sweeney, the director of the Southern African centre in Pretoria, says, 'The centre is set up to be like a family environment, with the players living in two houses with a lounge and games area. There are also two dogs. The teamwork is extremely good, and most of the players keep in touch long after they leave the centre'. The ITF funds the centres but also receives some funding for players through Olympic Solidarity scholarships.

Current ITF director of development Dave Miley at the opening of the ITF/FTB/East African Training Centre in Burundi in 2011

Cecilia Ancalmo, development officer for Central America, with wheelchair players in El Salvador

Development officer for West and Central Africa, Amine Ben Makhlouf, teaching in Mali

Part of the ITF's development work involves giving money to clubs and tennis centres in the form of 'facilities grants' to build or improve tennis infrastructure. But sometimes that money must be used to restore tennis facilities after natural disasters.

In the early years of this century, around $40,000 from the Grand Slam Development Fund helped to build a national tennis centre in El Salvador that featured 13 hard courts. But in 2005 Hurricane Stan ravaged the country, causing massive damage to the courts. The ITF gave a further grant to help with repair work, which the president of the El Salvador tennis association described as the money that enabled 'the rebirth of the tennis centre'.

In 2006 the Myanmar (Burmese) tennis association was given money from the Grand Slam Development Fund to install lighting at its ten-court national tennis centre in Yangon. Four months after the lighting was completed, Cyclone Nargis struck Yangon, damaging four courts, the association's office and – yes – the new lighting. The GSDF administrative committee agreed to a one-off grant to repair the damaged lighting.

THE ROLE OF AN ITF DEVELOPMENT OFFICER

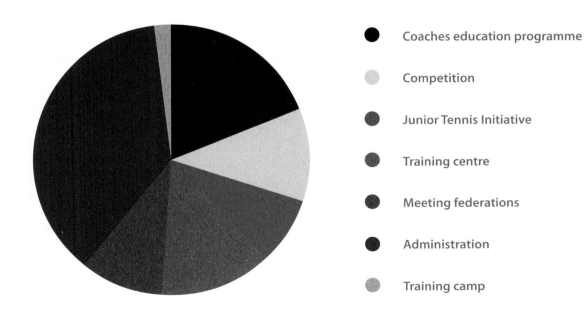

● Coaches education programme

○ Competition

● Junior Tennis Initiative

● Training centre

● Meeting federations

● Administration

● Training camp

A cornerstone of the development department's work is coaches' education. In the early 1980s, coaching tours were held in a variety of countries, ranging from Cyprus and Malta in the Mediterranean to India, and in January 1982 the ITF's first Worldwide Coaches Workshop was held in Delray Beach, Florida. It was attended by representatives of all the leading tennis nations, including Harry Hopman, Nick Bollettieri and Arthur Ashe. Since then, that coaches workshop model has been repeated at regular intervals, and today's workshop, now termed the ITF Worldwide Coaches Conference, attracts more than 600 coaches from around 100 nations.

As the main aim of the ITF's coaches education programme is to help nations become self-sufficient, the ITF doesn't certify coaches. Instead it provides approved syllabuses that are used by more than 100 nations to educate their coaches. National associations are encouraged to use the syllabuses as the basis for establishing their own national coach education and certification systems, which can then be approved by the ITF. So far, 12 nations have been approved at the highest level, and the number is expected to reach around 60 by 2015.

The approved coaches education programme has three levels of syllabus. Level 1 is aimed at those coaching beginners and intermediate players; Level 2 is for coaches working with advanced and high-performance players; and Level 3 was introduced to train coaches working with high-performance players who want to focus on more intricate details of areas covered in Level 2, such as biomechanics, fitness and sports psychology. Before 1993 ITF courses conducted by experienced coaches did exist, but they didn't lead to national certification.

Recognising that having coaching materials only in English would not help the growth of the game, the ITF now makes all syllabuses available in English, French and Spanish, and Level 1 and Level 2 ones are now available in more than 20 languages. The move towards coaching work in English and Spanish began in the 1980s, when the Spanish coach Miguel Crespo began working for the ITF; in 1997 Crespo became the ITF's development research officer based in Valencia, Spain. That year, he and development director Dave Miley wrote the Advanced Coaches Manual, which remains the ITF's best-selling coaching publication.

Legendary Australian player and coach Harry Hopman on court at the first-ever ITF Worldwide Coaches Workshop, held in Florida, USA, in 1982

Delegates at the 2009 Worldwide Coaches Conference in Valencia. Held every two years, the conference is the showpiece of the ITF's Coaches Education Programme, combining information on the latest sports science and practical on-court coaching presentations. The event is sponsored by BNP Paribas.

TOP RIGHT
Development officer for East Africa, Thierry Ntwali, running a Level 1 coaches education course in Burundi

BOTTOM RIGHT
Olympic Solidarity helped fund a Level 2 coaches course in Nigeria in 2010.

Delegates at the 2010 ITF AGM in Washington take part in a Play & Stay demonstration. The initiative was launched in the summer of 2007 and involves all the ITF major nations, the four Grand Slams, six regional associations, the Tennis Industry Association and tennis manufacturers, major coaching bodies as well as the ATP and WTA.

PLAY & STAY

Most development work is a question of setting up infrastructure, but the ITF is also responsible for marketing the sport of tennis, and there is a significant overlap between development and marketing. In recent years, the ITF has rebranded its marketing through development activities under the name 'Tennis Play & Stay', a campaign to demonstrate that when people play tennis in a way that's attractive and fun, they are most likely to stay with the sport.

The Tennis Play & Stay campaign has a core slogan of 'serve, rally, score', and associated key messages highlighting that tennis is 'easy, fun, healthy'. 'Serve, rally, score' is based on an approach to getting children and adults interested in tennis by getting straight to the point. From the first session, players are encouraged to serve, rally as much as they can, and keep score. Once they get the bug, then they can look for coaching to refine their technique, but the idea is to get them playing a recognisable tennis game – even with totally uncoached strokes – from the beginning. The key messages 'easy, fun, healthy' and 'serve, rally, score' are based on making new and potential players think more positively about tennis. Many people think tennis is difficult, certainly compared to other sports they may have tried, so the idea is to show them that it's relatively easy, can be great fun, and is a very good way to become and stay healthy.

ITF development director Dave Miley says, 'In a number of countries, the way coaches have been teaching tennis is based on methods that are 50 years old. It can be like teaching someone to play the piano by getting them to play scales for a year, and only then getting into playing pieces. People who play tennis want to play, not spend the first few months learning technique with little progress, or standing on a court watching others practise. There's also a perception in tennis that it's difficult – yes, it's difficult to do really well, but so is football, so we have to let people know that it's easy to play, even if you have to work hard to get better. But the campaign only works if it works at the micro level, which means in clubs and tennis coaching venues – we drop the stone, and the national associations then need to manage the waves'.

Roger Federer takes part in a Play & Stay promotional event at the Estoril Open in 2010.

ATP player Aisam Qureshi acts as an unofficial ambassador of Tennis Play & Stay, researching the viability of the programme for victims of the war on terror in Pakistan.

Research funded by the ITF and carried out by Babette Pluim and other associates of the ITF has highlighted that recreational tennis is good for one's health. A report by Pluim and four other authors, 'Health Benefits of Tennis', published in 2007 in the British Journal of Sports Medicine, shows that in one hour of recreational tennis, the average distance travelled is 2.3 kilometres, generating a heart rate of between 140 and 170. And with breaks between points, tennis creates 'interval training', which is very efficient for strengthening the heart muscles.

As a result, the report concluded that people who choose to play tennis appear to have significant health benefits, including improved aerobic fitness, a lower body-fat percentage, a more favourable lipid profile, a reduced risk of developing heart disease, and improved bone health.

In Myanmar, Burmese monks bless the children and their equipment ahead of the day's Play & Stay programme.

Tennis stopped traffic in Buenos Aires in March 2012 with the launch of the Tennis 10s tour by the Argentine tennis assocation. More than 50 red courts were constructed on Avenida 9 de Julio, closing seven lanes of the road for around four hours while 300 Tennis 10s players took part in a fun team competition.

Another sub-slogan of Tennis Play & Stay is 'Tennis 10s', an initiative aimed at introducing youngsters age ten and under to tennis in a way that is likely to make them want to stick with it. This is an updated form of what was previously known as 'mini-tennis', a form of the game aimed at children aged 6 to 11 in schools and clubs; it was launched in 1996 under the name 'Schools Tennis Initiative' and later referred to as 'Junior Tennis Initiative'.

One of the central themes of Tennis 10s is the emergence and proliferation of slower balls, a move that has also benefited adult beginners and has led to one of tennis's rare rule changes (see panel, opposite). It will take a decade or so for the full effects of players using the slower balls to work through to the full tour, but the hope is that they will allow juniors to develop their own styles rather than feel that there is only one way to play. ITF development officials believe the slower balls could bring back some one-handed backhands and possibly encourage more volleying. In 2012 the ITF launched 'Tennis Xpress', another Play & Stay programme that allows adults to learn tennis in an active and dynamic environment using the slower balls.

In 2001 an ITF task force was formed to look at how tennis could be introduced to new players in a way that made them want to stay with the sport. The team determined that slower balls make it a lot easier and more fun for starter players of all ages to learn, compared to learning with regular tennis balls. This tied in with anecdotal evidence that suggested regular tennis balls were not conducive to good learning. For example, as a junior, Justine Henin used soft balls in practice, but then had to adjust to the heavier yellow balls for matches; coaches in Sweden used slower balls for many years, and in the 1950s Czechoslovakian juniors coaches were found to be using punctured yellow balls to make it easier for youngsters to play lengthy rallies.

In 2004 Sandy Proctor of the British national association LTA coined the 'red, orange, green' terminology taken from traffic lights to indicate the progression in balls for youngsters: red as the slowest (75% slower than regular balls), then orange (50% slower) and green (25% slower). The ITF adopted this terminology and incorporated it into the Play & Stay campaign launched in 2007.

Since then, the use of red, orange and green balls has resulted in many nations reporting higher participation levels – sometimes even among adults who find slower balls easier for learning strokes – and scientific studies show that children have more fun, hit more balls and can use more advanced tactics than they can with standard yellow balls. And sales have reflected the trend: in 2008,

1.5 million softer balls were sold in the USA, a figure that rose to more than 2 million in 2009, with sales of 53–58 cm rackets (21–23 inches) increasing by 88 percent in one year.

This culminated in one of tennis's very rare rule changes in 2010. Since the start of 2012, a slower ball has been obligatory in all ten-and-under competition worldwide. Standard yellow balls are no longer allowed in any tournaments for these age groups – instead, clubs and tournament organisers have to have a red, orange or green ball on appropriate-sized courts.

Children try out the slower red balls at a Tennis 10s event organised by the Hellenic Tennis Federation in Athens

Retired player Martin Vassallo Arguello, who now runs a development programme at the Argentine tennis association, with kids at the Tennis 10s launch

Michelle Obama speaking at a USTA 10-and-under clinic at the 2011 US Open. The First Lady is behind the Let's Move! initiative (a partnership with the USTA) to encourage more children to live an active and healthy lifestyle.

More than 100 nations were running Tennis Play & Stay campaigns by 2011, some having used the logo in their national colours, and others having used their own top players and sponsors to make the promotional literature more attractive. An example of its success came in the South American 12-and-under championships, when Peru won with a team that included two girls from a socio-economic background not normally attracted to tennis, who had started tennis through Play & Stay initiatives.

In one important respect, the ITF's development work is much like charitable activity – there are always vastly more people who need help than there are resources to help them. To that extent, the ITF can only put in place pyramid-like structures it hopes will spread the encouragement of tennis throughout the world. But it's a model that has many admirers, including the International Olympic Committee president, Jacques Rogge, and the head of OIympic Solidarity, Pere Miro, who have both praised the ITF's development activity in public comments.

Miley says, 'Our work ranges from grass roots to Grand Slams, and the two ends of the spectrum are closely interlinked, albeit in a way that can't be quantified. The health of the sport depends on a lot of people playing, because when they play they want to watch, and because they play they want to buy things that make them play better (equipment, coaching, etc.). That's why decisions to fund junior clinics in parts of the developing world can ultimately benefit the Grand Slams, and all tennis's various layers of activity in between'.

In the USA, 5,000 courts already have blended lines drawn for junior courts. Within a decade, it's possible all courts will look like this.

Mayor of London Boris Johnson and UK Prime Minister David Cameron using the slower red balls at an International Paralympic Day exhibition in September 2011

Making friends through tennis: children of the Aspeca Orphanage in Kep, Cambodia, with Play & Stay equipment supplied by the ITF

"The International Tennis Federation is an excellent example of an international sports federation whose leadership is always striving to find new avenues in which to develop the sport. Since the late 1970s, the ITF Development Programme has allowed hundreds of players from a wide range of countries to qualify and compete at international level and, since 1988, at the Olympic Games. Today, this very comprehensive programme covering all aspects of tennis development is often cited as a model for other international federations."

JACQUES ROGGE, IOC PRESIDENT

IT'S EASY TO THINK OF THE ITF AS SIMPLY THE GAME'S GOVERNING BODY BASED
AT ITS LONDON OFFICES, RUNNING HIGH-PROFILE EVENTS LIKE DAVIS CUP
AND FED CUP. THAT'S JUST THE TOP OF THE PYRAMID. FURTHER DOWN THERE
IS A HIVE OF ACTIVITY ACROSS THE WORLD, WITH COUNTLESS VOLUNTEERS
AND LOW-LEVEL PROFESSIONALS DOING THEIR BIT TO ENCOURAGE PEOPLE
TO ENJOY TENNIS. HERE IS A SAMPLE OF SIX PEOPLE FROM ACROSS THE GLOBE.

Mario Carreras Aguero (Cuba) is a 57-year-old coach of young players (still widely known as mini tennis, now officially Tennis 10s) who has worked for most of his life developing a basis for tennis coaching in Cuba and making use of materials and advice from the ITF. He was 17 when the Cuban national school games came to his town, so he trained as an umpire, and then pursued a career as a physical education teacher. He spent his life in Cuba until 2008, often working against considerable obstacles. For the last four years he has worked at the Cuban Sporting Club in Panama, using his knowledge of developing the youngest players. Often his only means of transport has been a bicycle, though he has had to make use of long-distance bus services when he wants to monitor the development of his Tennis 10s programme. He says, 'To triumph in my camp and in all problems that life throws up, you need a key word: desire. Because to want to do something is to be able to do it'.

Mario Lucero (El Salvador) is a 55-year-old wheelchair tennis coach in El Salvador. He himself has been in a wheelchair since suffering a motorcycle accident at 16. His original sport was basketball, and he only discovered tennis in 1999 after receiving an invitation from the El Savador tennis federation. He knew nothing about tennis at the time but was instantly hooked, and since then has taught tennis to adults and children in wheelchairs. On Saturday mornings he meets with up to 12 players of all ages, teaching them not just about tennis but about overcoming their disabilities and adapting to life with physical limitations. He gets around in a 1985 car, and he pays for the petrol by repairing old electrical items. He says, 'In El Salvador the social problems are barriers, and I think my contribution has been a positive one: through tennis to get our boys away from the gangs and the drugs and to get them leading healthy lives'.

Manuel Maldonado (Guatemala) is one of Guatemala's most experienced coaches. He began at age 19 with adults and five years later started with kids. He now has 60–90 kids aged between 6 and 16. His effectiveness rose dramatically when he moved out of the capital, Guatemala City, and into the provinces after recognising that most of Guatemala's tennis activity takes place in the capital, but very little in the provinces. He is now responsible for eight provinces in the south of the country, and he has to travel by bus, sometimes up to two and a half hours to get to work, which means some days getting up at 4:30 a.m. in order to start coaching at 8 a.m. Not only does he not know how to drive a car, but he doesn't know how to work a computer, yet has a knack for inspiring young people. He says, 'The big difference I've seen in my 34 years working in tennis is the expansion in all the provincial departments of the country, not just in the capital. Before, only the kids from privileged classes in the capital could practise this sport. It's more exciting to work in the provinces because we find a lot of kids who just wouldn't have the chance to play tennis if we hadn't brought them the opportunity. They're enthusiastic, they always want to practise, they want to get better every day – I have mornings where they're waiting for me on court, eager to get on with the coaching, and that motivates my work a lot'.

Cheikh Sidia Berthe (Senegal) was one of the most prolific contributors to the development of tennis in Africa in the three decades before his death in 2008. An administrative director at a university, he discovered tennis relatively late but went on a course in the 1980s in Czechoslovakia, returning to Senegal enthused about promoting the sport of tennis through teaching it to youngsters. He spent all his free time – and sometimes more – coaching children and adults, often for no fee, and one of his early pupils was Yaya Doumbia (see page 140). This culminated in him setting up a tennis school in 1981, which grew rapidly. In spite of severe difficulties, within two years he opened a club, the Olympique Club in the capital Dakar, which has prospered and now has eight courts, plus squash courts, a fitness room and a swimming pool. He also served on the boards of the Senegalese tennis association and the African tennis confederation.

Yong Phui Chon (Malaysia) was 23 years old and selling noodles at a coffee shop in Kuching, on the island of Sarawak, when one of his regular customers gave him an old racket. When Yong came to use the racket, it became clear he was very gifted at tennis, and one of the regulars got him a job in the forestry department as they were looking for decent players to compete in an inter-departmental tennis tournament. Having landed himself a good job as a result of tennis, he began coaching during his free time, gaining his USPTR certificate after four years. He has now coached for 25 years, offering coaching at much lower prices than he could charge if he were in a big city. He has produced many outstanding tennis players who have won national titles and ITF junior tournaments, and some have become successful professionals and secured tennis scholarships to study in the USA. He says, 'I hope the training youngsters receive from me will mould them to be more disciplined, confident and mentally tough individuals'.

Anousith 'Khek' Phonesavath (Laos) was just 24 when he founded the first tennis club in Luang Prabang, Laos, and named it the 'Club Love Tennis'. Khek was self-taught, having learned as a child with a discarded racket and some old balls. After expressing an interest in setting up a club, a friend provided the facility, while Khek did all the work, drawing on his passion for tennis to become the club's coach. He now offers coaching to young children from disadvantaged backgrounds for free, encouraging them to become the best tennis players they can be. Many of these children attend coaching with no shoes and have to make do with discarded rackets from Khek and his friends, but they are in most cases passionate about the sport. He has tried to get funding from the Laos ministry of education and sports, but so far without success. To support himself, Khek works as a waiter in a hotel. He says, 'I hope some of my coaching will mean that the people I teach become coaches and they will continue my work, especially with children from underprivileged backgrounds. I have seen how tennis has helped some children avoid getting dragged into the world of drugs and crime, so I really want this work to continue'.

Left to right: Mario Carreras Aguero, Mario Lucero and Anousith 'Khek' Phonesavath

"TENNIS IS A LIFE-LONG SPORT,
SO WE MUST TAKE CARE OF VETERANS
AS MUCH AS WE TAKE CARE OF JUNIORS."

PHILIPPE CHATRIER
ITF PRESIDENT 1977–1991

CHAPTER 08

TENNIS FOR LIFE

THE ITF'S WORK FOR JUNIORS AND OVER-35s

IT'S EASY TO THINK OF JUNIORS AND OVER-35s AS SIMPLY THE AGE GROUPS
ON EITHER SIDE OF THE WORLD'S BEST AND BEST-KNOWN PLAYERS.
BUT THEY HAVE TWO VERY DIFFERENT ROLES. THE ITF'S WORK FOR JUNIORS
INVOLVES BOTH THE CREATION OF A BREEDING GROUND FOR THE NEXT GENERATION
OF TALENT AND THE NURTURING OF MILLIONS OF HOBBY PLAYERS WHO KEEP
THE SPORT GOING THROUGH THEIR ENJOYMENT OF IT AND THEIR SUPPORT
OF TENNIS-RELATED SERVICES. THE FEDERATION'S WORK FOR SENIORS
INVOLVES MAINTAINING A COMPETITIVE STRUCTURE FOR PLAYERS FROM AGE 35
INTO THEIR 90s, SO THAT THOSE WHO ASPIRE TO BE THE BEST DON'T
FACE DISCRIMINATION ON THE GROUNDS OF ADVANCING YEARS.

SENIORS

'Seniors' is the name given to players age 35 or older. Administratively, it is subdivided into Seniors – those age 35 to 59 – and Super Seniors, who are 60 and over (the last official age group is 85 and over, though a few sprightly 90-somethings have lobbied for a 90-and-over age group). It hasn't been called Seniors forever. At the start, the over-35s were known as 'veterans', and then 'vets', but neither was totally clear. In America, 'veterans' has strong ex-military connotations, while in many parts of the world, 'vets' are animal doctors. So in 2004 the ITF adopted the name Seniors, as it was felt to be universally understood (although the name veterans is still used, notably by the British seniors who call themselves 'Tennis Vets GB').

Structured tennis for the over-35s goes back for most of the ITF's 100 years, but it was not organised internationally until 1958. The US Lawn Tennis Association had a seniors committee from 1947, and there were various well-established tournaments for seniors scattered worldwide. But it was not until 1957 that a group of five people got together to form an international association to coordinate a transnational structure for veterans tennis. Italian Alessandro Loewy, Leon Dubler of Switzerland, Geza Wertheim of Luxembourg, Frenchman Luis Gautier-Chaument and Fritz Kuhlmann of Germany founded the Veterans International Tennis Association (the acronym VITA is Latin for 'life' – something the five founders were well aware of).

There is no age limit to compete on the ITF Seniors Circuit. The oldest age bracket is 85-and-over, although the increasing number of players still competing in their 90s could one day demand an additional age group. The seniors circuit runs just like its junior, wheelchair or men's and women's counterparts, with a player online entry and tournament management system (IPIN) and a 52-week rollover world ranking.

LEFT Italian Alessandro Loewy, the first president of the Veterans International Tennis Association. His experience in founding the Italian Amateur Veterans Tennis Association was vital to the creation of VITA. **MIDDLE** Fritz Kuhlmann, co-founder of VITA, was also president of the Badischer Tennis Verband, the most influential regional association in Germany. **RIGHT** Swiss Leon Dubler succeeded Loewy as president of VITA and like Loewy, was president of his national veterans association. Dubler donated the cup to VITA for the first international team competition, subsequently named the Dubler Cup.

VITA grew from the need to establish an official veterans tennis structure. Until the 1950s, the veterans tennis scene was made up of disparate events in a handful of countries. Activity continued to expand into new continents over the next 20 years and in 1979 the ILTF agreed to incorporate VITA into its own organisation, renaming it Vets Tennis. In 2004 it was rebranded as ITF Seniors for better promotion, marketing and development worldwide.

Fred Perry pictured in 1992 with the winning German team on one of his many visits to the Fred Perry Cup, the team championships for men age 50 and over

Dubler, a Swiss millionaire, gave his name – and the cup – to the first VITA-inspired competition, the Dubler Cup. This veterans team competition for men age 45 and over was run along similar lines to the Davis Cup. Italy won the first one, beating Germany in the final. Veterans tennis has various age groups, so the number of Cups and competitions is vast. The first women's event was the Young Cup for those age 40 and over, inaugurated in 1977, while a men's 55-and-over competition, the Austria Cup, was launched that same year, and the Britannia Cup for men over 65 came two years later. Among the total of 20 ITF-recognised seniors team competitions are the Fred Perry Cup and the Margaret Court Cup, and both tennis legends attended the competitions played in their names.

By 1979 VITA was supervising events in Europe, North America, South America and Australia, and was growing to the point where its links with the ITF were

becoming more intensive. It therefore seemed a natural progression for the association to be integrated into the ITF, and VITA was transformed into the ITF Veterans Committee. The first chairman of the committee was the Yugoslav Radmilo Nikolic, who spent 12 years as the ITF's veterans' supremo, assisted at staff level by Tony Gathercole, the first manager of veterans tennis, who worked out of the ITF's London headquarters.

By 1981 there were a number of team competitions, but demand for a world individual championships was growing. The initiative came from Otto Hauser, a member of the ITF veterans committee, who found a host nation, Brazil, and a venue, the Esporte Clube Sirio in São Paulo, for the first world individual seniors championships in 1981. The fact that the Dubler Cup was played in Argentina that year and the world individual championships were staged shortly thereafter meant 136 of the world's leading over-35 players took part.

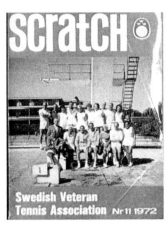

Jack Kotschack was the founding member of the Swedish Veterans Tennis Association and an early member of VITA. The Swede embraced the task of promoting veterans tennis through his self-confessed 'labour of love', *Scratch* magazine. *Scratch* began in 1961 as the official publication of the Swedish association, but such was its popularity that Kotschack began to add English articles about international veterans activities until its worldwide renown demanded an almost entirely English publication. *Scratch* was completely self-financed, written and edited by Kotschack.

LEFT Czech-born Argentinean Otto Hauser was undoubtedly responsible for the growth of veterans tennis in South America. He was invited to join VITA by Leon Dubler in 1969 and continued as an active member of the ITF Veterans Committee until his death in 1993. **RIGHT** Theo Sperry, left, established the first ITF Veterans Rankings published in 1981 and continued to be solely responsible for ranking calculation – a purely manual operation – until 1991.

"There is nothing like seniors tennis to keep one from growing old." LEON DUBLER

In the intervening 32 years, the world championships have grown into the biggest international event in tennis in terms of number of competitors and number of matches. The large number of different age groups means there are more competitions, and the change in venue each year poses a massive logistical challenge because there is no fixed infrastructure. So in 1994 the world individual championships were divided into two events: one for Seniors, the other for Super-Seniors. But in 2008 the two came together for a record-breaking all-comers championships in Antalya, Turkey, when the event saw 1,656 matches in its designated week (Wimbledon has around 650 main draw matches in a fortnight). The event was played on 88 courts across two clubs: 59 at the Ali Bey Club in Manavgat, and 29 at the Ali Bey Club in Belek.

In 1981 the ITF introduced individual singles rankings for seniors players. In 2010 a World Team Ranking was introduced, to mirror the Davis Cup and Fed Cup nations ranking systems; it takes into account the previous five years of each team cup. In 2011 a ranking system for seniors doubles and mixed doubles was introduced.

The Seniors and Super-Seniors World Individual Championships came together in one week for the first time in 2008, in Antalya, Turkey. The event saw a phenomenal 1,656 matches played on 88 courts across two clubs.

One of the active 90-somethings on the tour, Helene Salvetat of France.

PICK ON SOMEONE YOUR OWN AGE!

Although tournaments for seniors today can be run in age groups that span five years, in the early years there were sometimes large gaps between the different age groups offered at tournaments, which meant players faced opponents of a very different age. The former Wimbledon doubles champion Gardnar Mulloy complained when he reached 90 he had to play against youngsters of 85 as there was no 90-and-over age category. But that's nothing compared to one 93-year-old woman who found herself competing in a 75-and-over age group, and thus giving away nearly 20 years to some of her opponents.

THE GROWTH OF THE SENIORS CHAMPIONSHIPS

The table below shows the increasing number of world championship categories year on year since the introduction of the Dubler Cup in 1958. The ITF Seniors Circuit has grown to accommodate 20 team cups for men and women, plus 11 individual age groups for men and ten for women. That means a total of 72 world championship titles are on offer each year, as a team and across men's and women's singles, doubles and mixed doubles.

YEAR	EVENT	TOTAL PER YEAR
1958	Dubler Cup (men's 45)	1
1976	Young Cup (women's 40)	3
	Austria Cup (men's 55)	
1979	Britannia Cup (men's 65)	4
1981	Women's 40	8
	Men's 45	
	Women's 50 (singles)	
	Men's 55	
1982	Italia Cup (men's 35)	12
	Women's 50 (doubles)	
	Men's 60	
	Men's 65	
1983	Maria Esther Bueno Cup (women's 50)	14
	Jack Crawford Cup (men's 70)	
1984	Men's 35	15
1987	Women's 60	17
	Men's 70	
1988	Alice Marble Cup (women's 60)	18
1989	Von Cramm Cup (men's 60)	19
1991	Fred Perry Cup (men's 50)	21
	Women's 55	
1992	Maureen Connolly Cup (women's 55)	26
	Women's 35	
	Women's 45	
	Men's 50	
	Men's 75	
1993	Women's 65	27
1994	Margaret Court Cup (women's 45)	30
	Kitty Godfree Cup (women's 65)	
	Bitsy Grant Cup (men's 75)	
1996	Gardnar Mulloy Cup (men's 80)	34
	Men's 40	
	Women's 70	
	Men's 80	
1998	Althea Gibson Cup (women's 70)	35
1999	Women's 75	36
2000	Tony Trabert Cup (men's 40)	37
2001	Suzanne Lenglen Cup (women's 35)	38
2002	Queen's Cup (women's 75)	39
2005	Women's 80	40
2011	Doris Hart Cup (women's 80)	41

The Kitty Godfree Cup, donated by the Godfree family in 1994, for the women's 65s

Australia's Elizabeth Allan has won the most individual world championship titles in singles and doubles.

Gardnar Mulloy with the cup he donated

Lorne Main with his 2012 award for Outstanding Services to Seniors Tennis. Main is the most successful player in the history of the seniors circuit.

In many ways, the seniors circuit is the remnants of the old amateur tennis world, a tour of players who support themselves through day jobs but spend much of their leisure time (and leisure money) playing tennis. As a result, some of the international events were a little unpredictable. 'You never knew how many teams you'd get', recalls Tony Gathercole of the leading events for which he was responsible in the 1980s. 'Many people said they were coming but maybe they had a last-minute problem and didn't turn up, or others turned up without us expecting them. We also had to experiment a bit with the formats, because people had travelled a long way, so if they got to an event and then lost in the first round, they didn't get much for their travelling, so we began adopting round-robin formats so everyone got at least three games of tennis'.

By 2012 the ITF Seniors Circuit had 288 tournaments in 64 countries, up from 50 events in 20 countries in 1980, the first year the ITF was fully responsible for the circuit.

THE CHRISTCHURCH EARTHQUAKE

It takes a lot to stop keen tennis players from playing tennis, but the 2011 Christchurch earthquake was a natural disaster that took precedence over one of the larger tennis gatherings in the world. The quake struck one hour into the second day of the Seniors World Team Championships in Wilding Park, Christchurch. There were no casualties among the players, captains and officials in Christchurch, but the earthquake killed 185 people in New Zealand's second-largest city. The six categories of team championships being staged in the other venues, Ashburton and Timaru, carried on, but the four categories being played in Christchurch, along with the individual championships due to begin the following week, were cancelled.

A total of 177 players out of the 310 who had entered the Seniors World Individual Championships donated their entry fees to Canterbury Tennis, the host organisers, to help rebuild Wilding Park. Some players also organised fundraising events to help Christchurch, including the former American professional Gretchen Magers, who raised $6,500 through a pro-am tournament at the 2012 Seniors World Championships in San Diego. In addition, the ITF made a contribution of $25,000 to Canterbury Tennis.

ITF SENIORS CIRCUIT PARTICIPATION 2000–2011

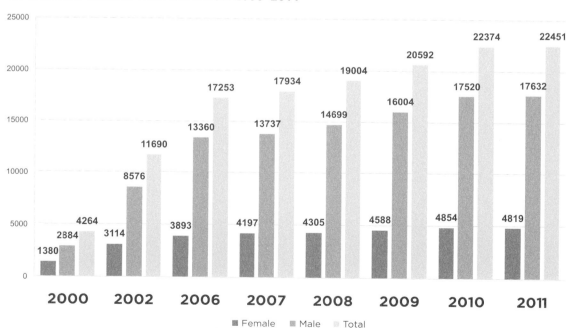

Judy Dalton and Gardnar Mulloy

Seniors tennis rewards the late developer, the player whose best years come after the age-18-to-35 period in which most professionals hit their peak. As such, many of the seniors champions are players unknown to the wider tennis world, and for a while the vast majority of former top professionals declined to play seniors tennis. But the number of former professionals who do enter seniors events – if only for one year – is growing. Among the names who made it as touring professionals and seniors stalwarts are:

Judy Dalton (AUS)
Wimbledon runner-up and seniors world doubles champion (1985) and seniors world individual champion (1997 and 1998)

Anders Jarryd

Anders Jarryd (SWE)
8 Grand Slam doubles titles and seniors world individual champion (2003)

Ann Jones (GBR)
Wimbledon champion and Great Britain seniors representative (1988)

Rick Leach (USA)
9 Grand Slam doubles titles and 4 years representing USA in seniors, including seniors world individual champion in doubles and mixed doubles (2012)

Frank Sedgman (left)

Lorne Main (CAN)
Monte Carlo champion and 13 seniors world individual titles in singles and 13 in doubles

Gardnar Mulloy (USA)
5 Grand Slam doubles titles and seniors circuit player into his 90s

Victor Pecci (PAR)
French Open runner-up and seniors world individual champion (2000)

Jeff Tarango

Mikael Pernfors (SWE)
French Open runner-up and seniors world individual runner-up (2002)

Frank Sedgman (AUS)
22 Grand Slam titles and seniors world individual runner-up (1991)

Jeff Tarango (USA)
French Open doubles runner-up and seniors world individual champion (2012)

Virginia Wade

Virginia Wade (GBR)
Wimbledon champion and Great Britain seniors representative (1988)

The winners of the 1985 Sport Goofy Tennis Trophy, an immensely successful joint ITF and Walt Disney world championships for players aged 14 and under and 12 and under. The 128 boys and girls competing in the finals at Walt Disney World, Florida, qualified by virtue of their results at established regional championships. From left, under-14 winners Michael Chang and Natalia Zvereva, and under-12 winners Monica Seles and Thomas Ho.

JUNIORS

John Barrett and Joe Block (Pepsi) present a young Andrea Jaeger with the winner's trophy for the 1979 Pepsi Junior Grand Slam tournament.

The ITF's work for juniors began in the mid-1970s, and much of the early credit goes to John Barrett, the former British player and Davis Cup captain who was instrumental in kick-starting the formation of an international junior circuit.

Barrett was running the BP International Tennis Fellowship, a British development programme for winners of official junior tournaments. In 1976 he realised that under-21 competitors needed to be competing internationally on a regular basis, so he started a points-based circuit and secured the American soft drink manufacturer Pepsi Cola as a sponsor. Thus the Pepsi Junior International Series was born, linking the most prestigious existing junior tournaments: the four Grand Slam junior tournaments (although the Australian Open junior event wasn't part of the series at the start) plus other events such as the Italian Open and the colourfully named Orange Bowl and Banana Bowl. For the

first three years, the circuit ended with the US Open junior event, but in 1979 it was expanded to 18 tournaments in 15 countries, culminating in a 'Masters'-like final held at Boca West in Florida in February 1980 as part of the Pepsi Grand Slam, an exhibition tournament.

At the same time Barrett was starting his international series, the ITF was setting up a Junior Competitions Committee headed by Enrique Morea. Its first major achievement was the establishment of a junior world ranking in 1978, which resulted in the first two junior world champions (Ivan Lendl and Hana Mandlikova, both from Czechoslovakia). The ITF felt it was the natural body to run the international junior series, and Barrett was looking for ITF approval for his series, so there was a natural coming together, with the ITF inviting Barrett onto its junior committee. The only casualty was Pepsi, which declined to pay the larger sums expected for a growing ITF global junior circuit.

> *"One of the first priorities of the ITF Junior Competitions Committee was the development of junior tennis in West Africa, which was extremely difficult because in many countries we were starting from scratch. The programmes initiated by the ITF developed rapidly, providing valuable opportunities for players in the region. In my opinion the future of our sport and our organisations finds itself increasingly dependent on the development of junior tennis."*

ENRIQUE MOREA, FIRST CHAIRMAN OF THE ITF JUNIORS COMMITTEE

The legendary Czech duo of Hana Mandlikova and Ivan Lendl (far left and far right), pictured with Chris Evert and Bjorn Borg, had the honour of becoming the first ITF Junior World Champions in 1978.

Roger Federer, age 17, wins the 1998 Orange Bowl, a Grade A tournament that carries equal weighting to the junior Grand Slams

JUNIOR WORLD CHAMPIONS TO PROFESSIONAL WORLD NO. 1s

Ivan Lendl	(1978)	Amelie Mauresmo	(1996)
Stefan Edberg	(1983)	Roger Federer	(1998)
Marcelo Rios	(1993)	Andy Roddick	(2000)
Martina Hingis	(1994)	Victoria Azarenka	(2005)

Martina Hingis, Andy Roddick and Victoria Azarenka as ITF Junior World Champions

The ITF Junior Circuit comes to prominence most of all at the four Grand Slam tournaments, when the world's top juniors get to share the stage with the world's leading players. The four Grand Slams are all Grade A tournaments on the ITF Junior Circuit, along with the Abierto Juvenil Mexicano, the Gerdau Cup, the Italian Open, the Osaka Mayor's Cup, the Orange Bowl and, every four years, the Youth Olympic Games. The boys' and girls' world champions also share a stage with the world's greatest players at the ITF World Champions Dinner in Paris in the second week of Roland Garros. For some, it's the start of their own careers at the top, while for others it can be the highlight of their playing careers.

EDBERG DOES THE GRAND SLAM

Stefan Edberg is the only player – male or female – to do the Grand Slam in juniors. He won all four major junior titles in 1983, completing the set by beating Simon Youl in the final of the US Open. In 2004 Gael Monfils went to the US Open with a chance of emulating Edberg's feat, having won the Australian, French and Wimbledon junior titles. Hampered by a knee injury, he lost in the third round to Viktor Troicki but still finished well ahead of his contemporaries as ITF Junior World Champion for that year.

YOUTH OLYMPIC GAMES

The ITF is part of the Youth Olympic Games, a version of the Olympics for athletes under 18, which began in Singapore in 2010 and will have its second (summer games) staging in Nanjing, China, in 2014. The Games are aimed at balancing sport, culture and education.

Tennis was one of 28 sports at the inaugural Youth Olympics. Tickets for the tennis event were sold out, reflecting the sport's popularity in the Games. A total of 38 countries were represented in the four draws (32-draw singles for boys and girls, 16 pairs in doubles), and the entries featured seven of the top ten boys in the ITF rankings and six of the top ten girls. Each sport had a nominated role model, and the recently retired Japanese player, Ai Sugiyama, was chosen to represent tennis.

The World Junior Tennis Finals 14 & under French boys and girls team in 1999. Seated far right is 14-year-old Jo-Wilfried Tsonga and third from right is 13-year-old Richard Gasquet. France won the boys' title that year, while a Russian team featuring Dinara Safina won the girls'.

In 2011 Korea became the first Asian nation in the 20-year history of World Junior Tennis to win the boys' title. Japan's Eiichi Kawatei, who was instrumental in the development of junior tennis in Asia, founded World Junior Tennis back in 1991.

JUNIOR TEAM COMPETITIONS

Unlike in the seniors circuit, where the team competitions came first and later spawned the individual events, the junior circuit began with individual events, and the team competitions followed. In 1985 the ITF began a youth team competition, the World Youth Cup for under-16s. Its inception owes much to the work of Eiichi Kawatei, arguably the most influential figure in the development of tennis in Asia in the ITF's first 100 years. Kawatei got the Davis Cup's sponsor, NEC, to support an under-16 team competition, with finals played in the Japanese city of Kobe.

In 1991 the competition added an under-14 age category called World Junior Tennis, which by 2011 had expanded to an astonishing 202 teams (boys and girls). There have also been two other junior team events, the Continental Cup for girls and the Sunshine Cup for boys, both under-18, but these were abandoned after the 2001 stagings, as interest levels from national associations were waning.

In 2002, when BNP Paribas took over from NEC as the Davis Cup's sponsor, the World Youth Cup was renamed Junior Davis Cup and Junior Fed Cup. Some of the greatest names of the modern era have played in this competition, among them Roger Federer as a 15-year-old in 1996 and Rafael Nadal as a 16-year-old in 2002. In fact, Nadal has an astonishing record of having won the World Junior Tennis team prize in the under-14s in 2000, the Junior Davis Cup in the under-16s in 2002, and the Davis Cup as an 18-year-old in 2004. (He couldn't win a team title in 2001 because his mother wouldn't let him travel to Chile just after the events of 9/11.)

Rafael Nadal (far right) and teammate Marcel Granollers (second from left) win the 2002 Junior Davis Cup for Spain

BRIDGING THE GAP

In recent years, various projects and initiatives have been launched to create links between the junior and professional circuits in order to facilitate what can be a difficult transition from the juniors to the professional game.

The Junior Exempt Project was launched for girls in 1997 and boys in 2006 and gives players who ended the year ranked in the Top 10 direct entry into the main draw of ITF Women's Circuit and ITF Men's Circuit (Futures) events – the level of the tournament into which a player can earn direct entry depends on the player's ranking. Girls have benefitted the most out of the feed-up Exempt Project so far, with 16 title winners from the project's launch through 2011. Four of those winners – Mirjana Lucic (1997), Katarina Srebotnik (1999), Michaella Krajicek (2005) and Caroline Wozniacki (2007) – won $75k tournaments.

From 2003 to 2011 winners of each junior Grand Slam singles title were offered a wildcard into main draw qualifying of that same Grand Slam the following year. Ukraine's Kateryna Bondarenko, junior Wimbledon champion in 2004, and Czech Kristina Pliskova, who won junior Wimbledon in 2010, both advanced through qualifying to make their debut in the main draw of The Championships the following years thanks to the scheme.

Katarina Srebotnik wins the 1999 ITF women's $75k tournament in Bratislava after earning a place in the main draw through the Junior Exempt Project

The ITF's Junior Tennis School began in 2008 with the aim of educating young players, their parents, coaches and officials on all aspects of a tennis career, both on- and off-court. In addition to an eLearning course, the ITF holds three educational forums during major tennis events each year, and supports the regional associations in the organisation of six to eight more. Experts such as sports doctors, journalists and former players are invited to speak at the forums.

With the vast majority of juniors unlikely to make it as touring professionals, the ITF's juniors work includes running a Junior Tennis School. As well as preparing those players who will be able to spend a few years on the tour for the rigours of their nomadic and unpredictable existence, the school also equips youngsters for the real world outside tournament tennis.

The Junior Tennis School was established in 2004 and has two main pillars: a series of educational forums and an online school with 17 modules.

One module is on career management and includes advice on planning for a life after tennis, or even a life after being a promising junior who never quite graduates to full tour level. Among the questions asked of juniors taking the career-management module are 'What are your gifts outside tennis?' and 'What do you care about more than anything else?' This is aimed at ensuring that even the most talented juniors don't think solely of becoming the next Roger Federer (even Federer has to think about life after tennis).

JUNIOR
TENNIS SCHOOL

"IF I WOKE UP TOMORROW
AND GOD SAID, 'YOU'VE DONE YOUR
TIME, HERE ARE YOUR LEGS BACK,'
I'D HAVE TO SAY 'BUT I'VE GOT A
WHEELCHAIR TENNIS TOURNAMENT
COMING UP IN LAKE TAHOE.
CAN I DO THAT FIRST?"

RANDY SNOW
WHEELCHAIR TENNIS PIONEER

CHAPTER 09

NO LIMITS

TENNIS FOR DISABLED PLAYERS

A NUMBER OF FORMS OF TENNIS HAVE THROWN A LIFELINE TO PEOPLE
WITH VARIOUS PHYSICAL CHALLENGES AND DISABILITIES, CONTRADICTING THE
IMPLICIT ASSUMPTION THAT THE BEST TENNIS PLAYERS ARE NOT ONLY VERY FIT,
BUT ESSENTIALLY ABLE-BODIED. WHEN IT COMES TO TENNIS FOR DISABLED PEOPLE,
THE ITF HAS THROWN MOST OF ITS EFFORTS INTO WHEELCHAIR TENNIS,
AND THE SPORT HAS LED TO SOME OF THE MOST INSPIRATIONAL
MATCHES SEEN ON THE GLOBAL CIRCUIT.

THE BIRTH AND GROWTH OF WHEELCHAIR TENNIS

Wheelchair tennis started in 1976 when Brad Parks, an 18-year-old who had become paraplegic after a skiing acrobatic accident early that year, teamed up with a wheelchair athlete, Jeff Minnenbraker, to develop tennis for players in wheelchairs. By 1980 they had an American national wheelchair tennis foundation; in 1981 the Wheelchair Tennis Players Association was formed; and in 1988 wheelchair tennis had spread sufficiently that the International Wheelchair Tennis Federation (IWTF) was formed. The ITF's development director Doug MacCurdy played a major role in bringing about the international federation, having followed the growth of wheelchair tennis since he first met Brad Parks in 1979.

The first prestige tournament for wheelchair tennis was the US Open Wheelchair Tennis Championships, which began in 1980 and by 1985 attracted both American and international players. As a way of warming up for the tournament, the IWTF organised a team event, the World Team Cup, the weekend before, largely to create international camaraderie, but it went on to become one of the mainstays of the wheelchair tennis year. Six men's teams competed in the first World Team Cup, and two women's teams were welcomed the following year.

Brad Parks introducing wheelchair tennis at one of his many clinics held across the USA during the 1980s

John Newcombe (pictured right with Tony Roche) invited Brad Parks to Australia to spread the word about wheelchair tennis.

New York Junior Tennis League
NEWSLETTER

VOL. 2 NO. 2   NOVEMBER 1982

National Champion Brad Parks Kicks Off Public School Program

Three hundred youngsters, half of whom were in wheelchairs and who had come from throughout the city, rooted enthusiastically for Brad Parks, National Wheelchair Tennis Champion, as he won 15 of 28 points from top ranked Eastern player Jon Molin, at Riverdale Sports Center on Friday, June 11. Parks was inspiring as he returned Molin's shots and approached the net to put away winners. Not only did Brad "defeat" Jon, but more importantly, he sent the message to the crowd of 300 cheering admirers—tennis is a game for everyone! The good-natured exhibition match was followed by a two-hour clinic during which every youngster in the center was able to hit forehands and backhands under the direction of Parks, Gordon Kent, Carol Cohen, and the N.Y.J.T.L. coaching staff. Hundreds of youngsters clamored for Parks' autograph.

Prior to the exhibition, David Dinkins addressed the audience, lauding cooperative efforts between the Board of Education, which provided tennis facilities, chaperons and busing for the handicapped, and the New York Junior Tennis League which raised $55,000 to provide coaches, racquets, balls, t-shirts, trophies, and a play-off tournament for the youngsters.

Other speakers included: Skip Hartman, President of N.Y. Jr. Tennis League, Dr. Alan Gartner, Executive Director of the Division of Special Education, Dr. Al Oliver, Director of Community School District Affairs, Dr. Steven Franse, member of the Board of Education, who presented "Partner in Education" awards to Skip Hartman, Robert Kelton, Robert Kelton Jr., and William Cooney at the Riverdale Sports Center. Henry Talbert of the U.S.T.A. congratulated the organizations and urged the youngsters to follow up on the court this summer. Denise Jordan, Director of Tennis for the Department of Parks, Mary Rowley, Executive Director of the National Junior Tennis League, and Eve Kraft of the U.S.T.A. Education and Research Center were also on hand. The United States Marines and the Talent Unlimited Band provided colors and music and the refreshments were catered by students from Park West High School's Culinary Arts class.

The gala event was held to officially an-

Each of the 180 handicapped youngsters hit forehands and backhands at the Riverdale opening event. Steve Schott of NYJTL (left) and Dr. Steven Franse (right), member of the Board of Education, showed the youngsters how to hit.

nounce the summer program, which was made possible by the interest of the Division of Special Education, Dr. Alan Gartner, Director, and Dr. Al Oliver, Director of Community School District Affairs, who saw the need to make better use of school tennis facilities in the summer. Dr. Gartner also saw the possi-

bilities for tennis with the handicapped, as it is a sport with an individualized standard of success.

Their ideas became reality as 16 coaches ran programs for 4000 children at 22 City sites in July and August. Included in the program was a schedule of regular clinics for special ed students who were transported to the sites by the Board of Education's special ed summer program. Coordinating the special ed programs for the League was Herb Turetsky, a teacher in the special ed division.

According to Dan Bergstein, one of the summer program directors, "The summer program was a great success. The Special Ed kids learned recreational skills (tennis) for the first time." Another staff member from the Board of Education felt that tennis was a way of communicating to the kids. Tom Lehman, Director of the Brooklyn District, said that over two hundred students with hyper and autistic backgrounds learned the game of tennis with amazing success. Jeannie Gee, Coordinator of Special Ed Division, reported that approximately 1000 special ed youngsters were given the opportunity to

National Wheelchair Tennis Champ Brad Parks and his sports chair makes it look easy.

(Continued on page 4)

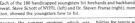

Parks collaborated with local tennis clubs, schools, and social and educational councillors to boost participation in wheelchair tennis in the U.S.

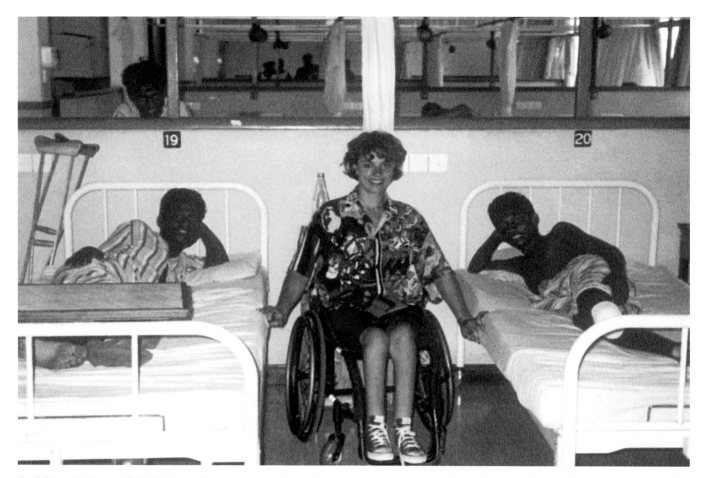

First full-time administrator of wheelchair tennis, Ellen de Lange, on a trip to Sri Lanka in 1993. De Lange was invited by the Sri Lanka Tennis Association to visit the army hospital and demonstrate the benefit of sport as part of the rehabilitation process. The trip was the start of a successful programme in Sri Lanka.

American Randy Snow, one of wheelchair tennis's biggest successes, also played a major role in building the sport worldwide through the ITF's Silver Fund activities as well as his own camps and clinics.

By the mid-1980s, wheelchair tennis was sufficiently international for it to have governing bodies in the USA, Europe and Australasia. The heads of these bodies – Brad Parks, John Noakes and Graeme Watts – were elected by the players, and met annually to discuss their wishes. A central issue at the time was that wheelchair tennis players wanted to be seen first as tennis players and secondly as disabled. That inevitably led to a formal approach to the ITF, led by Noakes in 1988, asking whether wheelchair tennis could become part of the ITF and requesting a change in the rules of tennis to recognise the two-bounce rule for use in wheelchair tennis.

Although it took nearly 10 years for the ITF to fully take over wheelchair tennis, links between the IWTF and the ITF intensified to the point where the two bodies came together to create a position of full-time administrator of wheelchair tennis, to be based at the ITF's offices in London. The first incumbent was the former world No. 2, Ellen de Lange, one of many Dutchwomen to have made a significant mark in the development of wheelchair tennis. In 1998, the ITF agreed to fully integrate the IWTF, which meant wheelchair tennis had its own department and committee alongside juniors and seniors.

By 1991 both the US Open and the World Team Cup had become such popular events that running them back-to-back was becoming impractical. And while the US Open would always remain in America, there were other nations expressing interest in hosting the World Team Cup. So in 1992 the event went to Europe for the first time as Belgium hosted it and moved to a different slot in the calendar. In 2010 it took place for the first time on the African continent, with South Africa staging the event in Pretoria with 360 competitors from 34 countries, and was broadcast live by South African television. In 2012 Korea ensured the World Team Cup was staged in Asia for the first time when it took place in Seoul. The 2012 staging saw the introduction of a qualifying tournament, a sign of the growing strength in depth of wheelchair tennis.

The World Team Cup has had two sponsors. From 1995 to 2009, it was sponsored by the American home health care and mobility products company Invacare (although in the early years the event carried the name 'Action', the brand name of Invacare's lightweight wheelchair that could be used for tennis), and since 2012 it has been part of the tennis sponsorship of the French bank BNP Paribas.

As wheelchair tennis grew, the strength in depth became greater, which in turn threw the spotlight on differences between types of disability as the ITF strove to keep a degree of equality in competition. In the 1990s separate tournaments began for 'quad' athletes, effectively those with upper-limb disabilities – in some cases, quads play with the racket taped to their hand if the hand lacks enough function to grip the racket adequately. Quad wheelchair events were first staged at the World Team Cup in 1998. Today, 50 percent of the ITF's wheelchair tennis tour includes a quad division.

Wheelchair tennis quadriplegic players, like David Wagner pictured here, are classified as those with a lower limb disability and one or more affected upper limbs. Despite the high level of disability and therefore a limited uptake to wheelchair tennis, a quad division was established in the 1990s as a need to differentiate between disabilities and retain equality in the sport.

The World Team Cup has grown from just six men's teams in 1985 to 52 teams from 28 countries in 2012; the quad division was added in 1998 and juniors in 2000.

Doubles medallists Germany, USA and France at the inaugural Paralympic Tennis Event in Barcelona 1992, which was the international breakthrough for the sport

Competitors at the 1954 Stoke Mandeville Games, the precursor to the Paralympics

Among the milestones for wheelchair tennis was the sport becoming part of a top-level tour event, the Lipton Players Championships in Key Biscayne in 1990. But perhaps the biggest breakthrough came at the 1992 Barcelona Paralympics, when wheelchair tennis became a full medal sport for the first time. The Paralympics had evolved out of a programme of research carried out at the Stoke Mandeville hospital in Great Britain in the years after the Second World War to use sport to help the rehabilitation of people with spinal cord injuries. The first International Wheelchair Games were held in London in 1948, and they went through a stage of being the Stoke Mandeville Games before becoming the Paralympics as part of a dual Olympic-Paralympic package that all cities bidding to host the Games must embrace.

Despite wheelchair tennis being an international sport from the early 1980s, there was a lot of discussion at the top of the game about whether it should be in the Paralympics. Brad Parks took some convincing that wheelchair tennis would benefit from Paralympic status, and as the founder of the sport and the head of it in the USA, his views carried a lot of weight. But others were strongly in favour, and the decision was taken to join the Paralympic movement.

As that battle was fought in 1988, able-bodied tennis and wheelchair tennis were one Olympiad apart, so when tennis returned to full medal status at the 1988 Seoul Olympics, wheelchair tennis featured as a successful demonstration sport in the Paralympics. It became a full medal sport at the Barcelona Paralympics in 1992, where Randy Snow of the USA and the Dutchwoman Monique van den Bosch won gold in both singles and doubles. The ground had been prepared a year earlier, when an exhibition match was staged between Arantxa Sanchez Vicario and one of the leading wheelchair players, Chantal Vandierendonck — it received massive exposure, including television coverage, and helped boost crowds the following year, when the Paralympics tennis event was staged at the Vall d'Hebron venue, which had hosted the Olympic tennis event just a few weeks earlier.

Quad athletes were admitted to the Paralympics in 2004, but apart from the distinction between wheelchair tennis and quad players, tennis is the only Paralympic sport not to have a classification by disability. In other sports, the original qualification of being wheelchair users has been expanded to include vision-impaired athletes, amputees, and sufferers from cerebral palsy and learning difficulties, but Paralympic tennis has just one medal winner in each event, so six in all (men's singles, women's singles, men's doubles, women's doubles, quad singles and quad doubles; quad events can feature men and women competing together).

Randy Snow is considered the most successful male wheelchair tennis player, but his greatest sporting feat came arguably in another sport. In 1984, the Los Angeles Olympics added a men's 1500 metres wheelchair race as an exhibition event, making it effectively the first Paralympic event to appear before a large audience. Snow went into heavy training, relocating to Houston, Texas, to train on the same track as Carl Lewis. Snow came in second and won a commemorative silver medal, and the 91,500 crowd gave the athletes a standing ovation at the end of the exhibition. The Texan went on to win gold medals in the 1992 Paralympics in Barcelona for singles and doubles tennis, and at the 1996 Atlanta Games he was a member of the bronze medal-winning wheelchair basketball team. He was inducted posthumously into the International Tennis Hall of Fame in 2012.

The women's singles final in Beijing in 2008 was one of the most exciting matches in Paralympic tennis history, after Esther Vergeer came close to losing her first match in over five years to countrywoman Korie Homan. Homan had match point against Vergeer, but the world No. 1 recovered to win her third successive singles gold.

Wheelchair tennis on the Grand Slam stage: the 2002 Australian Open became the first Grand Slam to integrate a wheelchair tennis event alongside its main event, with Wimbledon and the US Open following suit in 2005 and Roland Garros in 2007.

Tommy Robredo is tournament director of the Open Memorial Santi Silvas.

In 2011 Guga Kuerten established his own wheelchair tennis tournament on the NEC Tour.

INTEGRATION INTO THE MAINSTREAM

Much as wheelchair tennis brought gasps of amazement and admiration from tennis fans, the aim was always to make it part of the mainstream tennis family. This was why the emergence of, first, exhibition events and then officially sanctioned tournaments at the four Grand Slams was so important for the integration of wheelchair tennis. Wimbledon held an exhibition event in 2001, and by 2007, all four Slams were staging sanctioned wheelchair tournaments as part of their events. The majors now form part — albeit the most prestigious part — of the international wheelchair tennis circuit in a similar way to the role they have in the full able-bodied and juniors circuits.

In 2009 the ITF appointed six wheelchair tennis ambassadors: three former wheelchair champions and three prominent figures from the able-bodied game. The three past champions were Brad Parks, David Hall and Monique Kalkman (formerly Monique van den Bosch) while the three able-bodied ambassadors were Sven Groeneveld (who has coached Esther Vergeer), Tommy Robredo and Jonas Bjorkman. Gustavo Kuerten also acts as an unofficial ambassador, especially as he runs a wheelchair tennis event in his home city of Florianopolis in Brazil in memory of his late brother Guilherme, who had a learning disability.

Four examples of people for whom wheelchair tennis has offered a new outlook on life, if not a totally new life.

Chantal Vandierendonck (NED) A talented Dutch teenage player, she was driving from her home in the Netherlands to Belgium when her car skidded and she woke up in hospital a paraplegic. Her uncle had seen French players participating in wheelchair tennis on television and suggested she look into it. When she raised the subject with her coach, the Netherlands-based Englishman John Noakes, he said he knew nothing about it but was willing to give it a try with her. Within two years, Vandierendonck had won the US Open (winning all categories she entered in 1985), and became one of the leading players in the early history of wheelchair tennis.

Sabine Ellerbrock (GER) At the age of 30, Sabine was out running when her leg gave way. She had the injury assessed, and needed several operations over many years. Nothing seemed to cure the problem, and a foot infection resulting from one operation left her in a wheelchair. Her life disintegrated, and in 2007 she decided to end it all. But standing on the balcony of her parents' apartment in a high-rise building she planned to jump from, she decided life was worth fighting for after all. So she pulled back from the brink and wrote to various associations for disabled people. The first response came from the German wheelchair tennis association, so having played tennis as an able-bodied person, she took up wheelchair tennis. She first played wheelchair tennis competitively in 2009 and made an immediate impact on the NEC Wheelchair Tennis Tour, and by mid-2012 she had broken into the world's top five at the age of 36.

Kgothatso Montjane (RSA) Without two things – the end of apartheid in South Africa and the ITF's Silver Fund – Kgothatso would be unheard of outside her township of Seshego, near Polokwane. Born with a congenital deformity in both her legs and hands, Kgothatso, known in the wheelchair tennis world as 'KG', had undergone several operations before her lower left leg was amputated in 1999. When the ITF's Silver Fund was set up in 2001, it targeted South Africa, as the country had just two active wheelchair players (both white). These days it has nearly 500 registered wheelchair players, and Kgothatso profited from that growth. She won her first tournament in 2006 and has been South Africa's top woman player since then, breaking into the world's top ten and being voted South Africa's disabled sportswoman of the year in 2011. 'If Nelson Mandela hadn't come to power, my life would have been totally different,' she says. 'Wheelchair tennis has changed my life'.

Lucas Sithole (RSA) Involved in a train crash at the age of ten, Lucas was left a triple amputee, having lost both legs and half an arm. But he took up tennis, learning to hold the ball in the same hand as his racket for an unorthodox but effective service action. He has since travelled the world as a wheelchair player, representing South Africa in various international quad wheelchair competitions. In 2011 he broke into the top ten of the quad world rankings and was voted South African disabled sportsman of the year. 'I don't want anyone to feel sorry for me,' he says, 'I'm living my life to the fullest'.

Players and coaches take part in the Silver Fund programme at Kenyatta University Clinic in Nairobi, Kenya. Through the Silver Fund the ITF works with specific countries over a two-year period, sending out different ITF experts and player ambassadors to hold clinics, meet with local partners, set up development plans and talk to the media. The aim is that at the end of the two-year period the programme is self-sustainable and that opportunities exist for players to take part in international competition.

SILVER FUND

Wheelchair tennis celebrated its first quarter century in 2001 with the launch of the Silver Fund (marking the silver jubilee). This was an initiative aimed at providing wheelchairs and other tennis equipment, as well as infrastructure and advice in developing countries where money is not freely available. It had a starting boost of $15,000 from the ABN Amro tournament in Rotterdam and has regularly been supported by the Johan Cruyff Foundation set up by the former world No. 1 footballer.

One of its earliest success stories came from Sri Lanka, where the 20-year civil war between Singhalese and Tamils had left many soldiers with permanent injuries, but the army stepped in and began to pay disabled war veterans to train in wheelchair tennis. The ITF's wheelchair tennis manager Mark Bullock says, 'During one clinic I had over 100 disabled soldiers on three tennis courts, with just 12 chairs and 30 rackets to share between them. They were all very fit and active because they were professional soldiers, and it provided them with such direction and focus.'

Another success story comes from South Africa, where the dynamic chairman of Wheelchair Tennis South Africa, Holger Losch, has overseen the introduction of a programme catering to total beginners as well as elite players, and made WTSA into a self-financing association. In South Africa, wheelchair tennis is open to everyone irrespective of gender, colour or religion – in particular, it has moved from a whites-only pursuit to one where most players and coaches are now from townships where previously organised sport was largely unknown for disabled people. And South Africa has a handful of top-level wheelchair tennis players to act as role models.

The Silver Fund has also contributed to projects in Romania, Bolivia, Bulgaria, Moldova, Colombia, El Salvador, Kenya, Philippines, India, Indonesia and various other countries. A team from Kenya that took part in qualifying for the 2012 World Team Cup was able to do so as a direct result of support from the Silver Fund.

Wheelchair tennis is the most high-profile and well-developed variant of tennis for disabled people, and the variant into which the ITF has invested most of its efforts into. But there are others:

Tennis for deaf people.... this form of the sport is part of the Deaflympics, an IOC-sanctioned Olympic-style festival of sport for deaf people.

Tennis for blind people.... this is played on a badminton court with a foam ball that has a table-tennis ball embedded in it. The embedded table-tennis ball contains pellets or a bell that make a sound when the ball travels. Those with total blindness get three bounces, while those with partial sight get one bounce. This form of tennis is played indoors, but the ITF is experimenting with a felt ball in the hope of taking the sport outdoors.

Tennis for people with physical disabilities.... this is for people with upper-limb disabilities, like those who have had an arm amputated or are suffering from deformities (like victims of the thalidomide drug).

Tennis for people with learning disabilities.... sometimes referred to as 'intellectual disabilities', this has the same rules as able-bodied tennis, although matches sometimes consist of fewer sets. Learning-disabilities tennis ('LD tennis' or 'ID tennis') is part of the 'Special Olympics', a mass-participation sports festival for people with learning disabilities, and also one of seven sports making up the Global Games, an elite disability competitive event organised by the International Sports Federation for Persons with Intellectual Disability (known for short as 'Inas', formerly 'Inas-Fid').

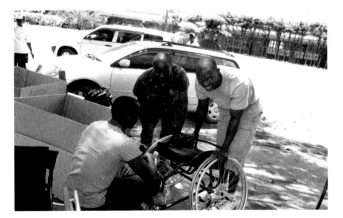

Putting together a low-cost motivation wheelchair, donated to a local Kenyan school by the Silver Fund programme

Former footballer and Silver Fund ambassador Johan Cruyff (right) receiving the Brad Parks Award on behalf of the Cruyff Foundation for its contribution to wheelchair tennis

There are two leading countries that have forced the pace in the growth of wheelchair tennis. At the beginning it was the USA, where the sport started, but the first 35 years of wheelchair tennis have been dominated by a string of high-quality players from the Netherlands. The stand-out is the women's world No. 1 Esther Vergeer, who remained unbeaten in 470 singles matches from February 2003 through her fourth Paralympic gold in 2012, but the World Team Cup roll of honour, especially on the women's side, testifies to the dominance of the Dutch.

So why has the Netherlands been so successful at wheelchair tennis? There are many reasons. The Netherlands has a wide-ranging social security system and a rehabilitation strategy for victims of accidents that is very strongly sports-focused. Dutch wheelchair athletes have always had good coaches and regular training opportunities, and because the Dutch tennis authority KNLTB embraced wheelchair tennis early, they have a good network of national tournaments. The Netherlands was already one of the most successful nations in the Paralympics in general (not just in tennis), so Dutch wheelchair tennis players had plenty of role models to look up to.

As the strength in depth of wheelchair tennis expands, the ability of one nation to dominate the way the Netherlands has will diminish. And 50 years from now, people will ask just how well Esther Vergeer would have done in a more competitive era, just the way they ask now how Bill Tilden would have fared against Federer and Nadal, or Suzanne Lenglen against Navratilova and the Williams sisters.

Dutch men and women lead the medal tally at the Paralympics; the women have achieved a clean sweep in singles at Atlanta 1996, Sydney 2000 and London 2012.

"Holland is a small country, we're only 300km from south to north and 200km from east to west. We're a flat country, we have more than 1,700 tennis clubs, and we have a very sophisticated structure which means you can play anywhere. Wheelchair tennis players can go to a club nearby and also play with able-bodied people."

EVERT-JAN HULSHOF, GENERAL SECRETARY, DUTCH TENNIS FEDERATION

Children get the chance to interview Dutch wheelchair tennis icons Chantal Vandierendonck and Maaike Smit at a clinic in 1996, part of the NEC Wheelchair Tennis Masters in Eindhoven. Kids' clinics are a regular part of wheelchair tennis tournaments in the Netherlands.

Considered to be the most dominant athlete in sport, Dutch wheelchair tennis phenomenon Esther Vergeer has raised the profile of wheelchair tennis not only in the Netherlands, but also worldwide. Her success has enabled her to establish and grow her own foundation which helps disabled children get into sport.

"IT'S SUNNY, IT'S EASY,
IT'S A WORLDWIDE GAME."

ALESSANDRO CALBUCCI

BEACH TENNNIS WORLD CHAMPION

CHAPTER 10

A LINE IN THE SAND

BEACH TENNIS

NOT A LOT OF PEOPLE KNOW THAT THE ITF IS ALSO THE GOVERNING BODY FOR BEACH TENNIS. THE FEDERATION TOOK RESPONSIBILITY FOR BEACH TENNIS, ITS LATEST 'ACQUISITION', IN 2008. AS WITH TENNIS, ITS ROLE IS TO ADMINISTER, REGULATE, STRUCTURE, DEVELOP AND PROMOTE THE GAME, AS WELL AS ORGANISE INTERNATIONAL COMPETITIONS. TODAY THE ITF PRESIDES OVER THE GLOBAL ITF BEACH TENNIS TOUR, WHICH HAD JUST 14 EVENTS IN 2008 BUT PASSED THE 100 MARK IN 2012 AND CONTINUES TO GROW RAPIDLY. IT'S A GOOD ANTIDOTE TO THE FEAR THAT VOLLEYING IN TENNIS IS A DYING ART, BECAUSE IN BEACH TENNIS THERE'S ONLY VOLLEYING – BUT IT IS A SPORT IN ITS OWN RIGHT, AND HAS ITS OWN FEDERERS, NADALS AND SHARAPOVAS, EVEN IF THEY AREN'T SUCH HOUSEHOLD NAMES (YET).

THE GROWTH OF BEACH TENNIS

With the growth in popularity of tennis over several decades, enthusiasts have looked for more convenient locations and ways to play the game. Often, a tennis court simply isn't available, so variations of the game have developed, most of them informally but a few in a more structured way, such as Padel (popular in Spain) and paddle tennis (USA).

For at least a century, holidaymakers have been spotted on the world's beaches hitting a ball back and forth with some form of bat, often little more than a table-tennis paddle. Sometimes it was a form of badminton. But in the last 20 years, efforts to formalise the variant of tennis played on a beach have been stepped up. Different forms developed over time, notably in Italy, Brazil and Spain, but it was the Italian version that became widely played in the early 1990s and was subsequently exported to other beach locations around the world.

Beach tennis is believed to have taken root in the Emilia Romagna region of Italy, a stretch of coast at the north of the Adriatic Sea that boasts around 1,600 beach tennis courts. But it has since established a strong and expanding presence in Brazil; the national tennis associations of Germany, France and Russia have recently embraced beach tennis with great gusto; and it has become a hotly pursued sport in places like Aruba and Mauritius, where there's no shortage of sun and sand.

The sport of beach tennis is a combination of tennis, beach volleyball and badminton. It shares a similar scoring system to tennis, is played on a beach volleyball-sized court, and has badminton's no-bounce rule. The ITF Tour currently only includes doubles.

Beach tennis's popularity stretches to countries such as Belgium, Japan, Gran Canaria and the Caribbean island of Aruba

This form of tennis, which is now officially known as beach tennis, is a combination of tennis, beach volleyball and badminton. It has badminton's no-bounce rule; beach volleyball's court dimensions (16 metres long by 8 metres wide, for doubles) albeit with a net that at 1.70 metres is slightly lower than for beach volleyball; and tennis's ball, albeit the low-pressure orange (Stage 2) ball used for junior tennis (see page 159). Beach tennis also shares tennis's scoring system of 15-30-40-game, but with a handful of default variations, such as the no-ad rule, the no-let rule, no second serve, and in doubles a serve can be returned by either player.

As beach tennis began to reach new regions, tennis rackets were initially used to play the game. However, as the original form of beach tennis used stringless bats, the ITF took the view that it should remain true to those origins and thus only sanction the use of paddle bats for official beach tennis events. Beach tennis now has its own paddle bats, largely made from carbon fibre or fibreglass with solid foam centre, but also admissible in wood (maximum measurements are 50 cm in length and 26 cm in width). Small holes made in the hitting surface are intended to improve weight distribution and reduce air resistance.

The ITF-approved Stage 2 orange ball, the slower ball used for 10-and-under tennis, is the official ball for beach tennis.

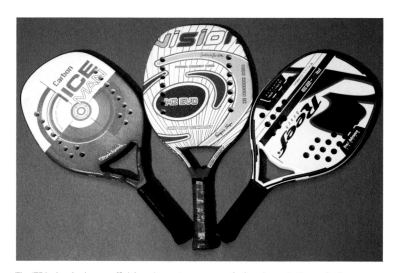

The ITF is developing an official equipment programme for beach tennis. Currently, the specifications on maximum length and width are monitored at all ITF Beach Tennis Tour events.

WHAT SHOULD I WEAR?

Beach volleyball has gained a reputation for its players showing a lot of flesh, so could beach tennis develop a similar reputation for attracting those who enjoy watching scantily clad sportsmen and women throwing themselves around on the sand? There are no limiting rules about clothing in beach tennis, although that doesn't mean there won't be one day. But for the moment, players can wear as much or as little as they want, which is usually whatever is most comfortable. That might seem an invitation to players to wear as little as possible, and bikinis are popular, but with fears about the power of the sun to cause skin cancers, maybe Anne White's infamous bodysuit worn at Wimbledon in 1985 will come into its own in beach tennis?

Italy, considered the forerunner of beach tennis, won the inaugural European Championships in 2007, which was organised by Tennis Europe and held in Olbia, Sardinia.

ITF BEACH TENNIS TOUR

ATP pro Andy Murray tries out beach tennis in Melbourne

Daniela Hantuchova and Shuai Peng took part in a beach tennis exhibition for the opening of the 2011 WTA Tournament of Champions in Bali.

The growth of the sport, initially in Italy but also in other countries, prompted those responsible for beach tennis to approach the ITF in the early years of this century, along the same lines as wheelchair tennis had approached the ITF a decade earlier. The only difference was that beach tennis was still so new it didn't have a world-governing body, so the ITF was able to step in and set global standards almost from the start. In 2007 the ITF conducted extensive research into the popularity and viability of beach tennis; the results made it clear that the sport was growing, and was becoming a serious form of tennis that needed a global governing body. That year, the ITF voted to accept beach tennis as a legitimate variant of the sport of tennis.

In 2008 the ITF Beach Tennis Tour was founded with 14 tournaments, mostly in Italy. The following year, the total was up to 23, and it has nearly doubled every year since, surpassing 100 in 2012. Beach tennis world rankings also came into operation in 2008, and in 2012 the first World Team Championship was held, with Moscow and the Russian Tennis Federation as its host. You may be struggling to think of which part of Moscow has a beach. It doesn't. Beach tennis doesn't have to be played on a beach, and the growing trend is for existing arenas to import sand and stage beach tennis events nationwide. This means that the record crowds so far witnessed for beach tennis – around 4,000 – are likely to be vastly exceeded as beach tennis becomes more popular and is staged in bigger tennis venues. Indeed, the French Tennis Federation turned court 13 at Roland Garros 2012 into a beach tennis court to showcase the sport.

So far, beach tennis hasn't attracted major sponsorship (certainly not tour-wide), but with tournaments paying prize money (over $250,000 in 2011), tournament organisers frequently enter into sponsorship deals or partnerships with local companies. There is also growing interest among television companies in broadcasting beach tennis, and as the product becomes more sought after, the potential revenue from television rights will grow.

And with the growth of beach tennis comes the growth of some star names. Because the ITF Tour only includes doubles, the biggest names tend to be pairs, and for the moment they are largely Italian. Perhaps the best-known doubles pair is Alex Mingozzi and Matteo Marighella, or one could make a case for the 2011 world champions Alessandro Calbucci and Luca Meliconi. The top women include Simona Briganti and Laura Olivieri, and if that's too many Italians, the leading Brazilian women are Samantha Barijan and Joana Cortez, who have reached 5th in the ITF world rankings.

How much beach tennis will develop in the coming years remains to be seen, but it is clearly growing at a considerable rate. The aim of those promoting beach tennis is not to rival regular tennis, but to offer a form of tennis that requires fewer facilities, as sandy beaches provide ready-made surfaces, so only the net, bats and balls are required. Expect it to grow, both on the beach and wherever large quantities of sand can be transported.

The Foro Italico in Rome staged the ITF Beach Tennis World Championships for the first three years, alongside the ATP and WTA event, before moving to Bulgaria in 2012.

ITF President Francesco Ricci Bitti with 2011 world champions Luca Meliconi and Alessandro Calbucci of Italy

The ITF signed tennis equipment manufacturer Topspin as international sponsor of the 2012 and 2013 Individual World Championships

FITNESS AND STAMINA

When it rains on a clay court, conditions can get heavy underfoot, but when it rains on the beach-tennis sands, the game can often get easier for the players. Beach tennis is played largely on dry sand, and moving quickly to the ball is a lot harder than it looks – it requires a high level of fitness and stamina. But a sudden burst of rain can make the surface much less fluid and therefore easier for feet to grip.

And occasionally there's more than a sudden burst of rain, like in 2011 when a beach-tennis event in Bermuda was badly disrupted by a hurricane. The nets were salvaged, but only just, and a number of the courts were flooded for several hours.

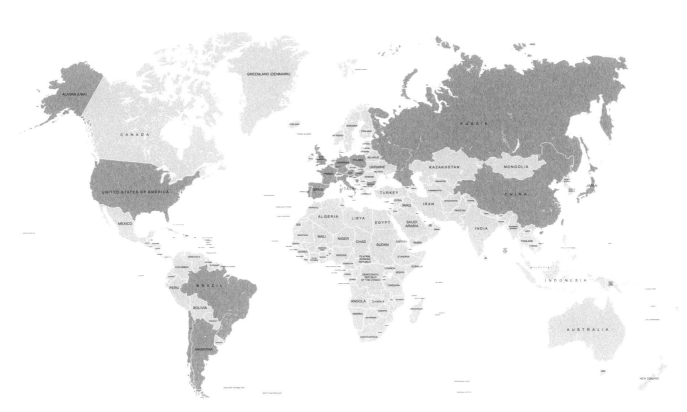

The ITF assumed responsibility of the development of beach tennis in 2008 and founded the ITF Beach Tennis Tour the same year, which has grown from 14 tournaments in Europe to over 100 worldwide in 2012. All regions – Europe, North America, Central America, South America, Asia/Oceania and Africa – are involved.

"THERE ARE TWO WORDS
TO SHOWBUSINESS.
MOST FORGET THE SECOND WORD."

MIKE DAVIES
THE FIRST ITF COMMERCIAL DIRECTOR

CHAPTER II

PAYING THE BILLS

SPONSORSHIP AND COMMERCIAL DEALS

THERE'S A NICE NOTION THAT GOVERNING BODIES OF A SPORT CAN COVER THEIR COSTS BY CHARGING MEMBER ASSOCIATIONS SUFFICIENT FEES TO COVER EXPENDITURES. THAT IS SIMPLY UNREALISTIC IN MOST SPORTS, AND ESPECIALLY IN A GLOBAL SPORT LIKE TENNIS, IN WHICH MANY NATIONAL ASSOCIATIONS EXIST ON VERY LITTLE MONEY AND A LOT OF GOODWILL FROM VOLUNTEERS. SO FOR TENNIS TO HAVE A GOVERNING BODY THAT CAN BE AS PROFESSIONAL AS TODAY'S GLOBALISED WORLD DEMANDS, IT NEEDS A SOUND COMMERCIAL BASIS TO BRING IN THE INCOME AND PROMOTE THE SPORT AND VARIOUS BRANDS LIKE DAVIS CUP AND FED CUP.

OUT OF SUCH A NECESSITY HAS EMERGED A VIRTUE – A COMMERCIAL OPERATION THAT DOES MORE THAN JUST BRING IN ENOUGH MONEY TO FINANCE THE ITF'S 80-MEMBER PROFESSIONAL STAFF. IT OFFERS A GLOBAL STAGE FOR COMPANIES TO INCREASE NAME RECOGNITION AND ATTRACT NEW CUSTOMERS. IT BALANCES THE NEED TO SHOW THE ITF'S TOP COMPETITIONS TO AS MANY TELEVISION VIEWERS AS POSSIBLE WHILE AT THE SAME TIME BRINGING IN MONEY FROM TV COMPANIES. AND IT BENEFITS THE SPORT OF TENNIS THROUGH WORKING WITH COMPANIES THAT ARE GIVEN 'OFFICIAL PARTNER' STATUS.

SPONSORSHIP OF DAVIS CUP

B By far the ITF's biggest operation in terms of income generation and promotion is the sponsorship of Davis Cup. It wasn't until 1981, with the introduction of the World Group format and all the publicity and controversy surrounding that change, that major companies became actively interested in sponsorship of the event. For potential sponsors, Davis Cup was now truly an international tournament. It was this commercial interest that allowed the then ITF president Philippe Chatrier to expand his staff from half a dozen administrators to an organised departmental structure headed by specialist directors.

Davis Cup is the ITF's biggest generator of commercial income – a report in 2008 estimated that for that year alone, the competition generated $53 million in commercial revenue; Fed Cup led the way as the first sponsored ITF competition when it formed an alliance with Colgate-Palmolive in 1976.

BNP Paribas's commercial relationship with the ITF started with its sponsorship of Davis Cup in 2001, which became title sponsorship the following year. Since then the bank has gone on to sponsor Fed Cup, junior Davis and Fed Cup, and the wheelchair World Team Cup as part of its global involvement with tennis at every level of competition.

NEC was the title sponsor of Davis Cup for 21 years and retains its commercial links with the ITF through its support of the NEC Wheelchair Tennis Tour and the NEC Wheelchair Tennis Masters.

Davis Cup has had just two title sponsors since 1981. The first was the Japanese electronics company NEC (Nippon Electronics Corporation), which became involved with the ITF through Fed Cup in 1980. But with Japanese firms discovering the benefits of sports and arts sponsorship at that time, the company embarked on a much bigger venture with Davis Cup, which was transforming itself into a more streamlined competition than it had been in the 1970s. The first year of NEC's sponsorship was the year the World Group was introduced (1981).

NEC's sponsorship meant the competition's official title for 21 years (1981–2001) was 'Davis Cup by NEC',

and the company's three-letter acronym became a distinctive feature at the back of the court at Davis Cup ties. The branding was in fact so successful that NEC became recognised as much if not more for its sponsorship of Davis Cup than for its own products. The branding of the company was particularly strong in Europe and North America, where sales of NEC products increased during the sponsorship period. But with changes at the top of the company in the late 1990s and a new strategy towards promoting the NEC brand, the company withdrew its sponsorship with effect from the end of 2001. However, it has remained involved with the ITF as sponsor of the NEC Wheelchair Tennis Tour.

NEC was replaced from the start of 2002 by BNP Paribas. This French-based bank was formed out of a contentious and at times bitter takeover battle between the Banque Nationale de Paris and the Paribas bank. The merger was completed in 2000, and, wanting its name ingrained across the world, the new bank stepped into Davis Cup title sponsorship; it is still there today with a contract that ensures the competition will remain 'Davis Cup by BNP Paribas' until at least the end of 2016.

BNP Paribas's slogan 'the bank for a changing world' – that is sometimes featured on courtside advertising boards – has helped the world understand what BNP Paribas's product is and the message behind it. They also top the global banking industry league table when it comes to the number of women in high-ranking functions. It should come as no surprise then that the French firm is also the title sponsor of Fed Cup.

Fed Cup has actually had a sponsor for longer than Davis Cup. In the 1970s it was sponsored by Colgate-Palmolive, and then from 1980 by NEC, but in general it brings in less revenue than its male counterpart. In 1995 the Fed Cup format changed, and the Czech KB Bank became the title sponsor from 1996 to 2000, with BNP Paribas taking over at the 2005 final.

A SPONSOR BEFORE A SPONSORSHIP DEPARTMENT

When the ITF signed up NEC to become the first title sponsor of the Davis Cup in 1981, the Federation didn't have a commercial department. NEC had been introduced to the ITF by the sports marketing agency West Nally, and all the negotiating was done with Philippe Chatrier (president) and David Gray (general secretary). Once the deal was settled, Chatrier appointed a former ITF board member, the Italian Paolo Angeli, to supervise the NEC sponsorship as a consultant to the ITF.

The ITF's first director responsible for commercial deals was Mike Davies in the mid-1980s. The role then fell to Christopher Stokes, before a commercial department was founded in 1999 under Jan Menneken, who still runs the department today.

Fed Cup became 'Fed Cup by BNP Paribas' in 2005 as the bank recognised the additional international exposure that the women's team competition could provide.

"The relationship between BNP Paribas and tennis is mutually beneficial, but it is above all a story of passion."

ANTOINE SIRE, HEAD OF BRAND, COMMUNICATIONS & QUALITY, BNP PARIBAS

The ITF sells international sponsorship rights for Davis and Fed Cup, and the 'package' of benefits for those companies includes on-court branding and visibility on other signage connected with the event. National associations hosting ties can enter into their own agreements with three domestic sponsors and a team sponsor. Car manufacturer Porsche (German Fed Cup team) and insurance company Mapfre (Spanish Davis Cup team) are examples of long-term team sponsors.

Although the lion's share of publicity goes to the title sponsor, Davis Cup also has up to six other international sponsors and partners and Fed Cup up to five. The pool of international sponsors has included companies based in 10 countries across the world. The ITF also has a long-standing partnership with Wilson Sporting Goods: the company supports both Davis Cup and Fed Cup, as well as activities like the ITF's Worldwide Coaches Conference, and provides shoes, clothing and accessories to the ITF development officers.

All national associations have assigned the right of sponsorship to the ITF, and in return receive a share of Davis Cup and Fed Cup sponsorship income. They can also recruit two domestic sponsors and one team sponsor. These sponsors cannot have courtside 'signage' space, nor can they eclipse any advertising for title or international sponsors.

Other ITF sponsors include Invacare and Camozzi, who have both sponsored wheelchair events, and the Johan Cruyff Foundation, which since 2003 has financed the Silver Fund, the ITF's initiative to promote wheelchair tennis in parts of the world where there is a demand for a wheelchair event but little money to encourage it.

WHAT DOES A SPONSOR LOOK FOR?

To part with a considerable sum of money as a Davis Cup or Fed Cup sponsor, a company wants to know that it is getting value for money. But how that is measured is an inexact science.

Audience figures for TV coverage play a big part; brief edited highlights on news and sports bulletins can also bring a brand name to the attention of millions of people; and hits on websites can give a good indication of an event's resonance. There are many different ways of assessing exposure, and forests of paperwork on how to assess what such exposure is worth in financial terms to a company.

And all that means that the ITF's commercial and event operations staff has a vital role in ensuring that the deals with sponsors are honoured. The event operations team, whose essential job is to make sure Davis Cup, Fed Cup and other events happen successfully, have a central role in monitoring the exposure for the sponsors. And for the commercial team, it's not just a question of agreeing a deal but also providing the information necessary for a sponsor to evaluate the value of its investment.

BNP Paribas's title sponsorship of ITF junior events exists alongside support from local sponsors, seen here on advertising hoarding for Junior Davis Cup and Fed Cup in Mexico

The World Team Cup, the Davis Cup and Fed Cup of wheelchair tennis, gained BNP Paribas as title sponsor in 2012.

Title sponsorship brings the added privilege of being able to 'borrow' the trophy from the reigning champion nation for various promotional purposes.

Selling the right to televise its events is an important source of income for the ITF and provides a vital means of exposure. More than 4,800 hours of Davis Cup coverage were broadcast in 164 countries through these deals in 2011, and the ITF's priority is to secure coverage on free-to-air, rather than subscription channels.

BROADCAST RIGHTS

The right to show a major event like the Davis Cup by BNP Paribas on television screens is another source of income, albeit one that has to be balanced with the need to make sure the competition – and the names of its sponsors – reaches a sizeable number of television viewers. Therefore the ITF's commercial department sells Davis Cup rights to television stations across the world. The most important broadcaster for a tie is the home team's rights holder, known as the host broadcaster, as it provides the 'feed' that goes to all the other rights holders across the world. The live feed is part of a package that includes English language commentary, score and caption graphics in the Davis Cup's branded typeface and logo, a feed of interviews conducted on- and off-court, and a highlights programme for broadcast after a Davis Cup weekend.

Davis Cup television rights are sold on a country-by-country basis. This means that transnational channels, such as the pan-European channel Eurosport, can only get Davis Cup rights in countries where it has a specific national 'window' (for example, Great Britain). Television rights are also sold in two parts: a deal covering matches involving that country's Davis Cup team, and a deal covering the most prestigious ties in the competition that don't involve the national team, which in effect means the World Group.

INTERNET VIDEO STREAMING

In the early years of the Internet, the ITF only allowed live television coverage of the Davis Cup in certain areas, mostly where there were no television rights deals. Internet coverage in those areas with TV deals was not available, or was 'geoblocked' as it's known in the trade.

But at the start of 2012, geoblocking of Internet video streaming stopped, which means that almost anyone anywhere in the world can now watch live coverage of the Davis Cup and Fed Cup world groups, as long as they have access to a computer with a decent Internet connection. There is a fee for watching, but that is more to protect the television rights holders than to bring in large sums of additional income.

There are frequently balancing acts to be found between the income the ITF could receive and the number of viewers who get access to a Davis Cup event. For example, a new cable or satellite channel might offer a sizeable sum of money for Davis Cup rights in an attempt to attract new subscribers, but its potential audience reach is likely to be quite small, even if the event proved very popular. A rival bid for much less money but with a much bigger audience would present a tricky decision. In general, the ITF favours greater exposure, partly so as to give more prominence to the brand names of the sponsors, and partly because of the Federation's general remit to spread awareness of the sport of tennis.

Similar arrangements apply to the Fed Cup and other such ITF events as Junior Davis Cup and Fed Cup and wheelchair championships, although as the demand for an event lessens, the less the ITF can earn from broadcast rights.

The deciding match of the 2011 Davis Cup final between Rafael Nadal and Juan Martin del Potro, televised by La 1 TVE, had an audience of 4 million and a 32.6 percent share of the audience, making it the most watched Davis Cup tie in Spain of all time.

The ITF is also responsible for radio commentary rights. Although there is less demand for these, a broadcaster cannot simply set up radio commentary at a Davis Cup or Fed Cup tie without the ITF's permission. The ITF funds its own radio-style commentary at the Davis Cup final – and the Fed Cup final in certain years – which is broadcast on DavisCup.com. It also produces nightly podcast radio shows called 'Straight Talking' during World Group weekends.

The ITF provides live radio commentary, with input from players and other guests, via the official sites for the finals of both Davis Cup and Fed Cup.

The ITF also distributes sound bites to radio networks worldwide

NON-COMMERCIAL PROMOTIONS

The ITF also engages in non-commercial promotions to increase the brand recognition of its products, and to recognise those who have contributed to them. The best two examples are the Davis Cup Commitment Award and the Fed Cup Heart Award.

In the run-up to its centenary, the ITF introduced the Davis Cup Commitment Award, an honour designed to recognise the commitment to the Davis Cup shown by the most loyal players. Any player who has played more than 20 ties in the World Group and zone groups I and II are recognised, and players participating mainly in zone groups III and IV are eligible for a commitment award after 50 ties. The

award was launched at the 2012 Davis Cup final, and followed by a series of award ceremonies at which national associations present commitment awards to any of their players who meet the 20-tie or 50-tie criteria.

The Fed Cup Heart Award is a few years older. Started in 2009 as a joint initiative between the ITF and BNP Paribas, it identifies a number of players each year who have given outstanding service to their country in Fed Cup competition. The first recipient was USA's Melanie Oudin; other winners include Kimiko Date-Krumm, Francesca Schiavone, Jelena Jankovic, Victoria Azarenka, Andrea Petkovic, and Petra Kvitova.

Li Na was a 2012 recipient of the Fed Cup Heart Award, a non-commercial initiative between the ITF and BNP Paribas which recognises players who have shown outstanding commitment to Fed Cup. Players are rewarded with a donation to a charity of their choice.

Ahead of the last two Olympics, the ITF has funded the publication of souvenir books featuring prominent players: *Journey to Beijing* (2008) and *Aspire, Inspire* (2012).

DavisCup.com had 27 million page views in 2011, an increase of 50% on the previous year; both DavisCup.com and FedCup.com also have Spanish-language counterparts with growing audiences.

"EQUIPMENT INNOVATIONS ARE EXERTING
A SIGNIFICANT AND INCREASING INFLUENCE
ON TENNIS. THE OBJECTIVE OF THE
ITF TECHNICAL CENTRE IS TO ENSURE THAT
AN APPROPRIATE BALANCE BETWEEN
TECHNOLOGY AND TRADITION IS MAINTAINED."

STUART MILLER
DIRECTOR, SCIENCE AND TECHNICAL

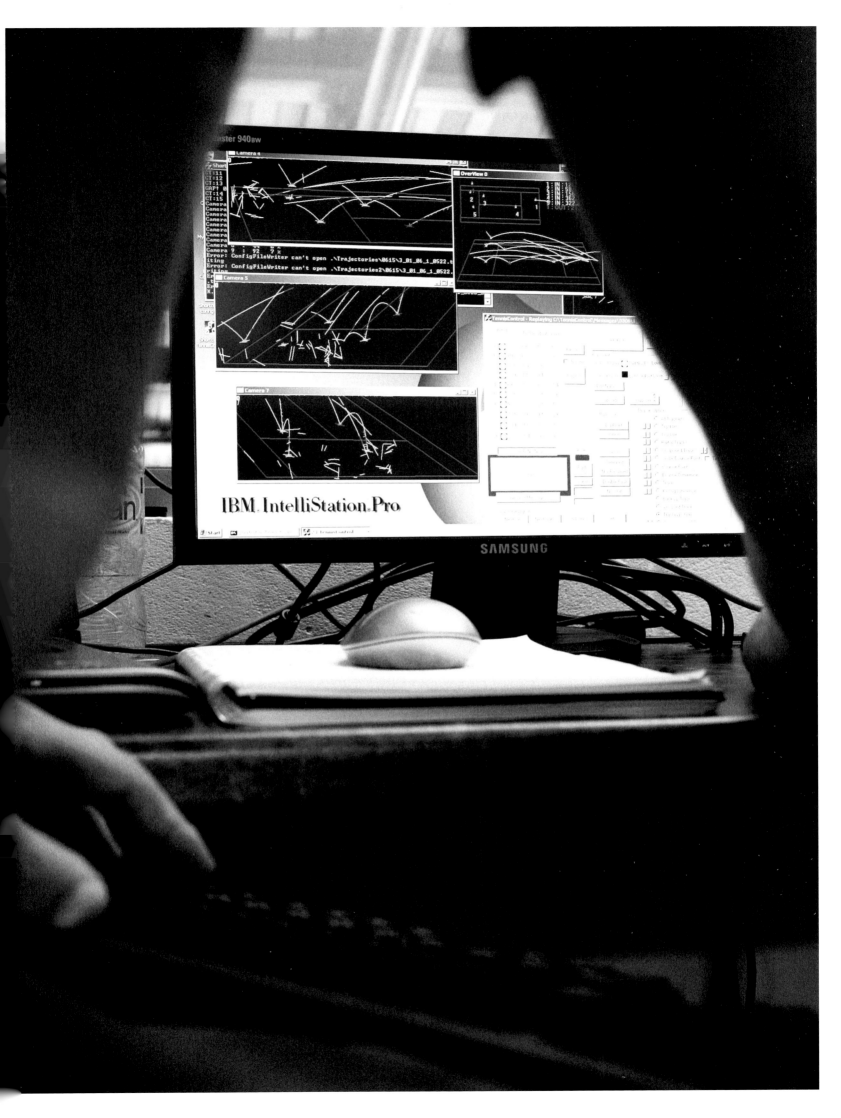

CHAPTER 12

TENNIS AT THE CUTTING EDGE

THE ITF'S WORK IN SCIENCE AND TECHNOLOGY

ALL SPORTS INVOLVE SOME ASPECT OF TECHNOLOGY THESE DAYS.
EVEN THE PURE SPORTS THAT REQUIRE ONLY PHYSICAL SPEED, STRENGTH OR
ENDURANCE INVOLVE HIGH-TECH FOOTWEAR AND TECHNOLOGICAL AIDS TO
ACHIEVE TOP-LEVEL FITNESS. SO A SPORT LIKE TENNIS THAT
REQUIRES RACKETS, BALLS AND SURFACES IS GOING TO BE RIPE
FOR TECHNICAL INNOVATION, AND WITH SUCH COMES A CORRESPONDING NEED
TO ENSURE THAT ADVANCES IN EQUIPMENT DON'T CRUSH THE NATURAL HUMAN
COMPETITIVENESS OF THE SPORT. THE ITF HAS ITS OWN SCIENCE
AND TECHNICAL DEPARTMENT, OF WHICH 'THE LAB' IS THE NERVE CENTRE.
BUT THE TECHNICAL ARM HAS ONLY EXISTED FOR 17 YEARS, THE PERIOD IN WHICH
THE TECHNOLOGY OF THE SPORT HAS EVOLVED THE FASTEST IN THE COURSE
OF THE ITF'S FIRST CENTURY.

THE EVOLUTION OF THE TENNIS BALL

Take the evolution of the tennis ball. The first rules of tennis that came into effect in January 1924 stipulated the size, weight and elasticity of the ball. But how do you measure these things? Size is easy: you just have a couple of rings, and if the ball passes through the larger one and doesn't pass through the smaller one, it passes the test. Weight is also easy: you put the ball on a scale. But what about elasticity?

At first, elasticity was measured just by dropping the ball from a certain height – normally 2.54 metres (100 inches) – onto concrete at a temperature of 20°C (68°F) and measuring whether it bounced up to between 53 and 58 percent of the height from which it was dropped. But in 1925 a major new device was invented that provided the first test for the 'deformation' of a tennis ball. Percy Herbert Stevens, an engineer who served on the Ball Test Committee of the British national association, the LTA, designed a machine that shows how much a ball deforms under a set load. The Stevens machine applies 8.16 kilograms (18 lbs) to a ball. It is a remarkable bespoke device that has remained largely unchallenged for more than 40 years.

The ILTF followed Stevens' invention with interest and invited him to demonstrate the machine at its 1925 general meeting. The minutes record: 'Mr P.H. Stevens with the aid of his diagrams gave a lucid explanation of the theory on which the proposal was founded. The meeting displayed considerable interest, and eventually the resolutions were passed, not only unanimously but with applause'.

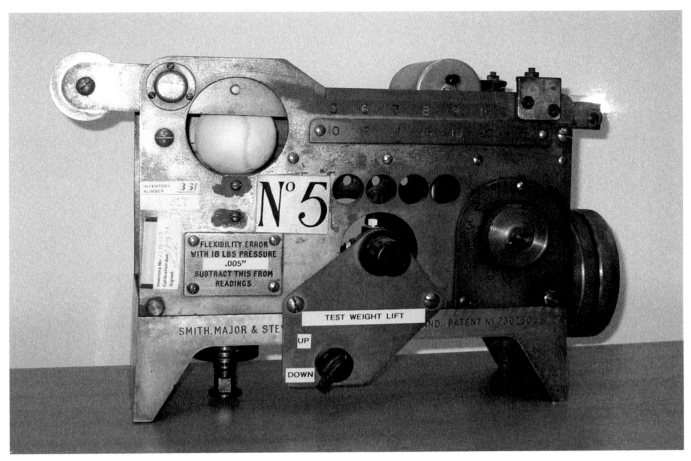

The Stevens machine, invented in 1925 by Percy Herbert Stevens to test the stiffness (deformation) of a tennis ball

To ensure tennis balls are the correct size, the ITF Technical Centre uses traditional ring gauges to assure each ball meets the necessary specification.

The automated deformation-testing machine replaced the Stevens machine to allow the ITF Technical Centre to test the large volume of balls submitted for approval as part of the ITF's ball approval programme (approximately 5,000 per year). The test measures how much a ball deforms under a 8.16 kg load. The ball is then compressed further before a second measurement is made.

IT'S NOT ROCKET SCIENCE....
OR IS IT?

In 2000 the ITF technical department reached out to scientists and researchers all over the world in staging the first Tennis Science and Technology (TST) congress. Contributions ranged from minute details about the impact of a tennis ball on racket strings to the environmental impact of tennis.

Among the contributions at the first TST congress was one from Rabi Mehta, a scientist with NASA in California (yes, a rocket scientist). Mehta had been studying lots of sports but admitted he had always been foxed by the motion through the air of a tennis ball. So he and Jani Macari Pallis from Cislunar Aerospace (another rocket scientist) set to work figuring out what happens with the fluff when a ball flies through the air.

They found a range of results, from the fact that the seam on a tennis ball does nothing to affect its flight through the air (unlike balls used in cricket and baseball), to the fact that the more used a ball is, the quicker it flies through the air – thereby suggesting a big server should use a more worn ball for first serves and a fluffier one for second serves.

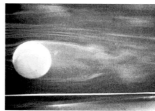

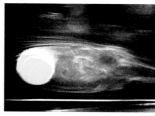
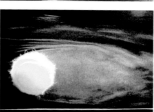

In 1966 the advent of 'pressureless' tennis balls meant the Stevens machine had to be adapted to perform a slightly different test. Conventional balls had relied on internal air pressure for part of their bounce, but for balls without that pressure, it became important to measure 'return deformation', or how well a tennis ball recovers from the crushing of the Stevens machine or a racket. That took measuring the elasticity of a ball to new levels of sophistication. It didn't end the need for the Stevens machine, which was adapted to measure return deformation, and the ITF continued using it until 1997, at which point testing for both forward and return deformation became automated (the ITF tests about 5,000 balls a year in its laboratory, so doing it by hand, as was required with the Stevens machine, became unwieldy). There may be only about 15 Stevens machines left in existence; the ITF owns two of them.

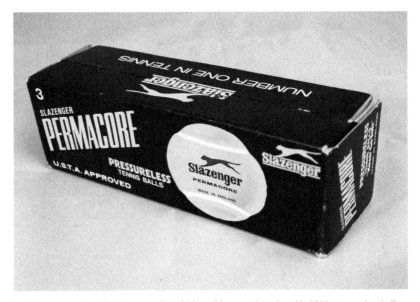

Pressureless balls, unlike pressurised balls, maintain their bounce over time due, in part, to their thicker rubber core. Introduced in 1966, pressureless balls tend to be used in tournaments at high altitude, where the thinner air means a regular pressurised ball bounces significantly higher.

A 'bazooka' air cannon capable of firing a ball at 100mph is used to simulate the effects of high-speed impacts. This shows the extent to which a ball compresses on a concrete surface before bouncing back.

The evolution of rackets – both the materials used and the advances in strings technology – has also created issues for the ITF to monitor.

Until the mid-1960s all rackets were made of wood, albeit increasingly composite blends of woods and resins based on scientific research. Then in 1968 Wilson brought out the T2000 aluminium racket, designed by the French player and entrepreneur Rene Lacoste and marketed as a Lacoste racket in some European countries. Despite its notoriously small 'sweet spot', several players found it to their liking, the most successful being Jimmy Connors. Ann Jones also won Wimbledon with a T2000 in 1969. By the mid-1970s the first rackets using chemical components were used by the top players. Arthur Ashe won Wimbledon in 1975 using a Head graphite frame, though such rackets became increasingly amalgams of different materials, so the term 'composite' is more appropriate than 'graphite'. The last Grand Slam singles final to feature two players using wooden rackets was the Borg v McEnroe Wimbledon final of 1981.

Tennis received a massive jolt in the late 1970s, when a series of shock results were all linked to players using a revolutionary form of stringing involving knots that left the racket face looking a bit like a half-eaten plate of spaghetti. The 'spaghetti-strung' rackets imparted so much topspin that they threatened to ruin the game (see panel, opposite). The upshot was the first set of rules about racket design, which came into effect in July 1978. (Spaghetti stringing was sometimes referred to as 'double stringing', but the two terms are not interchangeable, as not all double-strung rackets involve the spaghetti-like knots.)

1870s/80s: Tilt-headed racket used by William Renshaw

1880s: experimental racket with diagonal stringing

1880s: Leather-faced lawn tennis racket

c.1895: Slazenger E.G.M racket used by R.F Doherty

1900s: Slazenger Demon with fishtail handle

c.1920: Spalding 'Slocum'

1920s: Hobbies Crescent Steel

1930: Hazell's Streamline Blue Star

1930s: Dunlop Maxply

1950: Dunlop Maxply Donisthorpe

1968: Wilson T2000 used by Jimmy Connors

c.1975: Arthur Ashe Competition racket by Head

SPAGHETTI STRINGING

One of the more bizarre technical controversies in the ITF's 100 years was the case of 'double-strung' rackets, or what became known as 'spaghetti stringing' (even though the two terms are not interchangeable).

In early 1977 some bizarre results were posted by players using rackets strung using a method pioneered by a German horticulturalist, Werner Fischer. Fischer's racket had three planes of non-intersecting strings, with only five or six cross strings, embellished with a system of knots and plastic tubing that made it look like the remains of a plate of spaghetti. The result was a massive increase in spin, to the point where a player needed only to gently brush up the back of the ball while playing a groundstroke to give the shot so much topspin that it bounced over the head of even the tallest opponents.

The ITF was alerted to the issue when a 40-year-old Australian, Barry Phillips-Moore, reached the last 16 at the Belgian Open, and the unfancied Frenchman Georges Goven made the French Open semifinals – both using spaghetti-strung rackets. It agreed to look at the technology, which was legal but clearly causing problems. Three months later at the US Open, an American journeyman, Mike Fishbach, ranked well outside the top 100, beat two top professionals, Billy Martin and Stan Smith, with a spaghetti-strung racket. Shortly after, Goven beat Ilie Nastase at a tournament in Paris, which prompted Nastase to use spaghetti stringing when he played Guillermo Vilas. It was to be the end of Vilas's 50-match unbeaten streak, but controversially so, as Vilas walked off court after losing the first set saying, 'This isn't tennis!'

The result was a rule introduced by the ITF in 1978 specifying that 'the hitting surface of the racket shall be flat and consist of a pattern of crossed strings connected to a frame and alternately interlaced or bonded where they cross'. That wording effectively outlawed spaghetti stringing (although not all forms of double stringing). Today's ITF technical director, Stuart Miller, says, 'The ITF's role is not to hold back the development of tennis, but to maintain the players' status as the primary determinant of the outcome of a match, rather than the equipment. What was different about the spaghetti-strung racket was that it was a revolution, not evolution. That made the decision easy. If it had been a slight increase in spin it would have been evolutionary and may not have been banned. It was probably one of the most important decisions ever taken'.

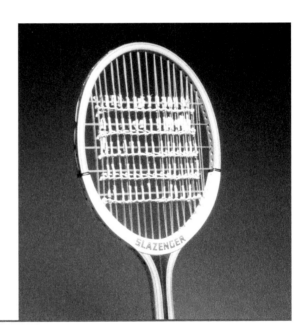

These first rules banned spaghetti stringing, but they set no limits on the dimensions of a racket. There was a convention that rackets were 27 inches long (68.6 cm) and the frame was nine inches wide (22.9 cm), but it was not a mandatory specification (as the net is 36 inches or 91.4 cm, it allowed two conventionally sized rackets to be placed on top of each other at right angles to measure the height of the net). But a year later Prince brought out its oversized racket, which prompted massive debate about how big a racket could legitimately be. As a result, the first racket specifications arrived in 1981, limiting frame length to 32 inches (81.3 cm) and width to 12½ inches (31.75 cm). The strung surface was also limited to 15½ inches (39.4 cm) long and 11½ inches (29.2 cm) wide.

That gave racket makers plenty of room to experiment with different sizes of frames, and a range of different frames appeared on the market. By the mid-1980s the first generation of big-hitters (Lendl, Becker, Edberg) was reaching the top of the game, and concerns grew that the sport was losing some of its variety because of the equipment. Yet advances in equipment technology were helping the club and public parks players to play better tennis. Therefore, in 1996 the ITF for the first time allowed recreational players to have bigger rackets than those taking part in professional tournaments, albeit only for a temporary period. From the start of 1997, the length limit for rackets used by professionals was reduced to 29 inches (73.7 cm), while non-professional players could continue using 32-inch (81.3 cm) rackets. But by 2000 the rule for everyone was 29 inches (73.7 cm).

1980s: The Ergonom
by Snauwaert and Depla

1993: The Handler
by Inova

1986: The Bergelin
8-sided racket

1998: The Limits by Wilson,
the maximum size allowed

2002: Wilson ProStaff 6.0
used by Pete Sampras

2006: Babolat Aero ProDrive
used by Rafael Nadal

The Racket

The racket shall consist of a frame and a stringing.

The Frame

The frame may be of any material, weight, size or shape.

The Stringing

The strings must be alternately interlaced or bonded where they cross and each string must be connected to the frame.

If there are attachments, they must be used only to prevent wear and tear and must not alter the flight of the ball.

The density in the centre must be at least equal to the average density of the stringing.

NOTE: The spirit of this rule is to prevent undue spin on the ball that would result in a change in the character of the game.

The stringing must be made so that the moves between the strings will not exceed what is possible, for instance with 18 mains and 18 crosses uniformly spaced and interlaced in a stringing area of 75 square inches (484 sq cm).

Sparked by the spaghetti-stringing controversy, the first official rules on racket design appeared in the 1978 Rules of Tennis.

SHOULD THE ITF HAVE BANNED ANYTHING BUT WOOD?

This was a question effectively raised by the letter sent to the ITF by 30 tennis 'grandees' coordinated by the respected British player and broadcaster John Barrett. Barrett's letter argued that a player cannot generate as much spin with a traditionally sized racket as with a modern racket. It didn't call for a return to wooden rackets, as this would have been impractical, but it implicitly begged the question about whether insisting on wood back in the 1970s would have allowed the game to preserve some of the variety Barrett and others feel has been lost.

We will, of course, never know, but what is clear is that racket makers were constrained by the limitations of materials. Until 1978 there was nothing in the rules to stop manufacturers from making a racket the size of a canoe paddle, but quite apart from the difficulty of playing shots aimed at the body with such a long racket, the wood wasn't strong enough to hold strings across too wide an area. The advent of composite materials that allowed for a much better power-to-weight ratio (lighter rackets that could withstand more force from strings and balls, compared with wood) also allowed for experimentation with larger sizes, so that was a direct result of using materials other than wood. But would it have changed the game from the way it's played today? No one knows.

Maybe there is an opportunity here for a rich tennis fan to offer two or more of the top players a lot of money to play an exhibition tournament with wooden rackets?

In 2003 a group of 30 experienced members of the tennis family, led by the former player, Davis Cup captain, broadcaster and tennis administrator John Barrett, wrote to ITF president Francesco Ricci Bitti, asking him to revert to the original maximum width of frame (see panel, above). Barrett and company argued that tennis was being reduced to a baseline slugfest, with players daring less and less to go to the net for fear of being passed by opponents whose rackets gave them an unfair advantage from the baseline over a volleyer.

The idea of reducing the frame from the permitted length of 12.5 inches (31.75 cm) to the traditional nine inches (22.9 cm) would reduce the 'sweet spot' and therefore bring more variety back into the game, they said. Barrett maintained that a side effect of the bigger rackets was that it was becoming

impossible to compare players from different eras because the equipment was so different.

The ITF looked into Barrett's arguments and concluded that it was the evolution of players and playing styles in combination with the evolution of the equipment, rather than the equipment alone, that was responsible for the speeding up of the game and improvement in baseline shots. 'We looked at the difference in topspin that could be generated by a 12.5-inch frame compared with a nine-inch frame', says the ITF's Science & Technical director, Stuart Miller, 'and found you could create as much topspin with a nine-inch frame. We therefore concluded that the style of play may well have changed irrespective of the equipment, so forcing manufacturers to revert to the nine-inch frame is unlikely to have made any difference'.

John Barrett, former player, tennis administrator and broadcaster. In 2003 Barrett challenged the ITF on its racket specifications, arguing that bigger rackets were killing the traditional serve-and-volley game.

There's a belief among tennis connoisseurs that the real changes to the speed and physicality of tennis in recent years have come not from rackets but from strings. Until about 20 years ago, top-level players almost always used gut strings, whereas these days the norm is either all synthetic or synthetic in the main strings and gut in the cross strings. The ITF has researched the impact of the most modern nylon and synthetic strings, and found that the newer, stiffer strings do enable a player to generate more spin than more elastic strings like natural gut. But as the game's governing body, it has to judge whether such differences are evolutionary or revolutionary, and so far the conclusion has been that technical advances in strings have been evolutionary (they have certainly had less sudden an impact than spaghetti stringing had in the 1970s) though the science and technical department is constantly monitoring progress and its impacts.

THE ITF SCIENCE AND TECHNICAL DEPARTMENT

The ITF has only had a technical department since 1996. Until then, much of the testing and monitoring of tennis technology was done by the British tennis association, the LTA, which had a technical department of sorts. The LTA worked closely with the British Standards Institute, which tested balls on behalf of the LTA; the US, French and Australian tennis associations had also been approving tennis balls for many years, but having the ITF's headquarters in London meant that the Federation's links to the LTA were closer.

In 1989 the ITF employed Tony Gathercole to run the veterans department and asked him to look after technical issues as well, a role that continued until the technical department was founded in 1996. The technical brief mostly involved ball testing; Gathercole sent prototype balls off for testing to the British Standards Institute, which approved them or rejected them the way it had for the LTA. Gathercole also coordinated a group that reviewed the evidence available on any issue at the time, for example, a tricky case of a double-strung racket. 'Much was based on anecdotal evidence from players and people in positions of authority in tennis', Gathercole recalls.

When Brian Tobin became ITF president in 1991, he believed that if anyone was going to take on a serious mantle of controlling the way in which the game is played, it needed to be the governing body. So in 1996 Andrew Coe was hired as the ITF's first head of technical, based at the Federation's HQ in Barons Court (next to London's other historic tennis venue, the Queen's Club). Coe was succeeded in 2001 by Stuart Miller, who remains in the post today. There was no room at Barons Court for the technical laboratory, so it was housed in a building in the nearby London district of Wandsworth. Once the ITF moved to its current offices in the London district of Roehampton in 1998, two squash courts in the basement of the building were commandeered and turned into what is now the nerve centre of tennis technological research.

LEFT The ITF's first head of technical, Andrew Coe, at the launch of the bigger tennis ball. Following a two-year experimental period, the 2002 Rules of Tennis were officially amended to allow the new ball, which was introduced to slow down the game. **RIGHT** Stuart Miller, today's ITF executive director of science and technical.

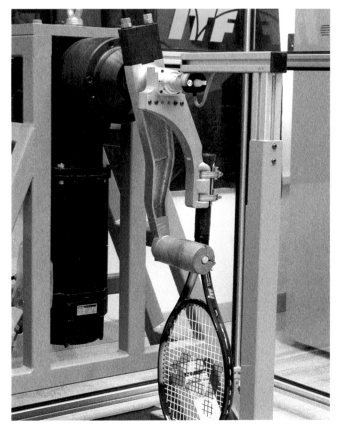

LEFT The Racket Power machine (nickname MYO) replicates a serve to measure the speed of the ball for impacts down the face of the racket. MYO is the Greek word for muscle. **RIGHT** To learn about the forces between a tennis shoe and the playing surface, the technical centre is developing a Sport's Shoe Tester (SST) to replicate typical tennis movements.

The 2003 ITF Tennis Science & Technology congress was notable for the first-ever official debate on automated line-calling systems. The panel from left to right: Gerry Armstrong (ATP official), David Mercer (broadcaster and ex-umpire), Sarah Gauci Carlton (Manufacturer, Cyclops), Mike Morrissey (ITF Administrator of Officiating), Georgina Clark (Vice President, WTA European Operations), Jeff Lucas (Head of IT, AELTC), John Rowlinson (Director of Television, AELTC).

The existence of an ITF technical department meant the Federation assumed responsibility for global testing of balls and administering rules about rackets, strings and court surfaces. By extension, it became the filter through which all tennis technical innovations had to flow. For example, the ITF had to develop a mechanism to ensure the Hawk-Eye electronic line-call review system was sufficiently accurate before it was given a licence to be used at tournaments, a mechanism that is applicable to all companies developing electronic review systems. The technical department has also had to build in variations on rules – for example, allowing for different balls to be used at altitude to ensure a level playing field in competition – and it supervised the research that led to the introduction of a new ball in 2002 that was 6 percent bigger than balls used up to that point.

In 2006 the name was changed from the technical department to 'science and technical', to reflect the growing role science was playing in the development of tennis technology.

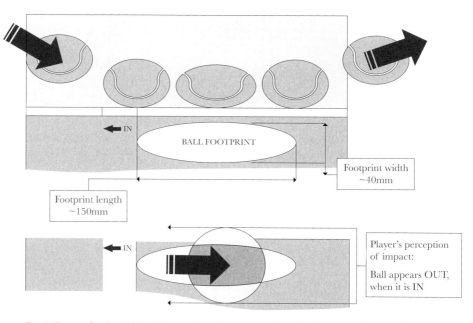

The challenges of making a line call are due to the ball compressing and sliding through impact, which lasts for just 0.005 seconds.

HAWK-EYE NOT THE FIRST

There is an assumption that electronic line-calling technology arrived with the Hawk-Eye ball flight tracking system in 2006, with only the 'Cyclops' service line 'eye' (introduced at Wimbledon in 1980) as a predecessor. But there was an electronic system used at the Australian Open in 1993.

Tennis Electronic Lines (TEL) was an Australian company that developed and marketed accurate line-calling technology. It worked by putting wires under the court surface along the exact position of the lines, and then impregnating all tennis balls with tiny magnetic particles invisible to the naked eye. When the ball landed, it sent a signal to a console held by the umpire, and if the ball was out, the umpire would call it.

The USTA tested TEL at the 1992 US Open but with a full complement of line judges in parallel (so no one knew it was being used), and Tennis Australia installed the TEL system on one of its outside show courts for the 1993 Australian Open. Problems with the court surface meant it couldn't be used on the first five days of the tournament, but then on day six it was ready for use. However, after just seven games of the first match, it was proving so problematic that it was turned off. The system was due to be used at the 1993 US Open, but in the qualifying tournament it was found that metal particles in certain tennis shoes interfered with the surface signals, and it was withdrawn from use before the main draws began.

The Hawk-Eye team manning the systems during a point at the 2006 Hopman Cup, where electronic line-calling technology made its official debut

One of the first achievements of the technical department addressed court classification. Millions of dollars were being spent on courts around the world, but some clubs and tennis centres were spending money without knowing how good the products were that they were getting. So from 1997 the ITF created a set of court-classification standards to which existing products and new entrants to the market had to adhere. The Federation was effectively saying to manufacturers, 'We're going to hold you to account for the quality of the products you install'. Some companies reacted defensively, and some revolted, but the ITF set a principle that has protected clubs, tennis centres and players over the years.

Recently, the ITF has developed a system of Court-Pace Rating (CPR), designed to measure the speed of a court and prevent nations from choosing surfaces for Davis Cup and Fed Cup ties that are either unfairly fast or slow. Any synthetic surface (grass and clay are excluded because they are inherently variable) can now be measured and given a classification based on the roughness and hardness. This is measured using a friction co-efficient for how much a ball grips the surface when it lands, and how high it bounces. Out of this, a rating between 0 and 100 is given – in practical terms, this tends to be between about 16 and 60, with 16 the slowest and 60 the fastest. The ITF allows home nations in Davis and Fed Cup ties to use surfaces rated between 24 and 50, but it will never give the exact rating – it will only say a surface is 'slow' (24–29), 'slow-to-medium' (30–34), 'medium' (35–39), 'medium-to-fast' (40–44) or 'fast' (45–50).

The Davis Cup and Fed Cup CPR rule came into effect in January 2008, and in January 2011 the ITF introduced a broader 'ITF recognition' scheme which takes assessment of courts further than just speed (such as condition, evenness of surface, etc). This means it can be of benefit to all tennis facilities as opposed to just those hosting Davis Cup and Fed Cup. More than 200 court surfaces are classified, and all testing is done either by the ITF or in ITF-approved laboratories.

COURTING VARIETY

In 2011 the ITF's technical department calculated that the amount of money spent on installing the world's entire supply of tennis courts was around $30 billion.

In 1996, when the ITF started its technical department, there were 12 classified brands of tennis court. By 2011 there were 220.

That doesn't mean there are that many companies producing courts – most companies have more than one brand – but it testifies to the explosion in available surfaces for tennis.

Court-Pace Rating measurements at Davis Cup using the Wassing Sestee and pneumatic tennis ball cannon. The ITF currently tests court pace at all Davis Cup World Group and play-off ties played on acrylic surfaces.

High-speed cameras are used to film players under match conditions. From the captured images, measurements of ball speed and spin, and racket speed and angle can be made.

WHAT OF THE FUTURE?

If tennis is constantly evolving in technological terms, what developments can we expect next? Use of satellite systems, linked with smarter materials to make rackets, could allow for much more information to be provided to top-level and recreational players about how they are using their rackets. If such information – such as statistics about their swing, strength of grip, court position and other factors – were available at changes of ends, it could play a similar role to that of the captain in a Davis Cup tie, allowing players to rethink their tactics based on access to fresh information.

If the trend towards taller players in the professional game continues, the ITF may have to assess whether the equilibrium in the rules that allows for fair competition is being disturbed. If so, some rules may need to be changed to allow for the physiology of the players, although changing court size would be low on the priority list, given the impact it would have on all the courts around the world.

POSTSCRIPT

OFF THE ITF WALL

01

Participants in the ITF's veterans events generally have high expenses, so they either have to be moderately affluent or raise money to cover their costs through more creative means. One example of such creativity came when Russia brought a team to a veterans event in Germany and promptly unpacked several dozen tins of caviar which they proceeded to sell to other participants. With caviar much cheaper in Russia than elsewhere in Europe, they saw the chance to recoup their travel expenses via a profit margin that still offered buyers a good deal.

02

For much of the ITF's first 100 years, the issue of professionalism proved very troublesome, and until open tennis arrived in 1968, professionals were viewed with some disdain by the traditionalists running the game. In 1939 the ITF's general meeting considered a proposal for organising a Professional Championship of the World. This was rejected, and the reason is recorded as: 'because of the difficulty of dealing with the professional exhibitionists who will not submit to any kind of official control and who are interested in matches merely as a spectacle for the public'.

03

It was agreed in 1924 that the ITF could only be disbanded if an 80 per cent majority voted to dissolve it.

04

'The ITF house is the home of good people, good students, and good athletes' – sign hanging on a wall in the Regional Tennis Centre in Fiji.

05

How many Grand Slam nations are there? Answer: four. Or is it five? The four nations that host the Grand Slam tournaments – Australia, France, Great Britain and USA – have 'major voting status' in the ITF's voting structure. But in 1991 Germany became the fifth nation to be given major voting status, with 12 votes at the ITF's annual meeting. Although Boris Becker and Steffi Graf had both been ranked No. 1 by 1991, the main reason was Germany's economic strength as a tennis nation, and the fact that its premier tournament, the German Open in Hamburg, dated from the 1890s. No other nations have been admitted to major voting status since then.

06

Many people are interested in records, and a popular question is: what is the best-attended tennis match in history? The official answer is the 2004 Davis Cup final, in which 27,200 spectators crowded into one end of Seville's Olympic stadium to see Spain beat the USA. The unofficial answer normally given is the Billie Jean King v Bobby Riggs challenge match at the Houston Astrodome in 1973, which attracted 30,000. But Alex Olmedo tells the story of him and Butch Buchholz playing a professional match in a soccer stadium in Peru in 1959 which allegedly attracted 43,000 spectators. So really, nobody knows!

07

The minutes of the ILTF's general meeting from 1939 talk somewhat disturbingly about a near riot. Describing an incident in the 1938 Davis Cup challenge round, the minutes state 'A roar of indignation went up from the public, and it appeared for a moment that a serious situation might arise almost amounting to a riot'. So what caused such indignation among the public? A jump serve! Australia's Adrian Quist was foot-faulted against the USA's Don Budge for allegedly having both feet off the ground when his racket hit the ball. Arguing that the rule requiring one foot on the ground was too difficult to enforce, the president of the US Lawn Tennis Association, Holcombe Ward, moved that the prohibition against jumping on serve be abolished. There were 114 votes in favour and 72 against, but as the measure needed a two-thirds majority, it was defeated, and the foot-fault rule remained unchanged for another 22 years.

08

Players who resent having to attend Davis Cup draw ceremonies might be interested to know that when Boris Becker first represented Germany in March 1985, players didn't take part in the Thursday fanfare. In fact Becker, who was 17 at the time and keen to play for Germany against Spain in Sindelfingen, poked his head sheepishly round the door of the room where the draw was taking place and asked, 'Would it be all right if I watched the draw?' Shortly after, the ITF made player participation part of draw ceremonies.

09

The 1984 Federation Cup, in the Brazilian city of São Paulo, was one of the most colourful events the ITF has had to stage, but also a problematic one. The balls and ball kids' t-shirts were confiscated by customs officials – the balls turned up just in time, but new t-shirts had to be printed, and they were still wet when worn by ball kids on the first day of competition. In a separate development, the Chinese team landed late at the airport, the delay making their participation in the official opening ceremony questionable. To give them a chance, the band was asked to play more tunes while everyone waited for the Chinese, yet the band didn't have a large repertoire so kept having to repeat what little it could play. Eventually the tournament director ordered the band to stop, which prompted the question as to whether the Chinese team had arrived. 'No,' he screamed, 'I can't take any more of the band!'

10

In the late 1940s, the ILTF spent a lot of time debating whether there should be one serve or two when a player had missed his (or her) first serve, and the point was then interrupted by an external reason thereby causing a let. The US tennis community was strongly against a first serve, arguing that this would effectively give the server three serves. The US position was supported by 74 votes to 68, but the measure needed a two-thirds majority to trigger a change in the rules, so the motion was lost. The rule remains the same today: if a point is interrupted because of an external hindrance, the replayed point starts with a first serve even if the original point was played off a second serve.

11

'It has been argued that lawn tennis began in the Garden of Eden when Eve "served" an apple to Adam which was a fault.' – Opening words of an article by ILTF president John Eaton Griffith in *World Sports* magazine, October 1948.

12

The term 'Grand Slam' is believed to have been coined in 1938. It came originally from the card game bridge, and was used by Allison Danzig, the tennis correspondent of *The New York Times*, as Don Budge closed in on holding all four major titles in 1938. Somewhat less well known is that the four tournaments that are today known as the Grand Slams were officially designated in 1924. Until then, the ILTF had called Wimbledon 'the World's Championships on grass' and the French championships were 'the World's Championships on hard court'. But at the 1924 general meeting, the Federation abolished the names 'World's Championships' and designated the Australian, French, Wimbledon and US tournaments 'Official Lawn Tennis Championships'. The idea was that other tournaments would

apply to join, and some were accorded 'official championships' status within a few years, but the original four gained such prestige that they were considered the elite, a full 14 years before the term 'Grand Slam' was first used in tennis.

13

The story of Percy Rosberg, a Swedish coach in the 1970s and 80s, serves as an example of how coaches need always to be on the lookout for unconventional technique that works. Rosberg was being assessed by another Swedish coach, Roland Hanson, for his 'Level 3' qualification. When Hanson turned up to observe one of Rosberg's training sessions with four juniors, Rosberg explained that three of the four players looked really good while the fourth had 'crazy technique' but he had to leave him in the group because the player regularly beat the other three. The junior with the crazy technique was Bjorn Borg. As a footnote, Rosberg later coached Stefan Edberg and encouraged him to switch from a two-handed to a one-handed backhand, something he had felt was not appropriate with Borg.

14

If ever the Davis Cup were to be abolished, the cup itself would have to go back to the US Tennis Association. This was a condition insisted upon by the USTA when the Davis Cup nations voted to hand over ownership and commercial rights of the competition to the ITF in 1979.

15

The story of Martina Navratilova's emotional return to Prague in 1986 is documented on page 131 of this book, but the political overtones provided a dilemma for the ITF's communications staff. Navratilova's return was a massive event for the media, yet the Czechoslovak authorities refused to recognise her existence, other than giving her the visa that was part of their obligations as Federation Cup hosts. So the ITF arranged a photo call at the top of the official hotel, and invited half a dozen photographers to represent the hundreds of photographers on site. They were taken up in an elevator, each with numerous cameras belonging to their colleagues draped around their necks. The photos of Martina and the Prague skyline have been well used, but somewhat less known is the story of the elevator taking the photographers to the roof stopping and Navratilova getting in. They were unfortunately all too crushed to get a photo of her, and no one dared given that the chosen few were all supposed to be on their best behaviour.

ITF PORTRAIT GALLERY

THOUSANDS OF PEOPLE HAVE SHAPED THE ITF OVER ITS FIRST 100 YEARS. DRAWING UP A LIST OF THE MOST INFLUENTIAL IS FRAUGHT WITH DIFFICULTY, AS SOME PEOPLE WHO HAVE MADE A MAJOR CONTRIBUTION WILL BE ACCIDENTALLY OMITTED, WHILE OTHERS WHO HELD CERTAIN POSITIONS BUT DIDN'T CHANGE THAT MUCH WILL BE INCLUDED. BUT WITH THE USUAL CAVEATS THAT THE MOST INFLUENTIAL PEOPLE AREN'T ALWAYS THE MOST OBVIOUS, HERE IS A LIST OF THE PEOPLE WHO HAVE DONE MOST TO SHAPE THE ILTF AND ITF SINCE 1913.

ANGELI, Paolo (1929–2012) – The Italian administrator who oversaw the sponsorship deal with NEC that allowed for the professionalisation of the ITF. An executive in the electricity industry, he became an ITF board member in the 1970s and oversaw the hiring of the Federation's first generation of staff. After leaving the board, he was asked by Philippe Chatrier to remain with the ITF as a consultant to oversee the Davis Cup's first sponsorship deal. The sports marketing agency West Nally had brought the Japanese electronics giant NEC to sponsor the Federation Cup in 1980, and when that was extended to Davis Cup in 1981, NEC needed an ITF partner, selecting Angeli. He was also the first president of the European Tennis Association (now Tennis Europe) from 1975 to 1978.

BARDE, Charles (1882–1972) – One of the trio credited with forming the ILTF and four-times president of the Federation. Believed to be a lawyer by profession, he was general secretary of the Swiss tennis association from 1911 to 1918, and in that role he met with Henry Wallet and Duane Williams to get the ILTF off the ground. He was the Swiss association's vice-president from 1918 to 1927, and president from 1927 to 1957. He was elected to be ILTF president seven times: 1920, 1927, 1929, 1936, 1939–46, 1952–53, and 1958–59.

BARNETT, Bob (1908–1979) – Served as ILTF president when the first professional Grand Prix was launched. A former Australian national cricketer who had spent the Second World War in a Japanese camp, he settled in London working in the extraction business and was nominated by the Australian association LTAA to be ILTF president in 1969. He was one of the founders of the Grand Prix circuit, drafting the rules of the new professional tour.

BOROTRA, Jean (1898–1994) – Vice-president of the French Tennis Federation for 38 years (1930–68) and ILTF president from 1960 to 1961. Known best as a player, the 'Bounding Basque' as he was nicknamed became the most influential voice in French tennis after his playing days. He was originally a staunch defender of amateur tennis but became a convert to open tennis in the mid-1960s. A controversial figure after serving as sports minister in France's wartime 'Vichy government', he later became a member of the French parliament. He was inducted into the International Tennis Hall of Fame in 1976 along with the other three 'Musketeers' (Jacques Brugnon, Henri Cochet and Rene Lacoste) and in 1994 was a founder of the International Committee of Fair Play.

CHATRIER, Philippe (1926–2000) – Generally recognised as the most visionary, influential and effective president in the ITF's history (1977–91). He was in reality the first of the executive presidents, as opposed to a figurehead, and shepherded the ITF into a more professional era, even if he himself was always an honorary president elected for seven two-year terms (the last ITF president to serve two-year terms). Chatrier was a journalist by profession and became editor of *Tennis de France* magazine. He was a good junior player and captained the French Davis Cup team, but he was most effective as an administrator. He became vice-president of the French Tennis Federation (FFT) in 1968 and president in 1973, a post he held until 1993, during which time he raised the standing of the French Open. He was elected president of the ILTF in 1977, but while his role became full time, he declined to make it a salaried position. He fought for and oversaw tennis's return to the Olympics. He was president of the Men's Tennis Council from 1976 to 1985 but was unsuccessful in preventing the ATP from breaking away from the Council in 1988–89. His last years were dominated by the advance of Alzheimer's Disease, a condition many of his close associates believe was hastened by his disappointment at the collapse of the Men's Council. He was inducted into the International Tennis Hall of Fame in 1992, and in 1998 the centre court at Roland Garros was renamed the Philippe Chatrier Court.

DAVIES, Mike (b. 1937) – A player turned administrator who was one of the dominant behind-the-scenes figures in the first two decades of open tennis. After a successful playing career that saw him rise to British No. 1 in singles and reach the Wimbledon doubles final in 1960, Davies joined Jack Kramer's pro tour. After retiring, he became executive director of Lamar Hunt's World Championship Tennis in 1968, a position that put him on a collision course with the ILTF and traditional tournaments in the early 1970s. In 1981 he joined the ATP, first as marketing director and then as executive director, before joining the ITF in 1985, working as marketing director and general manager. He is widely credited with introducing the yellow ball and coloured tennis clothing, as well as securing some influential television deals for tennis. He was inducted into the International Tennis Hall of Fame in 2012.

DE KERMADEC, Gil (1921–2011) – A French player turned administrator whom Philippe Chatrier sent on a fact-finding mission to Africa in 1976, a trip that proved the start of the ITF's development work. The son of an acclaimed artist (Eugene de Kermadec), he worked as technical director of the French Tennis Federation under Chatrier, and among other things carved a niche for himself making small films about tennis, including some effective coaching videos with studies of some of the top players. A creative character, he was very close to the Danish player and later musician and filmmaker Torben Ulrich.

DE STEFANI, Giorgio (1904–1992) – A former top Italian player who turned leading administrator in the 1950s and 60s. He was runner-up at Roland Garros in 1932. In 1951 he was elected to the International Olympic Committee and campaigned successfully for tennis to be a demonstration sport at the 1968 Olympics, but he was unsuccessful in getting it reinstated as a full-medal sport. He served three terms as ILTF president in the 1950s and 60s, including the 1967–69 period when tennis went open. He was also president of the Italian Tennis Federation from 1958 to 1969.

GRAY, David (1927–1983) – One of the most influential ITF administrators, despite having less than seven years as general secretary and ending his career in failing health. Gray made his name as the tennis correspondent of the British newspaper *The Guardian* and in 1976 became the ILTF's general secretary (effectively chief executive). He is generally credited with having removed the 'Lawn' from the Federation's name, and he played a big part in restructuring the Davis Cup. But his biggest passion was in getting tennis back into the Olympics, for which he had developed a great respect as a journalist – indeed his last task before joining the ILTF was covering the 1976 Olympics. He was inducted posthumously into the International Tennis Hall of Fame in 1985.

GRIFFITH, John Eaton (1894–1985) – The ILTF president for four two-year terms who earned a reputation for being more respectful to players than was common in his time. A high-ranking official in the British public service, he became an influential figure in tennis through his links with the British LTA and the ILTF. He served as ILTF president in 1953-54, 1959-60 and 1963-1964. He was one of the early ILTF advocates for bringing sponsorship into tennis and played a role in setting up the open Grand Prix circuit. Known informally as 'Eaton' despite wanting people to believe his surname was 'Eaton Griffith', he used to hold a party for the non-British players at his house on the middle Sunday of Wimbledon. He is also rumoured to have bought the Fed Cup trophy, after contributions from several countries ensured funding for it.

HARDWICK, Derek (1921–1987) – The ILTF president in the mid-1970s who made his name as an ambassador for open tennis in the 1960s. Originally a farmer who was a British doubles champion, he became a leading advocate of tennis going open. When Wimbledon announced in late 1967 that its 1968 event would feature professionals – a highly controversial move that prompted the threat of excommunication – Hardwick travelled around the world to talk to tennis bodies about Wimbledon's decision; he also formed an alliance with the USTA president Bob Kelleher that helped persuade the ILTF to accept open tennis. A powerful personality in committee who often got his way on controversial matters, he was the last of the ILTF's 'figurehead' presidents. But he earned great respect from the players as a long-standing member of the Men's Pro Council (including as chairman from 1974 to 1977), and his death probably hastened the Council's demise. He was inducted into the International Tennis Hall of Fame in 2010, 23 years after his death.

HEYMAN, Allan (1921–1998) – The ILTF president at the time of the player boycott of Wimbledon who had many of the turbulent disputes of the early open tennis years on his watch. Born and raised in Denmark, he settled in England in his early adult years and became a high-ranking lawyer in the British legal system. Originally an opponent of open tennis, he negotiated a deal with World Championship Tennis in 1972 that unwittingly triggered the founding of the Association of Tennis Professionals. A member of the All England Club, he used the 1973 Wimbledon championships as a battleground for officialdom's ultimately unsuccessful fight with the players, which damaged trust between Wimbledon and the ITF for many years.

KELLEHER, Bob (1913–2011) – Player, Davis Cup captain and USTA president who had a significant role in persuading the ILTF to allow tennis to go open in 1968. Originally a ballboy as a kid at the Westside Tennis Club in Forest Hills, New York, he captained the US Davis Cup team to victory over the all-conquering Australians in 1963. In 1967 he became USLTA president, determined to change what he described as 'dishonest practices' in tennis, namely the under-the-table payments to amateurs. He toured the USA pleading for open tennis and helped persuade the ILTF to accept professionals in early 1968. A judge by profession, and a one-time assistant referee at Forest Hills, he was inducted into the International Tennis Hall of Fame in 2000.

MacCURDY, Doug (b. 1948) – The ITF's first development director and later general manager. An American who originally worked with the USTA, he put together a multifaceted worldwide development programme and visited around 160 countries, working with coaches, players and officials from national associations. From 1995 to 1998 he was ITF general manager while continuing as director of development. He left the ITF in 1998 but continues to be involved in a number of ITF development initiatives. An intrepid traveller with an ability to feel comfortable anywhere in the world, he received the ITF award for services to the game in 1998.

MARGETS, Juan (b. 1954) – A leading administrator from Catalunya and Spain who has been ITF executive vice-president since 1998. A national junior champion, he served in various functions at the Spanish tennis association and Tennis Europe in the 1980s, before serving on the ITF's Fed Cup, Davis Cup and wheelchair committees in the 1990s. He became the ITF's top administrator in 1998, and a year later became chairman of the Davis Cup and men's circuit committees; in 2009 his administrative role was recognised with the title chief operating officer. Among his achievements are overseeing the restructure of the ITF at the end of the 1990s into five departments, and bringing about the Davis Cup and Fed Cup nation rankings. His brother Miguel is a leading coach and was Spanish Fed Cup captain.

PENMAN, Derek (1915–2004) – A British volunteer who played a major role in persuading the leading tennis authorities to let tennis go open in 1968. When Wimbledon announced in late 1967 that its 1968 event would feature professionals – a highly controversial move that prompted the threat of excommunication – Penman and fellow Wimbledon, LTA and ILTF figure Derek Hardwick went around the world to persuade tennis bodies about the merits of Wimbledon's decision. He was a British delegate at ITF general meetings from 1975 to 1984 and was honoured by the ITF in 1988 for services to the game.

REAY, Basil (1909–1987) – The first paid employee of the ITF (jointly with Shirley Woodhead, overleaf) as secretary from 1973 to 1976. He was working as a schoolteacher in Egypt in 1939 when war broke out, and returning to England with impaired eyesight, he joined the British tennis authority the LTA. From 1948 to 1973, he was joint honorary secretary of the ILTF with a succession of French secretaries nominated by the FFT. In 1973 he became secretary in his own right and was paid for his duties. He was also secretary to the Davis Cup Nations. An abrasive character whose interpersonal skills were not always his greatest strength, he became known in his latter years for being very resistant to change at a time when tennis was embarking on its new professional era.

RICCI BITTI, Francesco (b. 1942) – The third of the 'modern' ITF presidents, elected in 1999 and subsequently re-elected three times. A member of the Italian national junior team, he obtained a doctorate in engineering and pursued a career with communications technology companies, while maintaining an amateur interest in tennis. He was the ITF's technical delegate at the 1984 Olympics and was president of Tennis Europe and the Italian association FIT in the 1990s. He resigned both presidencies in 1999 to prepare his change of the ITF constitution in 2000 that now prevents an ITF president from having a formal role with a national association. He was elected to the International Olympic Committee in 2006, the World Anti-Doping Agency's executive committee in 2008 and in 2012 was appointed president of the Association of Summer Olympic International Federations (ASOIF).

SAMARANCH, Juan-Antonio (1920–2010) – An aficionado of tennis who was International Olympic Committee president when tennis was applying to get back into the Olympic fold. Born into an aristocratic Catalan family, he served as a sports administrator and local government minister, and in the 1970s was Spain's ambassador to the USSR and Mongolia. He became IOC president in 1980 with a mission to make the Olympic movement financially viable and get the best athletes back in the Games. This, as well as his passion for tennis (having been the leading player in Barcelona's Real Club in the 1920s), made him receptive to approaches from Philippe Chatrier and David Gray to reinstate tennis as an Olympic sport. He was given the ITF's Philippe Chatrier Award in 2000.

TOBIN, Brian (b. 1930) – The second of the 'modern' ITF presidents (1991–99) but perhaps better known as the man who modernised the Australian Open. He was one of Australia's top ten players in the late 1950s and captained the Australian Federation Cup team in the 1960s alongside his career in banking. In 1983 he became president of the Lawn Tennis Association of Australia (now Tennis Australia) at a time when the Australian Open was in danger of losing its Grand Slam status. He teamed up with the state government of Victoria to ensure the future of the Australian Open at a newly built, state-of-the-art Flinders Park (now Melbourne Park). He became the first elected official of the ITF to enjoy a salaried position as executive vice-president in 1989 and was then the first president to serve a four-year term when elected to succeed Philippe Chatrier in 1991. Among his major achievements as ITF president were the establishment of the technical department and securing financial reserves for the Federation. He was inducted into the International Tennis Hall of Fame in 2003.

WALLET, Henry (birthdate unknown, d. 1926) – Co-founder and second president of the ILTF, and at the helm during the schism between the sport of tennis and the Olympic movement. In 1909 he founded the Central Committee for Lawn Tennis, effectively the tennis section of the Union of French Athletic Sports Societies (USFSA) and thus the forerunner of the French Tennis Federation (FFT), of which he was the first president. Wallet worked with Duane Williams and Charles Barde to launch the ILTF, and used the USFSA's offices in Paris as the venue for the first meeting of the Federation in March 1913. He was elected president in 1914 and again in 1924, the year of the Paris Olympics which saw tennis fall out with the Olympic movement. In 1920 he became the first president of the FFT when it was formed out of the ruins of the USFSA, and obituaries described him as 'the father of French tennis'.

WILLIAMS, Charles Duane (1860 -1912) – Credited with being the motivating force behind the foundation of the ILTF but died on the Titanic the year before his idea became reality. An American lawyer from Radnor, Pennsylvania, he and his family moved to Geneva, Switzerland, in 1891. There he spent a lot of time promoting tennis, and in the course of that work met up with Charles Barde and Henry Wallet. By the time he discussed with Barde and Wallet the idea of an international umbrella organisation to group the burgeoning national lawn tennis–governing bodies, his wife had moved back to America, and he and his son, Richard Norris Williams, were sailing home on the SS Titanic in April 1912 when it sank. Both father and son are said to have jumped into the frozen water, but a falling funnel landed on Williams Snr and his body was never found. Williams Jnr went on to become US national champion and a Davis Cup winner.

WOODHEAD, Shirley (b. 1936) – The ITF's first staff member, jointly with Basil Reay, and later succeeded David Gray as general secretary. She began working for the ILTF through her job (and Reay's job) at the British LTA but became assistant secretary to Reay in 1973. Promoted to director level in 1984 at the same time as a new generation of directors was created, she effectively ran the ITF's administration until she left in 1987.

ITF PRESIDENTS

From 1913 through 1938, a chairman was appointed for each annual general meeting of the ILTF, until a proposal put forward by the Committee of Management that the ILTF should be headed up by a president and shall hold office for a full year was approved. France's Pierre Gillou, one of the founding members of the Federation, was elected as the first ITF president.

1913	Dr Hans Behrens	Germany	1948-49	Mr John Eaton Griffith	Great Britain
1914	Mr Henry Wallett	France	1949-50	Dr Russell Kingman	USA
1919	Mr Paul de Borman	Belgium	1950-51	Mr Roy Youdale	Australia
1920	Mr Charles Barde	Switzerland	1951-52	Mr David Croll	Netherlands
1921	Mr Paul de Borman	Belgium	1952-53	Mr Charles Barde	Switzerland
1922	Mr E Raymond Clarke	South Africa	1953-54	Mr John Eaton Griffith	Great Britain
1923	Mr Alfred Taylor	Great Britain	1954-55	Dr Russell Kingman	USA
1924	Mr Henry Wallet	France	1955-56	Mr Giorgio de Stefani	Italy
1925	Dr John Flavelle	Great Britain	1956-57	Mr Roy Youdale	Australia
1926	Mr Maurice Rances	France	1957-58	Mr Robert Watt	Canada
1927	Mr Charles Barde	Switzerland	1958-59	Mr Charles Barde	Switzerland
1928	Mr Paul de Borman	Belgium	1959-60	Mr John Eaton Griffith	Great Britain
1929	Mr Charles Barde	Switzerland	1960-61	Mr Jean Borotra	France
1930-31	Mr Maurice Rances	France	1961-62	Mr Roy Youdale	Australia
1932	Dr Hans Behrens	Germany	1962-63	Mr Giorgio de Stefani	Italy
1933	Mr Paul de Borman	Belgium	1963-65	Mr John Eaton Griffith	Great Britain
1934	Mr Louis Carruthers	USA	1965-67	Dr Paulo da Silva Costa	Brazil
1935	Mr Giorgio Uzielli	Italy	1967-69	Mr Giorgio de Stefani	Italy
1936	Mr Charles Barde	Switzerland	1969-71	Mr Bob Barnett	Australia
1937	Mr Paul de Borman	Belgium	1971-74	Mr Allan Heyman	Denmark
1938	Dr Hans Behrens	Germany	1974-75	Mr Walter Elcock	USA
1938-39	Mr Pierre Gillou	France	1975-77	Mr Derek Hardwick	Great Britain
1939-46	Mr Charles Barde	Switzerland	1977-91	Mr Philippe Chatrier	France
1946-47	Mr Paul de Borman	Belgium	1991-99	Mr Brian Tobin	Australia
1947-48	Mr Pierre Gillou	France	1999-present	Mr Francesco Ricci Bitti	Italy

MEMBER NATIONS 2013

AFRICA

Algeria

Angola

Benin

Botswana

Burkina Faso

Burundi

Cameroon

Cape Verde Islands

Central African Republic

Chad

Comores

Congo

Congo, Democratic People's Republic of

Cote D'Ivoire

Djibouti

Egypt

Equatorial Guinea

Eritrea

Ethiopia

Gabon

Gambia

Ghana

Guinea-Bissau

Guniee Conakry

Kenya

Lesotho

Liberia

Libya

Madagascar

Malawi

Mali

Mauritania

Mauritius

Morocco

Mozambique

Namibia

Niger

Nigeria

Rwanda

Senegal

Seychelles

Sierra Leone

Somalia

South Africa

Sudan

Swaziland

Tanzania

Togo

Tunisia

Uganda

Zambia

Zimbabwe

ASIA

Afghanistan

Armenia

Azerbaijan

Bahrain

Bangladesh

Bhutan

Brunei Darussalam

Cambodia

China, Peoples Republic of

Chinese Taipei

Hong Kong, China

India

Indonesia

Iran, Islamic Republic of

Iraq

Japan

Jordan

Kazakhstan

Korea, Democratic People's Republic of

Korea, Republic of

Kuwait

Kyrgyzstan

Lao, Democratic People's Republic of

Lebanon

Macau

Malaysia

Maldives

Mongolia

Myanmar

Nepal

Oman

Pakistan

Palestine

Philippines

Qatar

Saudi Arabia, Kingdom of

Singapore

Sri Lanka

Syria

Tajikistan

Thailand

Turkey

Turkmenistan

United Arab Emirates

Uzbekistan

Vietnam

Yemen

EUROPE

Albania

Andorra

Austria

Belarus

Belgium

Bosnia Herzogovina

Bulgaria

Croatia

Cyprus

Czech Republic

Denmark

Estonia

Finland

France

Georgia

Germany

Great Britain

Greece

Hungary

Iceland

Ireland

Israel

Italy

Latvia

Liechtenstein

Lithuania

Luxembourg

Macedonia

Malta

Moldova

Monaco

Montenegro

Netherlands

Norway

Poland

Portugal

Romania

Russia

San Marino

Serbia

Slovak Republic

Slovenia

Spain

Sweden

Switzerland

Ukraine

NORTH AMERICA

Anguilla

Antigua and Barbuda

Aruba

Bahamas

Barbados

Belize

Bermuda

Bonaire

British Virgin Islands

Canada

Cayman Islands

Costa Rica

Cuba

Dominica

Dominican Republic

El Salvador

Grenada

Guatemala

Haiti

Honduras

Jamaica

Mexico

Nicaragua

Panama

Puerto Rico

St Kitts & Nevis

St Lucia

St Vincent & Grenadines

Trinidad & Tobago

Turks and Caicos Islands

US Virgin Islands

USA

OCEANIA

American Samoa

Australia

Cook Islands

Fiji

Guam

Kiribati

Marshall Islands

Micronesia, Federated States of

Nauru

New Zealand

Norfolk Islands

Northern Mariana Islands

Palau, Democratic Republic of

Papua New Guinea

Samoa

Solomon Islands

Tahiti

Tonga

Tuvalu

Vanuatu

SOUTH AMERICA

Argentina

Bolivia

Brazil

Chile

Colombia

Curacao

Ecuador

Guyana

Paraguay

Peru

Surinam

Uruguay

Venezuela

THE PHILIPPE CHATRIER AWARD

In 1996 the ITF introduced an award to recognise 'long and outstanding service to the game', in essence, contributions to tennis that go beyond on-court achievement. It was aptly named after Philippe Chatrier, who had ceased to be ITF president five years earlier and who was in the early stages of a degenerative disease that was to end his life four years later. The award is the highest accolade the ITF can bestow:

1996 – Stefan Edberg

The Swedish six-time Grand Slam singles champion won the award in the year he retired, as much for epitomising sportsmanship as for his successes in Grand Slams and Davis Cup.

1997 – Chris Evert

The American had been retired for eight years when she won the award, by which time she had established herself as a respected voice of tennis analysis through television work.

1998 – Rod Laver

The only man to do a 'pure' (calendar-year) Grand Slam in the open era, Laver was honoured for both his ground-breaking individual exploits and dedication to Davis Cup.

1999 – Nicola Pietrangeli

It's highly unlikely anyone will break Pietrangeli's record of 64 Davis Cup ties, but the Italian was honoured for his post-career work as well, including captaining Italy's Davis Cup team.

2000 – Juan Antonio Samaranch

In his final year as IOC president, Samaranch was given the award in recognition of his support for tennis, in particular its return to the Olympics in 1988.

2001 – NEC

The Japanese electronics corporation was given the award at the end of its 21 years of sponsorship of the Davis Cup, a ground-breaking deal that allowed for the professionalisation of the ITF.

2002 – Jack Kramer

Kramer's award was a sign of healing relations between the ATP and ITF, but also recognition of Kramer's work with Chatrier in the 1960s to establish the first 'Grand Prix' professional tour.

2003 – Billie Jean King

King's massive body of work in tennis, from player to Fed Cup captain, from campaigner to ambassador, and general icon for tennis and women's rights, was recognised by the ITF.

2004 – Yannick Noah

Noah was honoured as much for his charitable work for 'children of the Earth' and the promotion of it through his music exploits as for being the last French men's champion at Roland Garros.

2005 – Tony Trabert

Trabert was honoured for straddling the amateur and professional eras, and after his playing days ended, for becoming a respected Davis Cup captain and television commentator.

2006 – Margaret Court

One of only three women players to achieve a 'pure' Grand Slam, Court was honoured for both her playing exploits and continuing to help the development of tennis after retiring.

2007 – John McEnroe

A choice that would have seemed inconceivable in his early playing days, McEnroe was recognised for his undying passion for Davis Cup and his insightful television commentating.

2008 – Neale Fraser

The Australian might have won the award just for his playing exploits and leading Australia to four Davis Cup titles in 24 years as captain, but he was also a long-time ITF board member and ambassador.

2009 – Martina Navratilova

Player, icon and social campaigner, Navratilova used her acceptance speech to make a number of recommendations for rule changes in tennis and attacked the practice of 'grunting'.

2010 – Gustavo Kuerten

A popular winner in Paris after his three Roland Garros titles, the likeable Brazilian also won the award for his work with handicapped children following the death of his handicapped brother, Guilherme.

2011 – Guy Forget

The soft-spoken Frenchman was honoured in recognition of his unstinting devotion to the Davis Cup cause, and also for being one of only two men to have captained Davis Cup and Fed Cup winning teams.

2012 – Arantxa Sanchez Vicario

The bubbly Barcelona native returned to the city of three of her four Grand Slam singles titles to receive the award that recognised her longstanding commitment to Fed Cup and Olympic tennis.

ROLL OF HONOUR

The accolade of Honorary Life President, Vice President or Counsellor is given to those members of the board who have left an indelible mark in their long service to the ITF in leadership and administration and in other areas of the sport. As honoraries they are not entitled to vote, but their contributions remain a valuable part of each annual general meeting.

Honorary Life Counsellor

Mr Anthony Sabelli (URU)	1949
Mr Robert Gallay (FRA)	1949
Mr Antoine Gentien (FRA)	1961
Mr Pierre Geelhand de Merxem (BEL)	1973
Mr J S Harrison (GBR)	1974
Mr Basil Reay (GBR)	1976
Mr Padma Bhushan R K Khanna (IND)	1977
Mr W Harcourt Woods (USA)	1979
Mr Leslie E Ashenheim (JAM)	1982
Mr Stan Malless (USA)	1983
Mr Laszlo Gorodi (HUN)	1984
Mr Joseph Carrico (USA)	1985
Dr Paolo Angeli (ITA)	1986
Mr Hunter Delatour (USA)	1987
Mr Alvaro Pena (COL)	1987
Mr Radmilo Nikolic (YUG)	1989
Mr J Randolph Gregson (USA)	1989
Mr Gordon Jorgensen (USA)	1991
Mr David Markin (USA)	1992
Mr Enrique Morea (ARG	1992
Mr Geoff Paish (GBR)	1993
Mr Jim Cochrane (GBR)	1995
Mr Robert Cookson (USA)	1995
Mr J Howard Frazer (USA)	1997
Mr Francesco Ricci Bitti (ITA)	1997
Mr Jean Claude Delafosse (CIV)	2000

Mr Walter Elcock (USA)	2001
Mr Fathi Farah (TUN)	2001
Mr Jan Francke (SWE)	2001
Mr Ismail El Shafei (EGY)	2002
Mr Harry Marmion (USA)	2003
Mr Eduardo Moline O'Connor (ARG)	2005
Mr Ian King (GBR)	2006
Mrs Julia Levering (USA)	2009
Mr Jan Carlzon (SWE)	2010
Mr Franklin Johnson (USA)	2011

Honorary Life Vice President

Mr Roy Youdale (AUS)	1962
Mr Charles Barde (FRA)	1963
Mr Giorgio de Stefani (ITA)	1969
Mr John Eaton Griffith (GBR)	1969
Mr Jean Borotra (FRA)	1969
Mr Allan Heyman (DEN)	1979
Mr Derek Hardwick (GBR)*	1987
Mr Pablo Lorens (ESP)	1989
Mr Heinz Grimm (SUI)	2002
Mr Eiichi Kawatei (JPN)	2004

posthumously

Honorary Life President

Mr Philippe Chatrier (FRA)	1991
Mr Brian Tobin (AUS)	1999

ITF WORLD CHAMPIONS

Every year, the ITF honours those players – men, women, junior and wheelchair tennis – who have reached the echelon of their game that season through their combined results on the tour, at the Grand Slams and in international team competition. The trophy is presented to each winner at the ITF World Champions Dinner in Paris, during the French Open.

Year	Men's Singles	Women's Singles
1978	Bjorn Borg (SWE)	Chris Evert (USA)
1979	Bjorn Borg (SWE)	Martina Navratilova (USA)
1980	Bjorn Borg (SWE)	Chris Evert (USA)
1981	John McEnroe (USA)	Chris Evert (USA)
1982	Jimmy Connors (USA)	Martina Navratilova (USA)
1983	John McEnroe (USA)	Martina Navratilova (USA)
1984	John McEnroe (USA)	Martina Navratilova (USA)
1985	Ivan Lendl (TCH)	Martina Navratilova (USA)
1986	Ivan Lendl (TCH)	Martina Navratilova (USA)
1987	Ivan Lendl (TCH)	Steffi Graf (GER)
1988	Mats Wilander (SWE)	Steffi Graf (GER)
1989	Boris Becker (GER)	Steffi Graf (GER)
1990	Ivan Lendl (TCH)	Steffi Graf (GER)
1991	Stefan Edberg (SWE)	Monica Seles (USA)
1992	Jim Courier (USA)	Monica Seles (USA)
1993	Pete Sampras (USA)	Steffi Graf (GER)
1994	Pete Sampras (USA)	Arantxa Sanchez Vicario (ESP)
1995	Pete Sampras (USA)	Steffi Graf (GER)
1996	Pete Sampras (USA)	Steffi Graf (GER)
1997	Pete Sampras (USA)	Martina Hingis (SUI)
1998	Pete Sampras (USA)	Lindsay Davenport (USA)
1999	Andre Agassi (USA)	Martina Hingis (SUI)
2000	Gustavo Kuerten (BRA)	Martina Hingis (SUI)
2001	Lleyton Hewitt (AUS)	Jennifer Capriati (USA)
2002	Lleyton Hewitt (AUS)	Serena Williams (USA)
2003	Andy Roddick (USA)	Justine Henin-Hardenne (BEL)
2004	Roger Federer (SUI)	Anastasia Myskina (RUS)
2005	Roger Federer (SUI)	Kim Clijsters (BEL)
2006	Roger Federer (SUI)	Justine Henin-Hardenne (BEL)
2007	Roger Federer (SUI)	Justine Henin (BEL)
2008	Rafael Nadal (ESP)	Jelena Jankovic (SRB)
2009	Roger Federer (SUI)	Serena Williams (USA)
2010	Rafael Nadal (ESP)	Caroline Wozniacki (DEN)
2011	Novak Djokovic (SRB)	Petra Kvitova (CZE)

Martina Navratilova and Ivan Lendl

Steffi Graf

Roger Federer

Year	Men's Doubles	Women's Doubles
1996	Todd Woodbridge/Mark Woodforde (AUS)	Lindsay Davenport/Mary Joe Fernandez (USA)
1997	Todd Woodbridge/Mark Woodforde (AUS)	Lindsay Davenport (USA)/Jana Novotna (CZE)
1998	Jacco Eltingh/Paul Haarhuis (NED)	Lindsay Davenport (USA)/Natasha Zvereva (BLR)
1999	Mahesh Bhupathi/Leander Paes (IND)	Martina Hingis (SUI)/Anna Kournikova (RUS)
2000	Todd Woodbridge/Mark Woodforde (AUS)	Julie Halard-Decugis (FRA)/Ai Sugiyama (JPN)
2001	Jonas Bjorkman (SWE)/Todd Woodbridge (AUS)	Lisa Raymond (USA)/Rennae Stubbs (AUS)
2002	Mark Knowles (BAH)/Daniel Nestor (CAN)	Virginia Ruano Pascual (ESP)/Paola Suarez (ARG)
2003	Bob Bryan/Mike Bryan (USA)	Virginia Ruano Pascual (ESP)/Paola Suarez (ARG)
2004	Bob Bryan/Mike Bryan (USA)	Virginia Ruano Pascual (ESP)/Paola Suarez (ARG)
2005	Bob Bryan/Mike Bryan (USA)	Lisa Raymond (USA)/Samantha Stosur (AUS)
2006	Bob Bryan/Mike Bryan (USA)	Lisa Raymond (USA)/Samantha Stosur (AUS)
2007	Bob Bryan/Mike Bryan (USA)	Cara Black (ZIM)/Liezel Huber (USA)
2008	Daniel Nestor (CAN)/Nenad Zimonjic (SRB)	Cara Black (ZIM)/Liezel Huber (USA)
2009	Bob Bryan/Mike Bryan (USA)	Serena Williams/Venus Williams (USA)
2010	Bob Bryan/Mike Bryan (USA)	Gisela Dulko (ARG)/Flavia Pennetta (ITA)
2011	Bob Bryan/Mike Bryan (USA)	Kveta Peschke (CZE)/Katarina Srebotnik (SLO)

JUNIORS

Year	Boys' Singles	Girls' Singles
1978	Ivan Lendl (TCH)	Hana Mandlikova (TCH)
1979	Raul Viver (ECU)	Mary-Lou Piatek (USA)
1980	Thierry Tulasne (FRA)	Susan Mascarin (USA)
1981	Pat Cash (AUS)	Zina Garrison (USA)
1982	Guy Forget (FRA)	Gretchen Rush (USA)
1983	Stefan Edberg (SWE)	Pascale Paradis (FRA)
1984	Mark Kratzmann (AUS)	Gabriela Sabatini (ARG)
1985	Claudio Pistolesi (ITA)	Laura Garrone (ITA)
1986	Javier Sanchez (ESP)	Patricia Tarabini (ARG)
1987	Jason Stoltenberg (AUS)	Natalia Zvereva (URS)
1988	Nicolas Pereira (VEN)	Cristina Tessi (ARG)
1989	Nicklas Kulti (SWE)	Florencia Labat (ARG)
1990	Andrea Gaudenzi (ITA)	Karina Habsudova (TCH)
1991	Thomas Enqvist (SWE)	Zdenka Malkova (TCH)
1992	Brian Dunn (USA)	Rossana de los Rios (PAR)
1993	Marcelo Rios (CHI)	Nino Louarsabishvili (GEO)
1994	Federico Browne (ARG)	Martina Hingis (SUI)
1995	Mariano Zabaleta (ARG)	Anna Kournikova (RUS)
1996	Sebastien Grosjean (FRA)	Amelie Mauresmo (FRA)
1997	Arnaud di Pasquale (FRA)	Cara Black (ZIM)
1998	Roger Federer (SUI)	Jelena Dokic (AUS)
1999	Kristian Pless (DEN)	Lina Krasnoroutskaia (RUS)
2000	Andy Roddick (USA)	Maria Emilia Salerni (ARG)
2001	Gilles Muller (LUX)	Svetlana Kuznetsova (RUS)
2002	Richard Gasquet (FRA)	Barbora Strycova (CZE)
2003	Marcos Baghdatis (CYP)	Kirsten Flipkens (BEL)

Bob and Mike Bryan

Anna Kournikova

Marcos Baghdatis

Year	Boys' Doubles	Girls' Doubles
1982	Fernando Perez (MEX)	Beth Herr (USA)
1983	Mark Kratzmann (AUS)	Larisa Savchenko (URS)
1984	Augustin Moreno (MEX)	Mercedes Paz (ARG)
1985	Petr Korda/Cyril Suk (TCH)	Mariana Perez-Roldan/Patricia Tarabini (ARG)
1986	Tomas Carbonell (ESP)	Leila Meskhi (URS)
1987	Jason Stoltenberg (AUS)	Natalia Medvedeva (URS)
1988	David Rikl/Tomas Zdrazila (TCH)	Jo-Anne Faull (AUS)
1989	Wayne Ferreira (RSA)	Andrea Strnadova (TCH)
1990	Marten Renstroem (SWE)	Karina Habsudova (TCH)
1991	Karim Alami (MAR)	Eva Martincova (TCH)
1992	Enrique Abaroa (MEX)	Laurence Courtois/Nancy Feber (BEL)
1993	Steven Downs (NZL)	Cristina Moros (USA)
1994	Benjamin Ellwood (AUS)	Martina Nedelkova (SVK)
1995	Kepler Orellana (VEN)	Ludmila Varmuzova (CZE)
1996	Sebastien Grosjean (FRA)	Michaela Pastikova/Jitka Schonfeldova (CZE)
1997	Nicolas Massu (CHI)	Cara Black (ZIM)/Irina Selyutina (KAZ)
1998	Jose de Armas (VEN)	Eva Dyrberg (DEN)
1999	Julien Benneteau/Nicolas Mahut (FRA)	Daniela Bedanova (CZE)
2000	Lee Childs/James Nelson (GBR)	Maria Emilia Salerni (ARG)
2001	Bruno Echagaray/Santiago Gonzalez (MEX)	Petra Cetkovska (CZE)
2002	Florin Mergea/Horia Tecau (ROM)	Elke Clijsters (BEL)
2003	Scott Oudsema (USA)	Andrea Hlavackova (CZE)

The Junior World Champion Singles and Doubles award was combined in 2004.

Year		
2004	Gael Monfils (FRA)	Michaella Krajicek (NED)
2005	Donald Young (USA)	Viktoria Azarenka (BLR)
2006	Thiemo de Bakker (NED)	Anastasia Pavlyuchenkova (RUS)
2007	Ricardas Berankis (LTU)	Urszula Radwanska (POL)
2008	Tsung-Hua Yang (TPE)	Noppawan Lertcheewakarn (THA)
2009	Daniel Berta (SWE)	Kristina Mladenovic (FRA)
2010	Juan Sebastian Gomez (COL)	Daria Gavrilova (RUS)
2011	Jiri Vesely (CZE)	Irina Khromacheva (RUS)

Julien Benneteau and Nicolas Mahut

Michaella Krajicek and Gael Monfils

Anastasia Pavlyuchenkova

WHEELCHAIR TENNIS

David Hall

Shingo Kunieda

Esther Vergeer

Year	Men's	Women's
1991	Randy Snow (USA)	Chantal Vandierendonck (NED)
1992	Laurent Giammartini (FRA)	Monique van den Bosch (NED)
1993	Kai Schrameyer (GER)	Monique Kalkman (NED)
1994	Laurent Giammartini (FRA)	Monique Kalkman (NED)
1995	David Hall (AUS)	Monique Kalkman (NED)
1996	Ricky Molier (NED)	Chantal Vandierendonck (NED)
1997	Ricky Molier (NED)	Chantal Vandierendonck (NED)
1998	David Hall (AUS)	Daniela di Toro (AUS)
1999	Stephen Welch (USA)	Daniela di Toro (AUS)
2000	David Hall (AUS)	Esther Vergeer (NED)
2001	Ricky Molier (NED)	Esther Vergeer (NED)
2002	David Hall (AUS)	Esther Vergeer (NED)
2003	David Hall (AUS)	Esther Vergeer (NED)
2004	David Hall (AUS)	Esther Vergeer (NED)
2005	Michael Jeremiasz (FRA)	Esther Vergeer (NED)
2006	Robin Ammerlaan (NED)	Esther Vergeer (NED)
2007	Shingo Kunieda (JPN)	Esther Vergeer (NED)
2008	Shingo Kunieda (JPN)	Esther Vergeer (NED)
2009	Shingo Kunieda (JPN)	Esther Vergeer (NED)
2010	Shingo Kunieda (JPN)	Esther Vergeer (NED)
2011	Maikel Scheffers (NED)	Esther Vergeer (NED)

THE CUP HOLDERS

DAVIS CUP

Started in 1900 as a friendly challenge between the American and British men, today the illustrious Davis Cup has over 130 entries from nations of all strengths and sizes. It is the largest annual team competition in sport.

1900	USA	**1929**	France	**1960**	Australia	**1986**	Australia
1901	not held	**1930**	France	**1961**	Australia	**1987**	Sweden
1902	USA	**1931**	France	**1962**	Australia	**1988**	West Germany
1903	British Isles	**1932**	France	**1963**	USA	**1989**	West Germany
1904	British Isles	**1933**	Great Britain	**1964**	Australia	**1990**	USA
1905	British Isles	**1934**	Great Britain	**1965**	Australia	**1991**	France
1906	British Isles	**1935**	Great Britain	**1966**	Australia	**1992**	USA
1907	Australasia	**1936**	Great Britain	**1967**	Australia	**1993**	Germany
1908	Australasia	**1937**	USA	**1968**	USA	**1994**	Sweden
1909	Australasia	**1938**	USA	**1969**	USA	**1995**	USA
1910	not held	**1939**	Australia	**1970**	USA	**1996**	France
1911	Australasia	**1940-45**	not held	**1971**	USA	**1997**	Sweden
1912	British Isles	**1946**	USA	**1972**	USA	**1998**	Sweden
1913	USA	**1947**	USA	**1973**	Australia	**1999**	Australia
1914	Australasia	**1948**	USA	**1974**	South Africa (w/o)	**2000**	Spain
1915-18	not held	**1949**	USA	**1975**	Sweden	**2001**	France
1919	Australasia	**1950**	Australia	**1976**	Italy	**2002**	Russia
1920	USA	**1951**	Australia	**1977**	Australia	**2003**	Australia
1921	USA	**1952**	Australia	**1978**	USA	**2004**	Spain
1922	USA	**1953**	Australia	**1979**	USA	**2005**	Croatia
1923	USA	**1954**	USA	**1980**	Czechoslovakia	**2006**	Russia
1924	USA	**1955**	Australia	**1981**	USA	**2007**	USA
1925	USA	**1956**	Australia	**1982**	USA	**2008**	Spain
1926	USA	**1957**	Australia	**1983**	Australia	**2009**	Spain
1927	France	**1958**	USA	**1984**	Sweden	**2010**	Serbia
1928	France	**1959**	Australia	**1985**	Sweden	**2011**	Spain

FED CUP

The strength in women's tennis grew to such an extent that by the 1960s there was a real demand for an international team event open to all, not just to USA and Great Britain like the Wightman Cup.

Year	Country	Year	Country	Year	Country	Year	Country
1963	USA	1976	USA	1989	USA	2002	Slovak Republic
1964	Australia	1977	USA	1990	USA	2003	France
1965	Australia	1978	USA	1991	Spain	2004	Russia
1966	USA	1979	USA	1992	Germany	2005	Russia
1967	USA	1980	USA	1993	Spain	2006	Italy
1968	Australia	1981	USA	1994	Spain	2007	Russia
1969	USA	1982	USA	1995	Spain	2008	Russia
1970	Australia	1983	Czechoslovakia	1996	USA	2009	Italy
1971	Australia	1984	Czechoslovakia	1997	France	2010	Italy
1972	South Africa	1985	Czechoslovakia	1998	Spain	2011	Czech Republic
1973	Australia	1986	USA	1999	USA		
1974	Australia	1987	West Germany	2000	USA		
1975	Czechoslovakia	1988	Czechoslovakia	2001	Belgium		

JUNIOR DAVIS CUP AND FED CUP

The junior equivalent of Davis Cup and Fed Cup for players aged 16 and under was launched by the ITF in 1985 as the World Youth Cup before it was renamed in 2002. Both events are held alongside each other.

Year	Davis Cup	Fed Cup	Year	Davis Cup	Fed Cup
1985	Australia	Czechoslovakia	1999	USA	Argentina
1986	Australia	Belgium	2000	Australia	Czech Republic
1987	Australia	Australia	2001	Chile	Czech Republic
1988	Czechoslovakia	Australia	2002	Spain	Belarus
1989	West Germany	West Germany	2003	Germany	Netherlands
1990	USSR	Netherlands	2004	Spain	Argentina
1991	Spain	Germany	2005	France	Poland
1992	France	Belgium	2006	Netherlands	Belarus
1993	France	Australia	2007	Australia	Australia
1994	Netherlands	South Africa	2008	USA	USA
1995	Germany	France	2009	Australia	Russia
1996	France	Slovenia	2010	Japan	Russia
1997	Czech Republic	Russia	2011	Great Britain	Australia
1998	Spain	Italy			

AUTHOR'S NOTE

How should one celebrate the ITF's centenary? That has been a question at the heart of the work that has gone into compiling and writing this book.

It would be easy to fall into the trap of writing a historically dry book that gets rather lost in processes and administrators, but neither the ITF nor I felt that would be appropriate. It would also be easy to try and chart everything that has happened in the ITF's first 100 years and produce an encyclopaedic record of every step the Federation has taken. The editor and I have read enough ITF reports and minutes to be able to do this, but while such a book might grace a tennis historian's bookshelves, how often would it come off the shelves and actually be read?

Instead, what we have tried to produce is a colourful celebration of the sport of tennis as overseen by the ITF during its first 100 years. As such, I hope you will find this book as varied, interesting and fun as a good tennis match or tournament should be. Celebrations should be joyful occasions, and while much joy emerges out of sadness and adversity, a book that celebrated this centenary without taking pleasure in the sport of tennis would be misjudged. I therefore unashamedly celebrate the good things about tennis in these pages, without denying some of the difficult growing pains that have led the ITF in particular, and the sport in general, to where they are today.

One person's name on the book hides an army of people who contribute to it, and to this end I am eternally grateful to all those who have helped with the research and logistics. They include John Barrett, Mark Bullock, Gianni Clerici, Frank Couraud, Tim Curry, Monica Escolar Rojo, Richard Evans, Jane Fraser, Heinz Grimm, Tony Gathercole, Michael Guittard, Marshall Happer, Mark Harrison, Richard Jones, Billie Jean King, Doug MacCurdy, Dave Miley, Stuart Miller, John Noakes, Tip Nunn, Janet Page, Nick Parr, Sandra Perez, Johnny Perkins, Christophe Proust, Prue Ryan, Luca Santilli, Audrey Snell, Christopher Stokes, Shirley Woodhead and Rachel Woodward. I am indebted to the book, edited by the late Dennis Cunnington, which celebrated the ITF's 75th anniversary in 1988. And special thanks go to my ever-patient editor, Emily Forder-White, and the ITF's head of communications, Barbara Travers, who had the confidence to entrust me with the task of writing this book.

Most of all, thanks should go to everyone who has contributed to the ITF over its first 100 years, for without their efforts, neither this book nor the centenary would exist.

CHRIS BOWERS

ACKNOWLEDGEMENTS

The author and the ITF would like to gratefully acknowledge assistance from the following publications as sources of information and suggestions for further reading:

Abgrall, Fabrice, and Thomazeau, François. *La Saga des Mousquetaires – La Belle Epoque du Tennis Francais* (Calmann-Levy, 2008)

Bunting, Sarah. *More Than Tennis – The First 25 Years of Wheelchair Tennis* (Premium Press, 2001)

Cunnington, Dennis (ed.) *75 Years of the International Tennis Federation 1913-88* (ITF, 1988)

Deford, Frank. *Big Bill Tilden* (Gollancz, 1976)

Evans, Richard. *Open Tennis* (Bloomsbury, 1988); *The Davis Cup – Celebrating 100 Years of International Tennis* (Ebury Press, 1998)

Fein, Paul. *Tennis Confidential II* (Potomac Books, 2008)

Kriplen, Nancy. *Dwight Davis – The Man and the Cup* (Ebury Press, 1999)

Wancke, Henry. *The Story of the Federation Cup – The First 32 Years 1963-1994* (Abbott Media Services, 1995)

Wood, Sidney. *The Wimbledon Final That Never Was* (New Chapter Press, 2011)

The ITF would like to extend special thanks to the staff at the Wimbledon Lawn Tennis Museum and the Kenneth Ritchie Wimbledon Library, at the French Tennis Federation Museum, the International Tennis Hall of Fame and the Olympic Museum, and to tennis photographers Russ Adams and Michael Cole for access to their archives.

International Tennis Hall of Fame *www.tennisfame.com*
The International Clubs *www.ic-tennis.org*
The Association of Centenary Clubs *www.centenarytennisclubs.org*

PHOTOGRAPHY CREDITS

Asociacion Argentina de Tenis (AAT) 158, 159 (bottom right)
Russ Adams 24 (top), 60 (bottom), 63 (bottom), 64 (bottom), 67 (top), 69 (bottom), 73 (bottom), 74, 80 (bottom), 90, 110, 125 (bottom), 174 (bottom)
AFP 39 (bottom), 61 (bottom)
Associated Press 24 (bottom), 32, 78 (top), 215
Australian Tennis Museum 55 (top), 109 (top), 129 (bottom)
Siggi Bucher 209 (top)
Bettmann/Corbis 34 (top), 49, 55 (bottom right)
Reg Caldecott 185 (bottom), 189 (third from top), 193 (bottom)
Camerawork USA, Inc. 137 (bottom right), 151 (bottom middle), 209 (middle top), 211 (top)
Sergio Carmona 87, 117 (top)
Michael Cole 15 (top), 53 (bottom), 57, 60 (top), 61 (top), 62, 63 (top), 65, 73 (top), 79, 81, 92, 114 (top), 120 (middle), 130
Robert Davis 5, 139, 157, 161 (bottom right)
Corinne Dubreuil 15 (bottom), 135 (bottom), 137 (top), 148 (top and second from top), 212 (bottom)
Edwin Levick-FFT 51 (top)
Encyclopedia Titanica 16 (bottom left)
L'Equipe 97 (bottom)
Federation Francaise de Tennis (FFT) 16 (right), 221
Arne Forsell 25, 120 (top)
GEPA 99 (top left), 103 (bottom left)
Getty Images 31 (top), 33 (bottom left), 66, 67 (bottom), 68 (top), 108 (middle and bottom), 199 (middle)
Gordon Gillespie 192
Ray Giubilo 103 (bottom middle), 230-231
Chen Gong/Lu Guang 187 (bottom)
Hellenic Tennis Federation 159 (bottom left)
Imagellan 206 (bottom)
Imago 176 (top)
International Olympic Committee 31 (middle and bottom left), 33 (bottom middle and right), 39 (top), 47, 187 (top)
International Tennis Hall of Fame 12 (bottom), 14 (top), 17, 33 (top), 85, 107, 125 (top), 129 (top), 219 (top left and right)
Do-Won Kim 209 (bottom left)
LA84 Foundation 36 (top), 40 (top)
Carlos Lezama 119 (top)
Sergio Llamera 115 (bottom), 210 (top)
LOCOG 161 (bottom left)
Newspix 42 (top)
NY Daily News/Getty Images 55 (bottom left)
Brad Parks 180-181, 183 (bottom left)
Borislav Penkov 200 (bottom)
Laci Perenyi 41 (bottom left and right), 43 (top right), 46 (top)
Melinda Phillips 131, 132 (all except top right), 133 (top and bottom left)
Popperfoto/Getty Images 105
Professional Sport 40 (bottom), 68 (bottom), 71, 72, 76, 82-83, 86 (top), 89 (left), 93, 95, 97 (top), 126 (top), 128, 132 (top right), 223
Real Federacion Espanola de Tenis (RFET) 208 (bottom right), 209 (bottom right)
Robertus Pudyanto/Demotix/Corbis 199 (bottom)
Roger-Viollet/TopFoto 28-29, 35, 108 (top)
Hiroshi Sato 135 (top)
Slovak Tennis Association 178 (bottom)
Sports Illustrated/Getty Images 78 (bottom), 114 (bottom)
Giampiero Sposito 194-195, 197 (top), 200 (top and middle), 201
Srdjan Stevanovic 103 (bottom right), 117 (bottom), 177 (bottom), 179, 206 (top)
Sveriges Tennis Veteraner 169 *(Scratch)*
Tennis Magazine 141 (top)
Time & Life Pictures/Getty Images 11 (bottom), 53 (top)
TopFoto 186 (bottom)
Ullsteinbild/TopFoto 23
Underwood & Underwood/Corbis 51 (bottom)
USTA 69 (top), 88 (bottom), 160, 161 (top)
Stephen Wake 42 (bottom), 43 (top left)
Fernando Willadino 188 (bottom)
Wheelchair Tennis South Africa 189 (bottom)
Wimbledon Lawn Tennis Museum 11 (top), 12 (top), 13, 18, 31 (bottom right), 56, 109 (bottom), 127 (bottom), 220
WTA 80 (top)
Paul Zimmer 43 (bottom), 44-45, 46 (bottom), 77, 86 (bottom), 88 (top), 89 (right), 91, 94 (top), 96, 97 (second and third down), 98 (top), 112, 116, 118, 119 (bottom), 120 (bottom), 121, 122-123, 134, 136, 137 (bottom left), 147, 156, 165, 167 (top), 170, 171 (all except second from bottom), 175 (bottom), 176 (bottom), 185 (top), 188 (top), 189 (second from top), 202-203, 205, 207, 208 (top right), 211 (bottom), 212 (top), 213

All other images are property of the ITF

INDEX

INDEX

INDEX

INDEX